Passionate Women, Passive Men

SUNY Series in Modern Jewish Literature and Culture

Sarah Blacher Cohen, Editor

Passionate Women, Passive Men: Suicide in Yiddish Literature

JANET HADDA

State University of New York Press

Published by
State University of New York Press, Albany

Printed in the United States of America

For information, address State University of New York Press, State University Plaza, Albany, N.Y., 12246

Library of Congress Cataloging-in-Publication Data

Hadda, Janet.
Passionate women, passive men.
(SUNY series in modern Jewish literature and culture)
Includes bibliographical references and index.
1. Yiddish literature—History and criticism.
2. Suicide in literature. 3. Psychoanalysis and literature. I. Title. II. Series.
PJ5124.H34 1987 839'.09'09353 87-9911
ISBN 0-88706-595-3
ISBN 0-88706-597-X (pbk.)

10 9 8 7 6 5 4 3 2 1

Four people have lived in my heart for as long as I can remember: my grandfather, Siegmund E. Hadda, M.D.; my grandmother, Hertha Hadda, née Schlesinger; my father, George M. Hadda, M.D.—all of blessed memory—and my mother, Annemarie Hadda, née Kohn.

Each in a different way suffered greatly in and because of Hitler's Germany, and the lessons they taught me constituted a protest against this catastrophe.

Watching and listening to my father and grandfather, surgeons both, I learned about the beauty of cure, the sanctity of life itself, and the inevitable fragility of the human mind and body. My mother and grandmother encouraged me to discover my own path and follow it, even when they could not envision the outcome.

Most importantly, my parents and grandparents all taught me by example that strength and dignity stem from within and can never be destroyed from without. The ideas and perspective that inform *Passionate Women, Passive Men: Suicide in Yiddish Literature* reflect their values. Gratefully, and with love, then, I dedicate the following pages to them.

Contents

Acknowledgments	ix
Preface	xi
Chapter One: Introduction	1
Chapter Two: Setting the Scene	15
Chapter Three: The Women	23
Felye	
Esther	
Manye	
Shprintse	
Sheyndl	
Merl	
Chapter Four: Like Father, Like Daughter	101
Chapter Five: The Men	119
Shloymke	
Fliglman	
Kreynin	
Yasha	
Chapter Six: After the Holocaust	177
Notes	197
Index	217

Acknowledgments

I wish to thank those who have contributed to the inception, production, and completion of this book:

Dr. Jonathan Boyarin, then taking a class I was teaching, who one day asked: "Does *Shvayg Shvester* contain the first suicide in Yiddish literature?"—and thereby started a process;

My teachers and colleagues at the Southern California Psychoanalytic Institute, who have encouraged me in a mode of thinking and responding that I could not have imagined without them;

Three teachers from my days as a graduate student whose profound influence I have only belatedly realized: Professor Mikhl Herzog, who introduced me to Yiddish, Ms. Shoshke Erlich, who taught me to read and love Yiddish literature, and Professor Dan Miron, who instructed me in the coherent and disciplined articulation of that love;

My husband, Allan J. Tobin: always ready to talk, to listen and—when the subject matter became too grim—to cheer me.

Preface

Passionate Women, Passive Men: Suicide In Yiddish Literature is a study of fictional suicides. Since I am neither an historian nor an anthropologist, I have intentionally avoided direct comparison between the literary examples I discuss and actual instances of suicide.

At the same time, however, I believe that art and life do reflect one another. My study reveals how the early absence of a benign, responsive environment can result in catastrophe for the individual who must endure it. Not every failure of nurturing leads to suicide, fortunately. Nonetheless, I hope that my interpretations, albeit of extreme and fictional events, will prompt the reader to think beyond these confines.

CHAPTER ONE

Introduction

This study reflects my dual professional concerns: literary criticism and psychoanalysis. It is, first of all, the exploration of a little noticed phenomenon—the unexpectedly frequent occurrence in modern Yiddish literature of characters who commit suicide. Secondly, but not secondarily, it proceeds from a perspective that utilizes the methods and principles of modern clinical psychoanalysis.

I do not attempt here to study the actual role of suicide in Jewish life.[1] However, the ample presence of suicides in Yiddish fiction inevitably raises questions about the well-entrenched stereotype of suicide as virtually nonexistent amongst Jews, particularly in Eastern Europe before World War II.

The notion that Jews do not commit suicide has been given popular credibility by the words of Emile Durkheim in his famous study of suicide.[2] Yet, studies completed subsequent to Durkheim's, but still before World War II, corroborate an alarming rise of suicide among Jews of Eastern—as well as Western—Europe.[3]

Indeed, even a brief survey of the Yiddish press during the latter part of the nineteenth century and the beginning of the twentieth century reveals that suicide was by no means absent from Jewish society and that Jewish readers were fascinated by it. The Warsaw newspaper, *Undzer lebn,* for example, contains over fifty articles and references to suicide within the first six months of its publication, that is, between March and August of 1907. These articles include one devoted to the general subject of suicide in Warsaw, stating that during the years from 1897 to 1907 there had been 1,956 suicides in the city, eighty percent of which had occurred within the working class.[4]

Not all the victims discussed in the pages of *Undzer lebn* were Jewish; at the same time, the names of the dead are often clearly Jewish even when the fact of religion is not mentioned. Moreover, the paper's specific interest in suicide among Jews is underscored by the presence of fictional attention to the topic. Sholem Aleykhem's *Shprintse* appeared in *Undzer lebn,* for instance, as did reviews of two Y. Gordin plays.[5]

The evident attraction of suicide did not end in 1907 nor was it limited to *Undzer lebn.* A sampling of Yiddish periodicals published throughout the nineteen-tens and nineteen-twenties indicates the continuing popularity of published accounts, both fictional and actual. The Yiddish paper *Haynt,* for example, contained an article in 1926 bemoaning the rise of suicides in Warsaw. Documenting 191 suicides during September and October of that year, the article advocated curtailing easy acquisition of poisons.[6] The Yiddish literary journal, *Literarishe bleter,* in turn, published short stories and book reviews explicitly focusing on the subject of suicide.

Since literary and historical treatments of suicide are juxtaposed in Yiddish newspapers and periodicals, it is tempting to assume that both reflect the same perspective. This is not the case. The chronicled renditions often do not cite known or suspected reasons for the self-imposed death. Where they do, the root is generally an economic blow or an example of insanity.[7] In contrast, even a superficial perusal of the literary works at hand indicates that, while the urge to discuss these matters may have played a conscious motivating role in the minds of some authors, neither financial collapse nor mental illness emerges as an overarching thematic issue.

Rather, a different and curious factor unites most of the literary suicides created by Yiddish authors: it is their failure to marry or, in fewer instances, to remain married once they have forged that bond. Suicide is forbidden, whereas marriage is one of the covenantal obligations of Jewish existence. Thus, the writers who sympathetically fashion suicidal characters suggest, through them, a hierarchy: the positive significance of marriage outweighs the negative importance of suicide. That is, where the commandment to marry cannot be fulfilled, the prohibition of suicide must be relaxed.

What is it about the characters in these works of fiction that prevents them from achieving wedlock, that status so central to traditional Jewish life? The answer to this question again emerges in a peculiar although clear pattern. The men who ultimately commit suicide are chronically withdrawn or inert, a condition that renders them incapable of sustaining the demands of marriage or, in less traditional circumstances, of competing to win a desired woman. The women, for their part, are too willful to be tolerated by conventional standards. Most commonly, their intensity is directed towards pursuing an independent lifestyle, sometimes involving taboo sexual behavior.

A man who is considered too passive or a woman who is perceived as excessively passionate does not fit the narrow confines of Jewish traditional married life. They are thus outcasts of their society, and where the society is itself considered cut off from other social groups, they become truly isolated.

Yet the inability of a fictional young man or woman to be sufficiently malleable to the requirements of the surrounding milieu elicits another query: what could have happened to precipitate such a disastrous life path? In the following pages, I pursue a response to this complex problem.

Suicide is the culmination of a life that has gone awry. As such, it serves as a watershed, encouraging investigation of what led up to it. Because psychoanalysis concentrates on human emotional development, it is ideally suited to understanding the genesis and subsequent course of suicidal psychopathology.

In this book, I do not attempt to cover every aspect of suicide, nor are my references to psychoanalytic approaches exhaustive. In particular, I will not discuss the teachings of Lacan and his followers, whose writings are replete with philosophical formulation and abstract allusions to the process of psychoanalysis. Readers may observe a conceptual and technical similarity between the works of these French and American critics and my own. Notably, we agree in the conviction that a text is never an immutably fixed entity and in the use of the critic's associations to the text as an interpretive aid. The difference, however, concerns the tendency of Lacan and others to incorporate their own associations into the center of the works they interpret, thereby attempting to create a new text rather than an explication of the existing one.[8]

Similarly, I do not focus here on the formulations and vocabulary articulated by Freud to explain his clinical work. Unfortunately, literary critics frequently employ Freud's terms in a reified manner, because they fail to understand that he used them as indicators of invisible processes. These investigators seek evidence of oedipal conflict, phallic imagery and the like, disregarding the fact that these are tools to help understand pathology, rather than ends in themselves. Such interpretations crudely articulated have done a terrible disservice to the subtlety of psychoanalytic investigation.[9] Finally, I do not use the literary works under scrutiny as vehicles for analyzing their authors, although this, in another context, could be a fruitful enterprise.[10]

What, then, is the aim of this study? Put as simply as possible, I am concentrating on the behavior, thoughts, fantasies, and dreams of literary characters from the perspective of psychoanalytic clinical principles in order to illuminate the factors leading up to their suicides. My theoretical framework is for the most part post-Freudian.

As is well known, Freud saw the growing child's sexuality as the root of future health or illness. Although he recognized infantile oral and anal erotism, Freud viewed the oedipal struggle as the decisive arena for determining a child's fate. There, the child fights a murderous battle with the same-sex parent for possession of the opposite-sex parent. Freud understood the oedipal conflict as inevitable and its outcome as dependent upon internal, or intrapsychic, mechanisms. According to Freud, then, the suicides of characters in fiction would result from oedipal vicissitudes.[11]

Psychoanalytic ideas have changed a good deal since Freud's brilliant and provocative formulations. Perhaps the single greatest development has come with a shift away from his closed circuit drive theory of human nature to one that conceives of the individual, from birth, as responsive to, and affected by, others.[12] Consequently, psychoanalysts have come to recognize that the years preceding the emergence of oedipal strivings are filled with developmental meaning involving the growing child and its environment.

A new generation of psychoanalytic thinkers, including D. W. Winnicott, Heinz Kohut, and Margaret Mahler have argued persuasively that Freud's notion of successful oedipal resolution is itself predicated upon the achievement of a prior state of psychic integration. The oedipal situation is triangular, involving entanglement with both parents. In order for the child to fully engage in this complicated triadic relationship, a previous step must occur. That is, an experience of smooth functioning with only one person—a dyadic bond—needs to be firmly established. If this early attunement fails to occur, the oedipal period will probably not reach a completely fruitful outcome. Where the early parent-child relationship has gone awry, the child will suffer the failure to receive critically needed emotional supplies and will, as a consequence, be less apt to enjoy an untroubled growth into adulthood.

It has been my discovery—unexpected when I began this study—that the issue of primary nurturing is pivotal in the lives of Yiddish literary suicides. For, virtually every character who commits suicide has suffered emotional deficit at a tender age. Each one has experienced a home life marked by incompleteness, absence, or irrevocable loss. Sometimes the inadequacy is physical, caused by parental death or willful abandonment; at other times it is psychological, due to the inability of one or both parents to provide the sustenance necessary for a secure, cohesive sense of self to emerge. This underlying lack forms the deep basis for later social malfunction—especially for the inability to marry and the subsequent choice of suicide as a solution. Singleness and suicide are symptoms, signs pointing to the fundamental malaise that occurs when a child does not find an appropriate environment at the beginning of life.

When these ideas—which refer to human development—are directed towards literary characters, questions surface immediately. First of all, how is it possible to employ clinical ideas with fictional characters who do not engage with the literary analyst in the same way that a real person may do with a clinician? They are unable to substantiate an interpretation or reject it; they cannot contribute to an analytic situation by developing transference reactions; they do not manifest resistance.

A second question revolves around the availability of data: how can an interpreter formulate psychic development when the character has no actual parents and cannot answer historical questions?

The third question is perhaps best articulated in terms of value: of what use and benefit is a psychoanalytic interpretation of a fictitious person?

I have presented these questions in order of their complexity, with the most complex and urgent first. I will answer them in the opposite order starting with the issue of worth, which is clearly a matter of individual opinion and taste.

The major value of a psychoanalytic approach is that it adds new dimension to the effort of interpretation and, while this should not preclude other forms of investigation, a psychoanalytic, psychodynamic focus can offer special insights. Why is it, for example, that certain literary figures appear to be more real than others? How is it that a character created in a different age, with unfamiliar sensibilities, lifestyle, and problems, can seem consistently modern? The elucidation of psychodynamic functioning can aid the reader who identifies with a character in becoming more consciously aware of the phenomenon and its significance.[13]

The second question, concerning data, is not problematic when approached by way of a rule fundamental to both literary criticism and psychoanalysis: whatever appears in the text—and only that—is grist for the interpretive mill. Thus, if there is no mention of a mother and a relationship with her, it is not valid to invoke her. The process of psychoanalytic literary inquiry has been greatly harmed by critics who argue deductively, claiming that the presence of a particular trait or conflict in a character must be the result of a specific etiology. Such an approach, like the unbridled use of free association by the interpreter, distorts the text as an integrated whole.

Far from contradicting respected psychoanalytic technique, the refusal to base interpretations on anything other than presented material is entirely consonant with current clinical thinking. The subjective reality of the analysand or other patient, rather than any preconceived ideas on the part of the analyst, forms the organizing center of investigation. Thus, literary critical caution parallels the circumspection of the sensitive and careful analyst.[14]

The last question, involving the validity of applying clinical principles to fictional characters, is the most challenging of the three, although it is connected to the issue of available data. Fictional characters are certainly not real people; more importantly, they do not come to an analyst for a cure. They do not develop transferential relationships, they do not fight against their own resistance to painful insights about themselves. In this sense, the psychoanalytic approach has an entirely different purpose than when the subject is a living being, an unhappy individual seeking help.

At the same time, however, because they are the constructs of a mind that has an unconscious, characters may themselves reveal, through their behavior, conversations and dreams, deeper meanings than those of which the author is consciously aware.[15] Every dream that a character experiences, for instance, is at bottom the creation of the author, transmitted via a narrative voice, yet this does not guarantee that the author has created the dream with a conscious grasp of all its ramifications. In this way, characters possess an unconscious realm, although it is not of their own development. Fictional figures may thus present themselves to the literary critic much as individuals who come to a therapeutic session may, without realizing, expose unconscious aspects of themselves to the psychoanalytically trained clinician.

Indeed, the notion that the narrator, and ultimately, the author, stands behind and thereby invalidates the character, disregards an important clinical concept. Virtually all psychoanalytic theory accepts the idea that individuals acquire impressions about themselves based on how they were treated as young children. Whether they are termed introjects, imagos, or simply influences, these internal forces must be identified and explored through transference analysis. Nonetheless, they are understood as part of the individual, aspects to be evaluated, perhaps reorganized, but not exorcized. So, too, may the narrative function behind a character be envisioned as vital to the creation and yet ultimately separate from its final form.

Moreover, corroboration of literary works has a certain simplicity that real life analytic case histories do not possess; that is, the reader wanting to check the cogency of a literary interpretation need only return to the text. There—although perceptions may vary—dream material will always be the same, behavior will always be described in identical fashion, the sequence of events will never change. Case studies, on the other hand, are inevitably based on what the analyst heard and managed to record, and they are therefore inaccessible to the kind of investigation that a work of literature allows.[16]

Clearly, then, literary texts prove unusually appropriate for psychoanalytic insights. At the same time, doubts about applicability serve to underscore a deep-seated misunderstanding of what clinical psychoanalysis is all about. Partly because of its historical association with medicine, psychoanalysis is too often perceived as mechanical, impersonal. According to this notion, all analysts, given correct and sufficient information, should come up with the same diagnosis and treatment strategy for any particular patient, much as physicians the world over can recognize and cure smallpox.

Actually, however, the analyst working with an analysand resembles an interpreter struggling with a literary text more closely than not. In several respects, analytic work parallels the unraveling of a literary text: (1) both processes concern narratives; (2) both efforts will, of necessity, always remain incomplete; (3) both yield up information which is perceived selectively; (4) in both cases, the person perceiving the narrative will have a reaction to it based on his or her own life.

In fact, analysts Donald P. Spence and Roy Schafer go so far as to argue that the input of the analyst into the narrative of the analysand is similar in kind but of greater intensity than that of the literary critic with a text. In his essay, "Narration in the Psychoanalytic Dialogue," Schafer characterizes the dialogue as "two agents, each narrating or telling something to the other in a rule-governed manner."[17] He goes on to comment:

> The analyst's re-tellings progressively influence the what and the how of the story told by analysands. The analyst estab-

> lishes new, though often contested or resisted, questions that amount to regulated narrative possibilities. The end product of this interweaving of texts is a radically new, jointly-authored work or way of working.[18]

Schafer's position is clear—the analysand and the analyst work together to construct a cohesive story of the analysand's life, one that will ease pain and facilitate change. Above all, his formulation accentuates the mutability of analytic work, wherein the patient does not lie passively on the couch while "reality" is interpreted to him or her; rather, it is a mutual enterprise, the analyst constituting an integral part of the ongoing elucidation that the analysand makes of past and present experience.

Donald Spence proceeds in a similar vein as Schafer, but his conclusions are startling. When considered according to their broadest implications, they render questionable the validity of clinical case studies, the basis of analytic education and theoretical understanding. In essence, Spence argues that analysts are always tempted to build the patient's remarks and reactions into a coherent pattern, one that increasingly approximates a finished narrative. Because of this liability, the analyst often overlooks or forgets the fact that these data, culled and presented as a relatively smooth-running story, are merely interpretations and that another story could be told from the same material.

Spence models his argument on the relationship between the author and reader of literary texts. The author, he says, needs to translate his perceived reality into language for the reader, and the reader must translate the author's words back into perceived reality. However, since this kind of translation can only occur idiosyncratically, the reader is inevitably limited to an incomplete and imperfect approximation. The more skillful the author, the more successful the transmission is likely to be. A badly-written work, in contrast, forces the reader to be more active in furnishing associations and interpretations in order to make sense out of the text. From here, Spence makes the analogy with psychoanalysis:

> . . . a truly free and spontaneous piece of association corresponds to a hasty piece of writing and can only be under-

> stood by active and constructive listening. Thus it follows that evenly hovering attention is *not* the necessary complement of free association as Freud claimed on many occasions and as many analysts still like to assume; on the contrary . . . free association, to be understood in any depth, requires a certain kind of active and constructive listening in which the analyst is continually supplying meanings, choosing from a range of ambiguities and, in general, imposing his own context on the material.[19]

Thus, Spence contends, the more freely a patient associates in psychoanalysis, the more meaning and coherence the analyst is required to provide.

As might be expected, both Schafer and Spence eschew the corroboration of psychoanalytic truth from any external "facts," seeking it instead from within the context of the analytic situation. Schafer believes the notion of common sense to be critical, asserting that the validity of an analytic insight or interpretation depends upon whether or not it attains a common sense acceptability for both the analyst and the analysand. Spence is more circumspect, warning against the danger of a premature leap from data gathering to theory, since the narrative truth of one person's analysis is not the same as theoretical fact.

Neither Schafer nor Spence intends to undermine the validity of the psychoanalytic method nor to invalidate its results. Rather, both strive to demonstrate that there is no single truth in psychoanalysis, that the "facts" of psychoanalysis are interpretations. Therefore, far from violating the psychoanalytic method by employing it to help explain texts, the literary critic is potentially on steady ground: observing narratives, attempting to understand them through psychoanalytic eyes, finally offering interpretations.

Yet the equation of literary critic and analyst only works if the critic knows what the analyst does. The essence of psychoanalysis is in its method. Theories, although invaluable for organizing technique, rest in the end on practical perception, from which they are distilled. Without the experience of what it means to enter, analytically, the world of another human being, any attempt to achieve a similar result with fictional characters will be doomed to sterile—or, worse, to misguided—"applications" of theory.

I contend, therefore, that it is impossible for a literary critic to master in-depth psychoanalytic criticism without being familiar with the central issues of clinical practice. Well-formulated theory does help, of course, to advance suggestions about literature. These contributions, however, may remain analogous to those of the literary critic who works with texts in translation.

An important question remains: what, in some detail, will the psychoanalytic method imply in these pages? Put perhaps over-simply, it will imply the smooth and continuous flow between conscious and unconscious processes. Precisely for this reason, and because he understood the subjectivity of listening, Freud insisted on the necessity that psychoanalysts in training undergo formal analysis. Then the analyst

> must turn his unconscious, like a receptive organ, toward the transmitting unconscious of the patient . . . Just as the receiver converts back into sound waves the electric oscillations in the telephone line, which were set up by the sound waves, so the doctor's unconscious is able, from the derivatives of the unconscious which are communicated to him to reconstruct that unconscious which has determined the patient's free associations.[20]

Theodore Reik describes a similar phenomenon, calling it the reciprocal illumination of unconscious processes. He discusses how, when the analyst tries to understand the patient, something from the patient's unconscious can enter the analyst's mind, via unconscious processes. There, it is made conscious, and in this way becomes available to be illuminated subsequently to the patient. As he puts it:

> Whilst I was trying to fathom the quality of my patient's mental reactions, an experience of my own was illuminated and entered consciousness and the psychological comprehension that came so late and so tardily helped me in turn to comprehend much in my patient that had hitherto been only dimly conjectured.[21]

Both Freud and Reik take as a given the fact that the analyst will have undergone psychoanalysis and will be able to have easy access to the unconscious of the analysand. I postulate a similar process with regard to the authors' creations of their characters and the literary critics' interpretations of this material; that is, from the unconscious of the author to the construction of the character, from there to the unconscious of the critic, who, in reading the text, picks up signals that lead to conscious awareness and interpretation. It follows that personal experience with psychoanalysis can play a crucial role in psychoanalytic literary criticism.

Now, with a new and more flexible view of psychoanalysis and its pertinence for literary study, it is time to return to suicide in Yiddish literature. A point of caution must be raised here, concerning the cultural, social, historical milieu of the texts. Just as clinicians must see a patient within the context of his or her family structure and social milieu in history—because these parameters can influence the meaning of individual dynamics—so, too, do we need to understand a literary character within these confines. This does not mean that surprises never happen. Indeed, the entire premise of this book is that suicide, ostensibly considered taboo and unpardonable, is, at the hands of numerous authors, both accepted and forgiven. The importance of this phenomenon, however, would be hidden if not for the cultural environment that forbids suicide, simultaneously emphasizing the importance of married life.

There is one final similarity between the psychoanalytic method per se and its use to illuminate Yiddish literary suicides, and that concerns the method of data gathering. Paul Ornstein, in his introduction to Kohut's collection, *The Search for the Self,* talks about Kohut's paper on Thomas Mann's *Death In Venice,* published in 1957, and he says,

> Kohut presents a clear, vividly condensed outline of the plot to highlight his perception of the protagonist's predicament—the equivalent of a good clinical history gathered with an empathic introspective mode of observation. Kohut then uses every literary detail and formal characteristic of the narrative . . . as a point of interpretive entry into a deeper layer of Aschenbach's inner world to find the reasons for its inevitable crumbling.[22]

Similarly, I have, in the following interpretations, reconstructed plots to refer as closely as possible to the suicides that are my concern. Therefore, most works are not fully summarized in terms of their general content. Rather, as in the case history of a patient, my remarks are geared to a fuller understanding of the character's development. My goal throughout is to elucidate the early emotional deficits that Yiddish literary suicides have suffered, whether caused by physical or emotional insufficiencies. Again and again, these lacks prove to be major stumbling blocks, preventing the socially necessary achievement of marriage and Jewish family life.

CHAPTER TWO

Setting the Scene

The strongest proof that Yiddish authors were creating suicide victims according to a particular pattern emerges from a superficially surprising quarter: the least, rather than the most, sophisticated treatments of the subject. If works whose interest in suicide is clearly secondary nonetheless conform to an overall design, then the design itself must have considerable power.

This phenomenon is evident in two short works from turn-of-the-century Eastern Europe: *Fir doyres—fir tsavoes* [''*Four Generations—Four Wills*''] by Y. L. Peretz,[1] and Der Nister's *A tog-bikhl fun a farfirer* [''*A Seducer's Journal*''].[2] Peretz' story is a moral tale concerning the dangers of abandoning traditional Jewish values and practices. Der Nister's work, depicting the romantic, at times overwhelmed introspections of a young man about town, focuses more, perhaps, on criticizing an arguably bohemian life style. Nonetheless, it, too, implies that excessive freedom from restraint can only end badly.

These didactic goals notwithstanding, it would still be possible to create effective characters and describe their suicidal fantasies and behavior. The failure to do so is due in large measure to the quality of narrative distance that emerges from each work. In *Fir doyres—fir tsavoes* the vehicle of communication is a suicide note; in *A tog-bikhl fun a farfirer,* it is a series of journal entries. In both instances, the tone is thus confessional, virtually absent of dialogue, purposefully reflective rather than spontaneous, talky rather than deeply felt.

All the same, Peretz and Der Nister make plain the reasons for their characters' suicides. Moritz Bendetzon's son takes his life because he can find no niche, no woman, no activity for himself. The female lover of Der Nister's journal writer kills herself when, pregnant with his child, she discovers that he will not even acknowledge his paternity, let alone marry her. Moreover, in the case of Peretz' story, and probably despite his aim, an unmistakeable picture of early psychological deficit forms the center of young Moritz' malaise.

His is the last of four wills that comprise the story. A suicide note, it fulfills two roles—it is not only Moritz/*zun*'s final communication with the world, but also a kind of philosophical bequest. Peretz' device introduces Moritz/*zun*'s family even before the appearance of Moritz/*zun* himself. The progression is a predictable one: Reb Eliezer Khaykls and Reb Binyomin write pious, hortatory wills that revolve around the dispensation of books and charity, although Reb Binyomin's will is considerably more detailed, revealing his worry that he cannot trust his children to carry out their religious duties without very explicit instructions. Significantly, he warns his sons not to harbor strong desires for success in business, because "the greater the businessman, the lesser the Jew" (p. 237).

In the third generation, Moritz Bendetzon reveals that he has not followed his father's advice. He has indeed become a *groyser soykher* ["great businessman"] and a *klenerer yid* ["smaller Jew"]. Yet his will, despite its composition in Polish rather than Hebrew, indicates that Moritz still retains the desire to keep his wealth within the Jewish community, even though his bequests are to institutions rather than individuals and thus signify a break in the chain of direct inheritance. Of primary importance in this document is the fact that Moritz has changed his name to make it more European-sounding. However, obviously unwilling to abandon his heritage entirely, he has compromised, maintaining the patronymic concept in a translated form and refashioning his father's name, Binyomin, into Bendet. Perhaps most suggestive of the conflict-laden environment in which he lived and raised his son is the juxtaposition of two provisions in Moritz' will: (1) he sets aside money to ensure that *kadesh* ["Kaddish," the mourning prayer for the dead] will be said for him, and (2) he stipulates that his business in the future be called *Moritz Bendetzon-zayn zun* ["Moritz Bendetzon—his son"].

These instructions are much harsher than his own father's warnings, for whereas Reb Binyomin's admonition had left his son's dignity and independence unchallenged, Moritz Bendetzon's words are insulting and condescending. The father assumes that his son is too untrustworthy or vindictive to perform the basic filial obligation of reciting kadesh and, in essence, he removes the privilege from him. Worse than that, his business bequest, although superficially generous, serves to divest the younger Moritz of his very name. Thus, the father's final legacy to his son is rejection, ambiguously stated.

By the time Moritz/*zun* introduces himself through his suicide note, his milieu has been fairly well delineated. Raised within a collapsing framework, he bears some inevitable scars. There has been nothing in this man's life that he considers valuable. He blames his wealth for the too-easy acquisition of material possessions as well as for the elusiveness of deep personal connections. Without his surveillance, even without his desire, that fortune had continued to multiply like a cancer, constantly exacerbating his condition. And at bottom he was miserable because, in his estimation, too little had been required of him. His life had not contained the adversity that sparks the average human being: "often my heart cried within me: let me lack something, let me be *forced* to do something" (p. 239).

Moritz/*zun*'s perceptions are, to be sure, the understandable result of an economic and social situation that leaves him hungry for meaningful action. At the same time, however, his emptiness and frustration are signs of an individual wanting in self-esteem and inner vitality. His wealth seems destructive because it is one more instance where he cannot manifest his autonomy. It is as if the elder Bendetzon, reaching from beyond death, continues to infantalize his son.

Even the opportunity for gratification afforded by travel and education is experienced by Moritz/*zun* as a blight, for it merely intensifies his feeling of displacement: "and I saw many countries, and not a single one was mine; I admired many places, and I didn't love a single place . . ." (p. 240). In essence, Moritz/*zun* is a man who neither knows where he belongs, nor where he *should* belong. He puts it somewhat differently in his note, but his meaning is clear: "There was no world I could control . . . and that which I could have controlled, I found ready made; it had been left to me . . ." (p. 240).

Clearly, Moritz/*zun*'s rootlessness and lack of mastery are internal experiences, whatever external stimuli strengthen them. Thus, while he—and Peretz as well—explain them as consequences of soft modern living, there is a psychological side as well, based on his sensation that he does not truly, or fully, exist. This deep void within him, not the surrounding milieu itself, causes his isolation. He says as much himself, although, characteristically, he sees his unhappiness as a further sign of worthlessness:

> Everything—the smile on my friend's face, the kiss of red lips . . . the *kadesh* for my father . . . at best I paid for things; but giving, donating, this I was not taught . . . (p.240).

Moritz/*zun* suffers from his inability to establish satisfying relationships with others. He is too empty himself to give to anyone else, but he is also too abject to ask for, and accept, friendship and love. Thus, he skims the surface of his life, buffeted by what to him are uncontrollable forces. Certainly, he has not managed to marry and therefore cannot compose the sort of will left behind by his father, grandfather, and great-grandfather. In this way alone, Moritz/*zun*'s suicide note underscores the reason for its existence. By its departure from the legacies of the younger Bendetzon's predecessors, the note reveals that its author has much to leave, but no one to whom to bequeath it.

If Moritz/*zun* feels none of life's tumult, the unnamed woman who takes her life in *A tog-bikhl fun a farfirer* dies after plunging into the fray more deeply than she is able to tolerate. Her affair with the author of the journal is brief: their entire relationship spans from the beginning of April until July 20. The story's protagonist presents himself immediately as a ladies' man, albeit at first publicly shy towards—even intimidated by—the young woman who has been in his circle for several months and whom he has just begun to notice.

The budding romance is duly recorded, along with lengthy, metaphoric effusions about the weather. Over and over, the young man refers to his new flame as *eydl* ["refined''], *zoyber* [''clean, tidy''] and *reyn* [''clean, chaste'']. And yet, from the very beginning, something calculated protrudes from these apparently innocent remarks:

> She must live with genteel parents and belong to a well-regarded and pedigreed family. One can see it: something out of the ordinary—pure and refined. She must, moreover, be the child of older parents (that's what I want . . .) Oh, what softness and flexibility in a body . . . It's not a body—it's a violin! (p.45).

As the attachment between the couple grows, so does the sexual tension. The narrator expresses his joy as the two begin to hold hands and, finally, to kiss. The woman now visits him daily at dusk. It is late May and early June. In the midst of this increasing happiness, however, the narrator notes in his journal that he had interrupted the gentle tryst of a young couple talking at the well outside his window. Distressed, they had hastily parted, and he had understood the cruelty behind what, for him, had begun as the desire to play a little prank.

Clearly, then, the young man's affectionate feelings are accompanied, as well, by opportunism and a certain sadism, at least with respect to lovers other than himself. Thus, his subsequent behavior comes as no great surprise, for his ability to love fully has been questionable from the outset. The drama begins with the young woman's absence for three days in early June. Then there is an entry, on June 7, that clarifies her temporary disappearance as an attempt to master her passion and her return as the failure to do so.

The narrator recounts how, on the previous day, he had stood at his window, watching a violent storm. The young woman had appeared in the street, battling the weather as she negotiated her ways towards him, her body outlined against her rain-and-wind-swept dress:

> A wild storm of desire overtook me . . . my knees began to tremble and seemed to give way beneath me. She entered . . . We absorbed each other with a youthful storm of frenzy . . . and, without words or strength, fell upon the bed . . .

> The outdoors rested after the storm. Quietly, without speaking, she went out into the darkness (p.54).

The woman had returned to her lover for more exchanges of sexual intimacy, but, although she continued to abandon herself with him, he had found her distant, as if soul and body were disconnected one from the other. The union falters as she becomes increasingly miserable and he cools towards her when he can no longer stand her tears. The narrator records the first major breach in behavior on July 10: "During the entire time that she usually comes to me, I was not at home yesterday . . . How she looked at me today!" (p.56). There is no further entry until July 20, which describes the couple's last encounter. The narrator coyly omits the woman's words to him, as she sits dry-eyed on his bed and talks to him in a strange voice. Yet the implication of her message is clear, as is the devastating impact of his own response to her pleading question as to what they must do now: "I don't understand what has happened. What is *my* part in this?" (p.56).

The two never see one another again. The young man, in a cold continuation of his post-conquest withdrawal, does not—or cannot—miss his suffering lover. Eventually, he learns, via a neighbor gossiping to his landlady, that she has killed herself.[3] The final entry of the journal finds him making plans to move to a new apartment, telling himself that his wish to find new lodgings stems from practical considerations, rather than from the new way his landlady has begun looking at him. This last disavowal of his feelings merely accentuates the narrator's pattern of cutting himself off from any true experience of sadness, vulnerability, or, for that matter, love.

A tog-bikhl fun a farfirer differs in an important way from *Fir doyres—fir tsavoes*: in Der Nister's story, the narrator observes the increasing despair of someone else, albeit someone he purports to have known well. More significant, however, is the element the two works have in common. For, despite the explicit suicide that ends a life in each case, the stories both announce the act, rather than providing the kind of psychological exposition that would render the deed inevitable or even expected. To be sure, a pregnant young woman's suicide makes sense, as does the self-inflicted death of a man who has had everything in life but love. Yet in neither instance does the decision emerge from the integration of personality and experience. Rather, it is imposed from the outside, because the plot of the story requires such action.

This external authorial device is more easily observed in *A tog-bikhl fun a farfirer,* because the woman is secondary to the narrator, whose emotions and thoughts are central to the story. She never comes alive, serving instead as a foil for his behavior and ideas. Therefore, her existence is limited to those occasions when the narrator chooses to mention her; she has no autonomous motivations at all, let alone suicidal ones.[4]

The same is certainly not true of *Fir doyres—fir tsavoes,* where Moritz/*zun* speaks for himself and explains why it is that he needs to die. Thus, what he says and how he says it emerge as the central probable reasons for the failure of this story to move and convince. The problem with Moritz/*zun*'s suicide note is that it is too neat, too well-composed—in a word, too comprehensible. As the thanatologist Edwin Shneidman puts it:

> In order to commit suicide, one cannot write a meaningful suicide note; conversely, if one could write a meaningful note, one would not have to commit suicide.[5]

From the very outset of his note, Moritz/*zun*'s words are measured and reasonable:

> I 'Moritz Bendetzon-son' am quitting the world, not out of joy, nor out of heartache, but out of emptiness (p.239).

After this initial announcement, he goes on to comment: "Aristotle was a great sage; nature abhors a vacuum" (p. 239). Immediately thereafter he continues:

> The world is a terrible machine. Each little wheel has its own task, its own purpose. If it becomes ruined, or it is used up before its time, it leaves the machine of its own accord, it goes from something into nothingness (p.239).

This exaggeratedly logical, abstract discussion of emotions is not unusual in a person attempting to defend against inner chaos, when it threatens to overwhelm. In this case, however, Moritz/*zun* has given in to the collapse of internal meaning. He is without power, without a sense of himself. He is hardly involved with trying to hold himself together and continue limping through life. The discrepancy between his supposed emotional state and his patient, careful message causes the suicide itself to appear distant and literary.[6]

The characters who commit suicide in *Fir doyres—fir tsavoes* and *A tog-bikhl fun a farfirer* do so because they are alone within themselves. Moritz/*zun* is unable to escape his hopeless morass of self-deprecation and emptiness. The young diarist's lover knows that she cannot bear her child in solitude, rejected by him. If the stories lack vitality, it is not because these figures fail to suffer. Rather, they have been created as metaphors, powerful images of society gone awry. Although they may have tried, neither author manages to step inside the suicidal mind. In the pages to follow, this limitation will become ever more obvious, as authors—including Peretz himself—struggle to describe the kind of lives that bring individuals to the point of self-destruction.

CHAPTER THREE

The Women

Felye

Felye Faynshteyn, the protagonist of H.D. Nomberg's *Shvayg, shvester* [''*Be Silent, Sister''*][1], is an unusual Yiddish literary suicide. For, unlike virtually all the other characters who kill themselves, Felye—and *Shvayg, shvester* itself—is concerned almost entirely with the issue of whether or not to take this decisive action, rather than with the events that may lead to self-destruction. Perhaps as a consequence, there is not much information in this work about Felye's early existence. Nonetheless, even without such data, the story makes clear her unhappy family life, the hatred she bears towards her own sexuality, and the direct connection between these two factors and her suicide.

The very first line of Nomberg's story reads: ''Felye Faynshteyn always kept a little bottle of cyanide with her'' (p.91). The reason for this strange form of self-defense is at first revealed obliquely:

> Some years previously, the last time she had been so terribly tricked and so deeply insulted, she had decided firmly that—enough! She could no longer endure the eternal torment; with her own hands she would have to break the chain of suffering that would continue to stretch unceasingly as long as she lived (p.91).

Evidently no longer able to endure her unhappiness, Felye had once prepared herself for death; she had written a suicide note and arranged herself in bed, the poison lifted to her lips.

But at that very point, at the moment of relinquishing her life, she had experienced the opening of a new, protective world—that of death as a safety valve:

> . . . in the mystical brightness of her head a clear thought slowly sketched itself: "I am dying peacefully, happily and with joy." And onto this thought a new one spun itself. "If one can die so peacefully and happily, what's so frightening about life? Why hurry?" (p.94).

From then on, she had found comfort in the notion that she could, at any time, choose to destroy herself. This thought was more than the memory of a mystical experience for Felye; it provided her with a sense that she was extraordinary, even unique, that she had perceived the essence of life, that she was powerful. Having discovered the juncture at which life and death are one, she had gained the courage to live, because her suffering had suddenly acquired a new dimension of meaning.

Thus, with her feelings of violation and outrage lulled, Felye was able to continue living, but her self-control was precarious, necessitating that she rigidly monitor her behavior. To others, this effort appeared as a mysterious listlessness, a demeanor that suggested a person burdened by some enormous secret tragedy:

> In her presence, people moved sedately and spoke softly. Anyone who laughed was shocked by his own voice . . . her simple speech about simple homey things made a peculiar impression, as if beneath it were hidden some great secret (p.95).

More important, Felye was forced to conceal certain things from herself as well as from others: her sexuality, her desire for love, her need for the warmth and support of family. In part by dressing with special care and by strictly censoring her reading, she had, indeed, managed to achieve this self-avoidance temporarily:

> She did not like colorful clothing; she herself wore either black or—at home—white; she had so cleverly patterned her blouses and covered them with folds that they concealed her

> bosom; and there were all sorts of novels and love poems which she could not bear because they made a revolting impression upon her, as if someone had handled a holy object with shameless vulgar hands (p.96).

Not even at home had Felye been able to relinquish or modify her aura of aloofness, separating herself, instead, from her mother and her younger sister, Anna:

> She became a stranger in the house. Neither her ailing mother nor her sister spoke a superfluous word to her . . . (p.95).

On the few occasions when she had felt obliged to summon up speech—as, for example, upon encountering her sister engaged in a fit of distressed weeping—her words were phatic, cool, peculiarly incongruous: "Only seldom did it happen that she sat down next to her sister, stroked her hair, and asked how late it was" (p.96).

Ironically, her relationship with her sister, and the concomitant emergence of feelings she cannot tolerate, finally pushes Felye over the edge. The problem begins with her perception that her younger sister—a beautiful and successful young woman—is nonetheless enduring the same romantic misery as she herself had suffered. She finds the resurfacing of buried hurt nearly unbearable—but, at first, not sufficient to encourage more than a flirtation with suicide.

Then Felye does something that she had heretofore avoided: she confides in Anna. She confesses that the dreadful insult had occurred when a boyfriend, the latest in a series of unsatisfactory suitors, had suddenly embraced and kissed her in a taxi while taking her home. The next day, Felye is found dead, having left behind an enigmatic message.[2]

In sharp contrast to Moritz/*zun*'s introductory words in *Fir doyres—fir tsavoes,* Felye makes her point with agonizing directness:

> I am dying, sister. Actually I died long ago (p.100).

After stating that she is dying by choice and wishing her sister well, Felye continues:

> If you ever happen to suffer as much as I have, tell no one of your suffering. Guard it in your heart, so that it is hidden and holy, and be silent, sister, be silent! . . . (p.100).

The key words in this note are *farborgn* [''hidden''] and ***heylik*** [''holy'']. In her lifetime, Felye had indeed attempted to rise above the ordinary, to be holy. But, as she unburdens herself to Anna, Felye's anguish pours forth not because the reliving of the carefully guarded secret had once again brought it to life, but rather, because in recounting the episode, she is forced to admit: ''This is foolish, banal'' (p.99). Such a bitter realization might have been enough to destroy the uncertain balance of her existence, her sense that she had captured the essence of life, and had thereby rendered herself unique and invulnerable, but there is an additional assault to the framework she has constructed: Anna understands her sister and wishes to commiserate. The collapse of Felye's world is now complete. Felye's response to the benevolent words of Anna is that they caused her to be ''deeply insulted,'' just as the boyfriend's kiss had done before. She is offended and infuriated by what she assumes is a suggestion that her misery is commonplace. Unable to endure the reality that she has invented her defilement, that in fact her original agitation had stemmed from her ambivalent feelings about the embrace and that, in her conflict, she is not perfectly pure but rather perfectly human, Felye goes through with her self-destruction.

Felye's suicide note contains another important clue to her emotional state at the end of her life. This is her instruction that should her sister ever suffer as much as she, Felye, has, she should cover up her pain. Here, Felye seeks to regain and maintain a sense of superiority over her younger sister. In one statement she both denies the possibility that her sibling had been capable of comprehending her plight and empathizing with her and establishes herself as her sister's future guide, even after death. Thus Felye, who has been unable to see beyond one narrow aspect of life, that is, whether or not her unique purity has been attacked, manages to right things for herself once again—but this time she has to die in order to do so.

In the end, the cause of Felye's tragedy is that she could not accept herself as a sexually approachable woman. Her self-constraints expose the fact that she was not unaware of erotic excitement; instead, she was terrified of it and needed to avoid it at all costs. When it had once—or on one final occasion—burst through her defenses, she had wanted to die rather than live with herself under such circumstances. Her reprieve was the fantasy that, indeed, she was asexual, holy, even ghost-like. But once reminded that she is, after all, a woman like her sister—albeit incapable of enjoying that reality—she is engulfed with rage at both her sister and herself. Viewed in this light, Felye's suicide is a final attack of her own sexuality and, by dint of her suicide note, that of her sister as well.[3]

Esther

At first blush, Esther, the protagonist's daughter in Dovid Bergelson's *Der toyber* [''*The Deaf Man*'']{4} seems like a guilt-ridden woman. Specifically, her guilt—and her shame—stems from the fact that she has indulged her sexual impulses without the sanction of marriage. It is Esther's misfortune to work as a cook for the same mill owners who employ and exploit her father. When she enters into a liaison with the son of the house, that relationship causes her to become the butt of crude amusement among the other workers. Her position, plus the implication that she is pregnant, apparently lead directly to her suicide.

A closer look, however, reveals that the deeper tragedy for Esther is not her immediate plight but rather her father's failure to respond to her cry for help. Esther is a shadowy figure, presented through the haze of her father's deafness and difficulty in communicating coherently. Since early childhood and the death of her mother, he has been her only parental tie. He, and therefore his opinion of her, are thus of particular significance. *Der toyber* catalogues, not Esther's concerns about her sexuality, but rather her father's obsession with that issue. Unable to view her as his frightened and needy child, he talks to her vaguely about Mendl Bik, the mill-owner's son, and shows disapproval over her marriage prospects when she informs him of a humiliating proposal she has received via a matchmaker. It is after this last conversation that Esther, evidently convinced that she can never regain dignity, even—or especially—with her father, takes her own life.

The deaf man is an isolated and distant individual. Near the beginning of *Der toyber,* he is injured in a work-related fall. This casualty exacerbates what had already been a state of decline; he never fully recovers his health, and his hearing loss becomes increasingly debilitating.[5] He has no friends, almost no contact with others. Moreover, the accident precipitates an inundating depression:

> On his own, it seemed, he no longer thought about life or death, [he] lay in bed with an indifferent and pale face . . . It seemed by now to be all the same, whether or not he ever got up from bed again (pp.120–121).

Esther seems to need him most during just this period, yet he fails to buttress her. Quite the contrary, he lets her down miserably on several occasions; after three unsatisfying encounters with him, she resorts to suicide.

Even beforehand, however, the father had learned that Esther was in danger. *Der toyber* opens with the sentence:

> At the beginning of Autumn, something once again occurred between Mendl, Vove Bik's tall and handsome son, and Esther, the deaf man's twenty-two year old daughter (p.113).

Subsequently, he witnesses others making fun of Esther behind her back and discovers, through a local busybody, that Esther is in love with Mendl. The narrative voice[6] explains that:

> He had in mind to go there to her, to Bik's kitchen, and to tell her something necessary. But exactly at that time the dismal accident happened to him. Apparently, it was already destined that way (p.117).

The deaf man's faltering and inactivity are not anomalous; in fact, they characterize the general flavor of his relationship with his daughter. Each time they meet, he attempts to mention something to her but is unable to articulate what he would like her to know. Instead, he treats her with silence or thinly coated disdain.

The first instance occurs soon after his accident. Esther calls on him, wearing a new jacket, looking at him through eyes recently grown darker and more serious. During the visit, she bursts out crying and although he finally realizes that he wants to warn her against unrealistic hopes, he does not relay this to her. Esther leaves in despair, smacking her lips together "as if with that smacking she wanted to say: 'Not much of a father . . . whose advice she will hear here' " (p.122).

Nonetheless, Esther comes to her father again, this time attempting to convince the people attending to him—in his own home—that he deserves better care. The deaf man lies in bed, thinking once more of the important matter he wants to discuss with her. What comes out instead is a vague allusion to his dead wife, a comment he immediately regrets because he realizes that Esther will not be comforted by the notion that only someone she has never known can come to her aid. And, indeed, this is exactly Esther's reaction:

> She looked at him with such wonder, as if she wanted to ask him: 'What use is she now, that dead mother in the old cemetery?' (p.124).

Matters go from bad to worse. When Esther offers her father some butter cake that she has baked, he accepts, reciprocating with a double message: "Bik knows what's good." And, finally, he formulates what he had wanted to say in the first place. Referring to the original rumor, according to which some employees had approached the Bik house, intending to attack Mendl for firing them, and had "noticed something," he claims:

> It's wrong . . . what the workers saw that night . . . And what else? He doesn't believe them, not Bik and not that son of his. He doesn't believe them at all (p.124).

In this way, the deaf man compounds the insult he had inflicted with his comment about Esther's butter cake. There, he had used ambiguity to slight her; here it is halfhearted denial. But in both cases he manages to avoid noticing Esther's obvious and desperate need of support.

The last time father and daughter meet, he has gone to visit her at Bik's house, planning to ask her "a necessary thing." But, when he arrives, he sees Mendl hurrying from a corner of the kitchen. He loses his train of thought and "in his deaf head a suspicion rambled around: 'Mendl is an ugly fellow . . . really an ugly fellow' " (p.126). On this occasion, Esther feeds her father a potato and announces that the matchmaker has been to call. For the first time since his accident, the deaf man revives, only to wilt again when he learns who has been proposed. He counters, using the same adjective that had come to his mind about Mendl: "But that's a very ugly match . . ." Esther concurs: "Yoylik is a scoundrel . . . An Odessa scoundrel." Yet, instead of comforting her, Esther's father munches his potato, addressing what will be his final words to her: "Yes, yes, a scoundrel . . . definitely a scoundrel" (p.127).

After this unfortunate example of disharmony the deaf man dreams:

> He is looking out of the highest window of the mill and sees Mendl in the courtyard, chasing the non-Jewish woman who cleans the office. She is running away in fear, falls on the ice and is afraid; any minute Mendl will catch her. And to the side stands Schultz, the miller, holding his sides and laughing as he shouts: "Catch her! . . . catch, catch!" And suddenly he, the deaf man, sees that Mendl is not running after the non-Jewish woman who cleans the office, but after his Esther. He is actually gripped with horror. Esther, fleeing, stretches out her arms and screams in fear. If he weren't deaf, he would hear a heartrending scream (p.127–128).

By morning, according to the narrator, the dream has been forgotten, although the deaf man learns, from his tenant, that he had roared in his sleep. When he gets up and goes out, it is only to discover that Esther is dead.

The deaf man's dream is pivotal to understanding the complicated sort of relationship he maintains with his daughter, since it provides clues to issues he cannot face in his waking life.[7] The manifest content, the plot part of the dream that can be related like a story, contains numerous elements taken almost without distortion from the dreamer's experience. When he had noticed the other workers making fun of Esther, he had been looking out of a window on the top floor of the mill; Schultz had been with Mendl and had made a crude gesture at Esther's expense; later, the deaf man had remembered a "joint sin" committed by Mendl and Schultz, involving a pregnant, non-Jewish woman from a neighboring village.

Why is it, however, that the deaf man does not remember his dream the next day? The answer to this lies in the latent content, in the aspects of the dream that require interpretation because they have to do with deeply buried yet significant material. Perhaps the most obvious feature of the dream, one never expressed by the deaf man in his waking life, concerns the extent to which he sees his daughter as a victim of the Bik family. He identifies with her; thus, just as she screams when she is chased and about to be harmed, so, too, does he scream in his sleep (and so, too, was he physically hurt because of the Biks). In this way he seems to admit—in his unconscious—that she is innocent; in any case, the wish is evident that she be as blameless in her suffering as he believes himself to be in his.

At the same time, however, the deaf man denies the connection between the two of them and instead views Esther as a non-Jewish woman, someone quite alien to himself and his way of life. Furthermore, by introducing a new version of his waking reality, i.e., a non-Jewish woman but not a pregnant one, he may be expressing his fear that Esther is indeed pregnant, something completely inimical to his expectations of her, something he wants to push away.

The issue of Esther's sexuality is central to the attitude her father takes towards her. This, too, is revealed through his dream, where he is watching, not a love affair, but rather a scene of explicit violence and lust. His reaction to seeing her pursued is one of horror, perhaps indicating not only his sympathy for her, but also his inadvertent recognition of her sexuality. This interpretation is reinforced by two factors: (1) the deaf man does not hear his daughter scream, and (2) he neither remembers his dream nor is able to discuss Esther's straits with her directly and sympathetically, choosing instead to deprecate her obliquely. The failure to hear Esther's scream, although Schultz's taunts are distinctly audible to him, may be explained as the deaf man's inability to accept that Esther's response to Mendl might have contained some desire on her own part. Moreover, he, the father, cannot tolerate the voyeuristic pleasure he experiences by observing her in this activity. It is simply too exciting for him and causes the abrupt end of his dream. The reason that Esther's father is incapable of clear thoughts about his daughter's situation thus appears to be at least twofold, perhaps threefold: he identifies with her as a maligned individual; he finds contemplating her as sexually active unendurable, since she has chosen to do it in a manner unbecoming of a good Jewish daughter and with a man whose values he despises; he cannot abide her behavior because it dangerously arouses him.

The deaf man's reaction to Esther's death, and the little that is revealed about his relationships with other women, suggest that his anger at female sexuality and its power over him is pervasive and deeply rooted. This is not to deny the aspect of his rage and misery that grows out of his moral beliefs; nor should his desire to avenge the insult inflicted upon his family be ignored—the narrative is both too complex and too veiled to allow for that. Rather, his behavior must be viewed from the perspective of where and how he expends most of his energy.

The deaf man cannot cry when he sees his daughter's corpse, although he resists being separated from her and begins to drag her with him when he is forced to leave Bik's house. Suddenly, though, he sees someone at the door of the kitchen and remembers "the dream, the courtyard of the mill, Mendl, the non-Jewish woman, and Esther" (p.131). Abruptly, he relinquishes the plankboards holding Esther's body and runs off, without pursuing any definite destination. The next day, however, there is evidence of his whereabouts during the previous night:

> That was so strange and wild.
>
> At the Bik household they had forgotten to drive the cow into the stable for the night, so they found her very early the next morning with her tail cut off, outside near the courtyard door . . .

> The tail had been chopped off high up near the back. Drops of blood still dripped from the wounded spot (p. 131).

While the deaf man's act is clearly vengeful, it is also violent in a specifically sexual way—a symbolic castration of his daughter, who had punished him with her choice of a lover and then compounded the insult by abandoning him. As a retroactive retaliation, it ensures that the cow will never be whole again, that she will never be perfect before a bull, i.e., ***bik*** (the Yiddish word for bull). The choice of Bik's cow helps the wrathful attacker assail his enemies while releasing his fury at Esther.

The deaf man's symbolic action is not a direct reverberation of his daughter's suicide. Rather, it is a response to her sexuality. This is the greater of two evils for him. Unable to mourn her death when confronted with it, the deaf man nevertheless wants to keep her with him. Only after he remembers his forgotten dream does he run away from her and perpetrate a deed that he could not, and no doubt would not, have inflicted on her personally. The dream brings back to him the realization of Esther's conduct and, now admitting it to consciousness for the first time, he punishes her. After he has vented his ire at her, he is then able to menace the Bik family—and, interestingly, he turns to the elder Bik, his own exploiter, as his target.

It takes several weeks before the deaf man surfaces as a suspect in the crime against the Biks' cow. By this time, he is in a state of severely diminished psychic organization, pondering long and hard before arriving at the formulation that Bik, who has been much on his addled mind, is "a rich pig" (p. 136). Going to Bik's house, he stands in the dark corridor, watching a motionless beam of light from the kitchen, almost as if hoping vainly for some comfort from his lost daughter; he had accepted that aspect of her personality. The realization of his bereavement helps a bit. Whereas he had previously recalled the tragedy in a confused and fragmentary fashion, he is now more lucid:

> Now he remembers that he had been at Bik's house, and seen him quite close up.

> And he remembers, furthermore: he is a deaf man, a Jew and a porter, who once had a wife, Leah, and a daughter—Esther (p.138).

Matters do not improve, however, as a result of this insight. He continues to hound Bik, whose family is frightened, and with good reason: the deaf man has been found lying in the snow, holding an ax, and someone has been observed climbing over Bik's fence late at night.

In the end, the deaf man combines his angers one last time, revealing again the depth and nature of his response to Esther. One night, his instability exacerbated by insomnia, he experiences a misperception born out of his own desires, a hallucination of wish-fulfillment; unable to sleep, he looks out his window:

> . . . a melancholy and unhappy cow was standing there looking in. Soon he recognized the cow. 'Vove Bik's cow . . .' (p.146).

The next day he is found dead, having killed not Bik's cow but someone else's.

Several aspects of this final episode in the deaf man's life stand out as curious: the projection of his own feelings onto the cow; the delusion that the animal belongs to Bik; his need to slaughter the cow. And, of course, he himself perishes, although the cause of death remains unclear.

Assuming that no act is unmotivated, although it may sometimes appear to be so, there are at least two plausible aims underlying the deaf man's action. Of these, the more obvious is a desire to chastise his daughter once again, while at the same time harming Bik. Implicit in this notion is the father's attempt to deny his daughter's suicide while simultaneously asserting his control over her; that is, on some level she is still alive to him, still punishable for her behavior. The second goal is more complicated than the first, but not inimical to it. It rests on the possibility that the deaf man has combined aspects of both himself and Esther in his vision of the cow. By killing that cow, he not only murders those common qualities but achieves a wished-for reunion with his daughter as well. These deep motivations would hardly be conscious, but the deaf man's subsequent death strengthens the likelihood that, despite his unacceptable aggression, he has acted—or given up—in order to achieve such a reunion.

The deaf man's physical violence towards females is not unprecedented. On one occasion after his accident, for example, he tries to attract the attention of his tenant, but the latter deliberately ignores him and his frantic attempts to appear pitiful to her. He entertains the fantasy of tripping her in order to be noticed, and imagines her amazement at realizing that he is even alive. This experience of non-recognition brings to mind a memory of his wife:

> That was how he used to look angrily and mutter at his wife Leah. Then, out of spite, she used to go to bed with her clothes on and then in response he would grab the plate of food from the table and suddenly hurl it onto the ground (p.123).

His fury at not being heeded is thus directly related to his sexual demands; he is angrily frustrated at being denied both kinds of comfort.[9]

Later, the link between rage and sexuality is reiterated in an unusual way. When the Bik family finally begins to suspect the deaf man of having mutilated their cow, others agree that there is something perverse and savage about him:

> Once the old clothes dealer's emaciated wife annoyed him, so he threw one of his boots at her head, then grabbed her beds, tables and benches and angrily hurled them outside (p.132).

To those speculating, this anecdote provides sufficient proof that the deaf man would be capable of maiming an animal as well. Their judgment is based on the connection they discern between the deaf man's violence and its outlet on female objects.

A pattern emerges: the deaf man feels a certain need for solicitude, which is somehow connected as well to sexual longing, at least insofar as it, too, remains ungratified. His outlet is aggression against those who seem capable of giving so much, yet provide so little.[10] He experiences these sensations, not only towards his wife and his tenant (with whom the sexual aspect appears submerged), but also—and perhaps especially—towards his daughter. Esther had taken it upon herself to help feed and care for him. Her death is, then, the removal of nourishment from his life. Furthermore, she had behaved in such a way as to inflame the sexual component of his response—thus the stimulus behind his symbolic castration of her. These factors help explain why the deaf man would both attempt to merge with the symbol of his child and at the same time murder it: the desire to regain a former state of closeness is mixed with rage at its absence in the present; in addition, the incestuous implication of that desire is unacceptable and must therefore he denied, even if it means destroying what he loves most.[11]

These possibilities shed light on Esther's tragedy because, despite her vague delineation as a character, she does take a lover, react to her father—and commit suicide. To the extent that she acts, her motives are open to investigation. Moreover, given her obvious, if problematic, bond with her father, some relation between his influence and her behavior must be expected.

Perhaps the most striking element of Esther's conduct is her romance with Mendl Bik. He is, of course, an attractive and powerful figure, one whose attentions or manipulations would likely be difficult to refuse. There is more to the story, however, because Mendl is also the scion of the family that has oppressed and maltreated her father for twenty years. The deaf man is filled with envy of the Bik family, coveting their luxury:

> . . . [he] thought that he, the deaf man, liked warmth, he also liked the head of a fish, hot fresh *khale* and a bit of fatty meat, the same fatty meat that Bik had once eaten right in front of him (p.128).

He feels weak and helpless before them, as evidenced in his conviction that he cannot succeed in gaining any compensation for his accident at the mill. Urged by the interfering Yosele to sue Bik, his response is:

> Bik . . . is so big and he, the deaf man, is so little . . . really little. Certainly the big one will be victorious over the little one (p.125).

Both envy and the sense of impotence are present when, eating Esther's butter cake, he comments that Bik knows what is good.

Esther nonetheless chooses to involve herself with Mendl. In part this may represent an attempt to achieve some of the material benefits that she has been denied because of the deaf man's poverty: now she can boast a new jacket when she comes to visit her father. At the same time, Mendl represents the very substance of her family's misfortune and degradation. By preferring to align herself with the Biks, for whom her father has toiled since she was a small child, she expresses her rejection of his essence and her own heritage.

Yet, however much she tries to escape, Esther remains ultimately dependent upon her father for solace and sheer acceptance. It is to him that she turns in the end, whatever role Mendl may have played in her misery and thoughts of suicide. The deaf man is unavailable, mainly because he himself requires so much care. Moreover, subject as he is to fits of violence when his needs are not satisfied, he would not have been much comfort to her even if she could have forced him to acknowledge her condition—as his subsequent attack on Bik's cow corroborates.

The deaf man's failure to ease Esther's agonized sense of doom is apparent in the near paralysis that characterizes every interaction between the two. This tragic disharmony is highlighted during their final meeting where, perhaps hoping against hope that her father will have a resourceful response to her wretched marriage proposal, she is once again forced to watch him eat her food and refuse her any sympathy whatsoever. In this larger context of empty gestures and isolation, Esther's suicide gains clarity as the act of someone who finds herself completely adrift, without a viable future, and finally denied even the limited support of which her father might have been capable.

Manye

Manye, in Y. L. Peretz' *Zindik blut* [''*Sinful Blood*''][12] bears a peculiar relationship to Bergelson's Esther.

Manye's situation—and her position in Peretz' story—differs on the surface from that of Esther. While still a school girl, she had encouraged a seductive flirtation with a teacher. When the adventure culminates in virtual rape, she runs away from home to sink into her iniquity, to become, literally, the property of men. She does not, however, commit suicide at this point. As she explains in the first person, epistolary narrative that Peretz employs, she takes her life only when she realizes that, at her death, she will be forgiven her sins by the Catholic Church, to which she has converted. Needing to ensure eternal damnation, she takes exactly the step cited by the church as uniquely unpardonable.

Part of the distinction between Manye and Esther is narrative: much less of Manye's conscious experience has to be inferred, since she reveals herself in the first person. Furthermore, although both works contemplate female sexuality, it is not possible to discern how Esther feels about Mendl or, for that matter, about men in general. She never says anything to shed light on the matter and she interacts directly only with her father. Manye, in contract, both expresses herself on the subject and reinforces her statements with action.

Despite these variations, however, Manye and Esther have one vital experience in common, and it is the most striking aspect of their tragedy: they both desperately seek parental help in a moment of crisis and fail to receive essential comfort and support.

The physical deserter in Manye's life had been her father, and, from the very beginning of *Zindik blut* it is clear that she has a good deal of hostile feeling towards men. When she asks for paper in order to write down her story, for example, her favorite nurse in the sanatorium where she is hospitalized for syphilis asks whether she is writing to a fiance. Manye replies that she views all men with equal fondness, then thinks to herself:

> Men only like things that are made up. If I have no one to speak to, let me for once write a word of truth about myself (p.25).

A little later, while she is recounting her sexual exploits to the titillated nurse, the latter implies that the tale must be fabricated. Denying this, Manye comments:

> I will not tell you any lies, nurse. Here, especially, I do not write or tell lies. Men make us into liars . . . (p.29).

Even the first sentence of the story exudes a sense of frustration and mistrust: "I have already been here for three days, and I still have yet to see a doctor" (p.24).

This first sentence provides an important clue to a critical issue in Manye's life, one that, more than any other, influences her reactions to men. She had never known her father, who had left home before she was born. Growing up betrayed and abandoned by the man who was to be her model of how to function with men, she cannot even be sure whether he is alive or dead. Not surprisingly, she decides that, in general, men dislike truth and cannot tolerate reality.

Not that Manye has ever forgotten her unknown father—in fact, she enjoys maligning him, or her notion of him. At the same time, she feels guilty because he is her parent and, even though she has never met him, she nonetheless identifies with him and sees him reflected in herself. Her tragic sense of connection with her father is outlined in the title of the story: she believes she has inherited his sinful blood. Manye's first perception of this unfortunate bond had occurred when she was still at school, beginning to fall in love, and had overheard the object of her affection discussing her with a friend of his:

> I heard the other one [the friend] say: 'Oh, do I love Manye!' He meant me, and the one whom I almost loved, answered: 'Well, the apple doesn't fall far from the tree' (p.28).

As a result of that experience, Manye had allowed herself to seduce and be seduced.

If Manye's father had appeared all bad to her—the epitome of evil—her mother, in sharp contrast, had seemed entirely good, even holy, incapable of a mistake or misstep. From her, Manye was convinced she had inherited her saintly face. Such is her idealization that even on her death bed, she fears mentioning her mother's name, lest it thereby be besmirched. Implied in this holiness is a denial of sexuality; small wonder, then, that after her encounter with the religion teacher, Manye had decided she could not go home. Certain that her sinfulness would be too much for her mother, she had run away. Before leaving, however, she had allowed herself to approach the house, where, through a window, she had observed her mother in prayer:

> Her lips certainly murmured: Papa-Father, merciful father, have mercy on us . . . have mercy, as a papa does with his child . . . Father in heaven . . . (p.30).

Unable to know for certain what her mother was saying, Manye had supplied the words as she imagined them. The reference to God as a father is not unusual in the Yiddish prayers traditionally recited by women.[13] Nonetheless, for Manye, the equation is more complicated. It suggests that her response both to God and to her father is an ambivalent mixture of hatred and disappointment, combined with the wish for protection. This is indeed the case.

Talking to her nurse about her illness, for example, Manye explains that, as a result of becoming sinful, she had sought God; her body may have been defiled, but she had wanted her soul to be pure. Despite the rejection of God by her peers and in her reading, she had clung to her Jewish faith:

> I began to pray, I observed all the fast days, on Yom Kippur I shut myself away, and didn't let anyone in . . . (p.27).

She had donated her clothes to other prostitutes, all the time praying only that she would not be afflicted with syphilis:

> Merciful Father, I am sinning, I have bad and sinful blood, punish me however you will, take me altogether, but not this, not this! (p.27).

Her supplication proving a failure, Manye registers her despair by railing against God. Yet, she cannot tolerate the loneliness of this position and turns her misfortune against herself, speculating that perhaps she is destined to be punished for having caused her mother to die of grief.

On another occasion, Manye recalls her life subsequent to leaving home and remembers being picked up by a strange man. She insists to the horrified nurse that he might have been her father, reasoning that, although he had attacked her sexually and ultimately sold her, he had nonetheless kept her for a time and nurtured her.

Manye's confessions have some makings of an unresolved oedipal struggle: the young woman's wish to be united sexually with her father, the fear that she has killed her mother, the ensuing guilt, terrible enough to require that the offender pay for her sins.[14] There is, however, another way of looking at the evidence which, while it does not preclude the presence of an oedipal conflict of some sort, nonetheless points elsewhere. Behind the young woman's seductive facade is an overwhelming need to be protected—not only from her sexuality, but, more importantly, from homelessness, death—above all, from her mother.[15]

Manye's thoughts about her father and about God occur at her moments of greatest isolation: when she has been sexually active, when she realizes that she cannot return home, when she is about to die and contemplates a reunion with her cold and distant mother. Each time, she longs for what she has never experienced before, a parental figure strong enough to counteract or neutralize the pain inflicted by her mother. It is almost irrelevant if cruelty or even taboo behavior accompany the attention. Manye is too desperate to care—anything is preferable to abandonment.

An inchoate acknowledgement that her mother neither understands her nor sympathizes with her lies at the root of Manye's idealization, which serves several purposes simultaneously. First, it is a way of splitting off the frightening rage she feels towards her mother for being so lacking in warmth and accessibility. Instead, she consciously experiences her mother as all good and her father as all bad. Second, this idealization helps her explain to herself why her mother is so remote. If there is something wrong with her—if she is capable of poisoning her mother's pure air with her sinful breath, as she imagines just before running away—then the anguish of her emotional deprivation need not stem from her mother's shortcomings. Thus she is spared the realization of how helplessly alone she really is.

Finally, by deciding that she is not worthy of being buried near her mother, Manye acts to avoid the superstitious possibility of being joined with her after death. By isolating herself, she need never confirm her suspicions about her mother: that the latter had been completely incapable of tolerating her sexuality and had indeed died because of it. After she had run away, Manye explains,

> She, my pious, holy one, found out, traced me, succumbed and died . . . / And she is buried in the cemetery here . . . / And I knew and I wasn't at her bedside . . . It was not I who shut her eyes . . . I didn't go to her funeral, I haven't seen her grave . . . / Couldn't, I can't, I mustn't! (p.31).

At the same time, Manye's neglect implies that, however unworthy she deems herself, she is also filled with unconscious anger towards her withholding and critical mother, therefore seeking to safeguard herself against an eternity of unhappy contact. Moreover, her vexation had been manifested long before, in the choice of her religion teacher as deflowerer. Beneath the conscious submission to her sinful blood, Manye had used this experience to convey two hidden ideas. First, her actions had proven that religious values did not prevent the simultaneous merciless exploitation of a younger and less powerful person. Manye's active seduction thus becomes a statement of outrage against her mother for her hypocrisy and harmful influence.[16] In this context, secondly, Manye's need to flee is motivated not only by her sense of worthlessness and miasma but also by her need to cast off a dreaded burden. For this reason, she refuses to communicate with her mother at the end of the latter's life and singlemindedly ensures that she is free of her forever, even after death.

Manye's tragedy is that, for as long as she lives, she carries her hurt and anger with her, no matter where she goes, and regardless of whether or not she has actual contact with her mother. She endures the impossible combination of attempting to establish a fantasy of a loving mother while at the same time protecting herself from the cruel aloofness that was reality. In the end, the struggle is too much for her, and she takes an overdose of morphine. This final act is not only a way of making certain that she will avoid any possible contact with her mother's peaceful and rewarded soul. It is also a defiant celebration of "sinful blood." Manye's last communication represents her catastrophic realization that a fantasy of the robust and involved father she has never known is ultimately easier to sustain than the dream of winning acceptance from an emotionally barren mother.

Shprintse

Sholem-Aleykhem's Shprintse, like the unnamed lover of *A tog-bikhl fun a farfirer,* appears only through the words of another character, in this case her father, Tevye the Dairyman. *Shprintse,* first published in 1907, recounts one of Tevye's greatest tragedies, the suicide of his beloved child.

The stories of *Tevye der milkhiker* ["*Tevye the Diaryman*"] were originally published over a period of twenty years, from 1895 to 1916.[17] Basically, they are vignettes portraying a poor—but not destitute—Jew who produces and delivers dairy products to wealthy people vacationing in the countryside. He is married to Golde, a fine Jewish wife who, remaining in the background (albeit vocally) most of the time, is nonetheless sorely missed by Tevye when she dies. Additionally, Tevye is blessed—though he considers it a mixed blessing—with seven daughters, and his interactions with five of them constitute the focus of his adventures. Their names: Tsaytl, Hodel, Khave, Shprintse, and Beylke. Tevye has two major problems: how, by means of dignified matches, to marry off his daughters; and how, without forfeiting their respect, to control them, for they have been raised by him to be willful and independent. The chief tension in the stories results from a merger of these two related concerns, as Tevye attempts to regulate, or at least understand, the love and marital choices made by his children.

Although the episode with Shprintse is self-contained and, in a way, separate from the other Tevye stories, it is also connected to the rest by dint of Tevye's unique monologue voice. In a manner reminiscent of psychoanalytic free association, Tevye meanders through the maze of his life, delivering his insights with verve and sensitivity. These stories, taken as a whole, reveal that Tevye, for all the kindness and interest he lavishes on his daughters, nonetheless fails to accept them unless they conform to certain implicit—and impossible—rules. Moreover, Shprintse's idea of committing suicide, while certainly not directly suggested to her by her father, is nonetheless made available to her by Tevye's unusually frequent references to death in general, and to suicide in particular.

Tevye talks compulsively about death. First, there are the indirect cases, in which he makes gratuitous or ironic mention of the subject, usually with reference to his own demise. At times, this is meant to be a joke, as when he says to himself: "Get up, kiss the *mezuze* [a small tube containing an inscribed strip of parchment, attached to the doorpost of premises occupied by observant Jews, and symbolically kissed by persons entering or leaving], slam the door and ***holokh leolomo,*** 'Went to his eternal home; died' . . ." i.e., leave without saying goodbye (p.184).[18] On other occasions, the humor barely covers Tevye's expression of anger and disappointment. One of the earliest instances of this appears in the story *Dos groyse gevins* ["*Grand Prize*"] where, speaking in a contemplative vein, he says: "A person toils, suffers; one might as well lie down and die—may it happen to the enemies of the Jews!" (p.15). Elsewhere he comments more directly about himself and his poverty:

> Did the world really care about him when he lay—God forbid, heaven preserve us, six feet in the ground, when he died

> three times a day of hunger, together with his wife and children? (pp.43–44).

At one point, lashing out at a relative who has just caused him to squander his nest egg, he pictures not only himself, but his entire family destroyed:

> I said, you took a whole house full of living creatures, pitiable innocent beings, poor things, and you slaughtered them without a knife (p.61).

These expressions may be understood merely as figures of speech; e.g., *koylen* "to slaughter" also has the meaning "to ruin"; but Tevye takes his words seriously enough to qualify them with such preventive formulae as "God forbid" or "heaven preserve." Somewhere, these comments assume their somber alternative, no matter how metaphoric he intends to be.

The phrase "lying in the ground," or "lying six feet in the ground" is particularly interesting, because Tevye uses it so often in his reflections, making it his response to a diversity of situations. Speaking to his tired horse, for example, he says: "I say: *shlimazl* ["unlucky creature"], crawl into the ground just like me, learn, too, what fasting on a long summer's day is like . . ." (p.18). On another occasion, Tevye asks for a reward that his donors find ludicrously modest: "And among the group there was so much laughter that I nearly buried myself in the ground" (p.32). When Tevye must decide whether or not he will allow himself to be shipped off to Palestine by his arriviste son-in-law, the literal and figurative definitions of this expression merge. Admitting that his wife is dead and that, therefore, he has no pressing reason to remain in Europe, Tevye muses:

> What are you establishing here and whom do you have here? Your Golde, may she rest in peace, is already lying in the ground anyhow, and you yourself, may it not be uttered, aren't you lying six feet in the ground? How long will you plod along in the world? (pp.185–186).

Yet, however playful Tevye's references to death and dying may sometimes be, they assume a different quality when he talks about his daughters. In those instances his utterances clearly go beyond mere figures of speech.

Although he adores his children, he is capable as well of implicating them in the death of their mother, not to mention laying at their feet his own expectations of a shortened life. At first, Tevye only hints at his offspring's guilt: "Let her [Golde] intercede in the other world for her daughters; she suffered enough for them, and maybe even left the world because of them, unable to stand the way they dispersed in every which direction" (p.168). Later, he becomes more direct, blaming his daughter Khave, who has converted in order to marry her non-Jewish lover, for causing Golde's death (p.219).

Tevye is more temperate when assessing his daughters' role in his own unhappiness. He tries, for instance, to keep his reaction to Khave's betrayal philosophical:

> Did Tevye have to be a classic Jew, made miserable all his life, plowing the earth with his nose, so to speak, raising children so that afterwards they would suddenly tear themselves away by force, falling away like a cone from a tree to be carried by wind and smoke? I think to myself: it's as if a tree grows, an oak in the forest, and then a creature with an axe comes along and removes one branch, and then another branch, and yet another branch. What is the poor tree without its branches? It would be better, you human being, to chop the tree down completely—and let that be the end of it. Why should a naked oak protrude in the forest? (p.136).

Tevye's meaning is clear: if my daughters insist upon straying from me, I might as well be dead myself. Moreover, in his misery about Khave, Tevye even contemplates taking his own life. As he puts it: "In short, when the holy book says: 'Against your will you live'—a person does not take his own life and it's not that way for nothing." Tevye wants to believe that no pain warrants the unthinkable act of suicide. "There is no sore in the world that does not heal," he claims, "and no sorrow which is not forgotten" (p.134). Yet immediately afterwards, Tevye reveals that he fills his head with philosophy ". . . in order to drive out the thoughts, that is, in order not to think about her, about Khave, that is. And, as if out of spite, who creeps into my head but she, Khave that is'' (pp.135–136). Tevye's wound has not healed at all. His comments about life are not hopeful, but rather bitterly ironic and resigned. His intellectualizations and denials represent unsuccessful defenses against his pain.

Tevye sometimes turns his sense of rage and defeat away from himself and onto his children. At those moments he contemplates, not his own death, but theirs. This attitude occasionally emerges through figures of speech, as when he twice compares his daughter Shprintse's lovesick demeanor to the extinguishing of a light—the very same term he uses to describe Golde's final decline.

At other times, his response is more directly aggressive. About to be reunited with Khave, who wishes to return to the family, Tevye rails out at her one last time, using the same tree metaphor as before, but with a new focus: "She is regretful?—I say—Too late! The little branch, I say, that has once torn itself away from the tree must, I say, become withered. The little leaf, I say, which has fallen off, must rot . . .'' (p.217). There can be no mistaking the hostility of these sentiments, and the attempt to render small, weak, and childlike the figure of his already humbled daughter. A moment later Tevye will tearfully embrace that prodigal, broken twig, but he thereby displays merely one side of his ambivalent love.

Thus, thoughts of suicide constitute one of Tevye's conscious methods for coping with his problems. Closely connected to these thoughts are notions of a passive death and fantasies of homicide. With great regularity such ideas are related to one or more of his daughters. This is not coincidental.

At first glance, Tevye's appraisal of his daughters appears inconsistent, especially when it comes to the matter of their gender. He is clearly proud of them when their behavior reinforces his own love of argumentation and intellectual commitment and, not by chance, when their actions indicate an identification with his own masculine self. Speaking of his daughter Hodel, to whom he is closest, Tevye extols her beauty and then says:

> And added to these troubles, she has to have a head too . . . she gulps books like stuffed cabbage. You will of course ask: What relation is Tevye's daughter to books, when her father deals in cheese and butter? Listen, I ask that same question of them, of the fine young *men,* I mean, the ones who don't even possess trousers—I hope I haven't offended you—and yet they have a yen for studying . . . [emphasis mine] (p.96).

Tevye delights in this brainy daughter and in her clever sisters. At the same time, however, he bemoans having spawned them at all, quoting scripture about the difficulties of parenthood and deprecating his children in a particularly furious manner when he describes how he was forced to hire a male to recite kadesh for Golde:

> What choice did I have, since God punished me, gave me no males, just females, just daughters and more daughters, no good Jew should know them! I don't know whether all Jews are made so miserable because of their daughters or whether only I am so terribly unfortunate that I have no luck with them? (p.170).

Tevye becomes fed up with his daughters when they conduct themselves in what he considers to be a typically female manner. Forced to leave his beloved home, he is near tears himself yet makes fun of his daughter, Tsaytl, because she has been weeping: "Aha, I think, my daughter has started wailing again, like a woman over the *Unsane toykef.*[19] These women, I'm telling you, are very serious. The minute anything happens, they cry. Tears are cheap with them!" (pp.215–216). The girls are praised by Tevye for being like him, and deprecated, even cursed, when they act in a manner identified by him as typical of women.

For their part, Tevye's daughters take after him in that they, too, are easily moved to talk about death, yet they do so in their own fashion. They are most direct and dramatic than he is, and their aim is to evoke his love and sympathy. They have seemingly internalized their father's tendency to view his relationships—particularly with them—in life and death terms, and they go him one better in ardor. After Khave has converted, for instance, she tries to reestablish contact with Tevye, to make him listen to her. Grabbing hold of his horse, she cries out: "Father! May I die if you move from this spot! I beg you, hear me out first, dear father! . . ." (p.137). But Tevye considers Khave dead already; moreover, he does not hear her out; thus, in her terms now as well as his own, she is, for all intents and purposes, rendered dead, discarded by Tevye. Ironically, Khave may in fact have responded to a cue from her father, since, immediately before her anguished plea, he describes her appearance in the following way: "She looks at me in a strange, wild fashion, her face dead . . ." (p.137). There is an expression, *toyt vi di vant,* literally "dead as the wall" which means "deathly pale," and this is undoubtedly what Tevye intends, but it is not what he says.

Much later, when Tsaytl is striving to soften her father's heart with respect to Khave, the fever of the moment reaches a pitch that makes Khave's earlier supplication sound mild by comparison. Tsaytl is lamenting the breach between Khave and Tevye. Tevye insists that the very mention of his daughter's name wounds him and he takes out his hurt on Tsaytl: "And I attack my daughter and give her a bitter end" (p.216). Kissing her father's hands, Tsaytl goes on to exclaim—"May things go badly for me, may I die right here on the spot if this time, she says, you push her away the way you did last time. . . ." And, a moment later, she repeats: "May things go badly for me—she says—may I die, if you don't forgive her, she says, because she is your daughter, just as I am." And Tevye's answer to this outpouring is, by now, familiar: "What do you want, I say, with my life: She is no longer my daughter! She died, I say, long ago!" (p.218).

Tevye's language—both spoken and not yet spoken—thus finds its reflection in the words of at least two of his daughters. Moreover, father and daughter fuel one another when they are involved in a confrontation. However, the suicide of Tevye's child Shprintse cannot be attributed to turns of phrase. This does not mean that Shprintse's decision is unrelated to her father, but only that clues to her behavior must be sought elsewhere, beyond Tevye's mode of conversation and defensive philosophical musings. Indeed, the answer is to be found in Tevye's own conflicts about his role as a man.

There is abundant evidence, from Tevye's words, that he is sensitive about the possibility of being considered unmasculine. One of his favorite phrases is "Tevye is not a woman"—usually used ironically as a comment upon his inclination to indulge in what he considers women's behavior, including crying, being unable to contain himself, speaking too soon. Just a moment before he makes fun of Tsaytl for crying about being forced to leave their home, Tevye says: ". . . my eyes filled with tears . . . If I weren't ashamed in front of my daughter, I would have had a really good cry . . . But Tevye is not a woman, so I control myself and pretend to be jolly . . ." (p.215). Earlier, when he describes having to part with his daughter Hodel, he recollects: "I alone conducted myself like steel and iron; that is, I wasn't really steel and iron; inside I was boiling like a samovar, but show that to anyone? Feh! After all, Tevye is not a woman . . ." (pp.116–117). But, he reports, in the end the scene had become so charged with loss and the memory of loving moments, that even he had finally broken down. Although he reveals this, he is unable to admit that he had wept: "Don't hold it against me that I . . . just like a woman . . ." (p.117).

Thus, Tevye knows that his behavior is not what he himself deems exemplary. At the same time, however, he feels proud of his unusual qualities. Reflecting on a heated discussion with Hodel, he comments: "For such a thing, a father would get angry at a child, would deliver a few slaps or let out all his angry, barren dreams. But Tevye is not a woman. I hold with the idea that anger is idolatry" (p.114). In other words, to be a good father in this instance means to be like a woman without feeling like one.

Tevye's dilemma is twofold. He feels the conscious desire to mother his daughters, but he considers it unacceptable to do so. At the same time, he resents them immensely, because, as females, they have license to be the way he wishes, but won't allow himself, to be. It is only when his children both behave like boys and yet remain dutiful as girls that he can tolerate them. Implied here is Tevye's wish that his children be both sons and daughters to him. He hopes that they will permit him to choose their husbands, and thereby their futures—granting him all the gratitude that is his traditional reward; at the same time, he does not want to cope with their sensitivities and weaknesses. Due to his own sense of softness and vulnerability, which he tries valiantly to suppress, he cannot bear to witness theirs, lest he succumb to a feared and hated emotional outburst.[20]

Tevye's real ambivalence towards his daughters emerges most clearly from his fantasies, in which, essentially, he kills them off. Here, Tevye reveals how much he would like to be free of his daughters, to return them to the watery place from whence they came, to have Golde reabsorb them:

> Various thoughts creep into my head, all kinds of figures and people, people long dead come toward me. And now I think of home, alas and alack! The house is completely dark; the kids, may they be healthy, are naked and barefoot, look at their father, poor things, at the *shlimazl,* to see whether he has brought home a bit of fresh bread, or maybe a roll; and she, my old lady, ever the busybody, grumbles: "I had to have children for him, and seven to boot—forgive my words, but one might as well take them and throw them into the river alive!" (p.18).

Tevye places the responsibility for wanting to be rid of the girls on Golde, rather than assuming it himself—but, of course, he is the designer of the reverie.

Tevye recounts a second fantasy that, although it, too, involves water, is more elaborate than the first. Moreover, it stands out because, in retrospect, it is prophetic. Tevye's beloved Hodel has come to break the news to her father that she is leaving home to join her husband, who has been banished for his insurgent political behavior. Tevye describes the event:

> "Are you listening, father? I have to tell you something. Today I am saying farewell to you . . . forever. . . ." That's what she says to me, so quietly it could barely be heard, and she looks at me with a strange sort of look, with a look I will never forget. And at the same time a thought flies through my head: "She wants to drown herself" . . . Why did drowning occur to me? Because, God forbid, such a thing had hap-

> pened: a girl not far from here got all involved with a village non-Jew and because of that village non-Jew . . . you already know what. So, out of misery, the mother became ill and died, and the father squandered his money and became a pauper. And the village non-Jew thought things over and married someone else. So she went to the river, the girl that is, and threw herself into the water and drowned herself . . . (p.113).[21]

Two aspects of this fantasy stand out. First is the fact that Tevye chooses to imagine his daughter Hodel drowning herself, especially when nothing in her behavior suggests any such inclination. Second is the fact that this occurrence, presumably real in someone else's experience, ultimately transpires in Tevye's life as well. In fantasy, however, the actual events are condensed: Khave gets all involved and marries a village non-Jew, and Shprintse, who is probably pregnant (although it is never clear), drowns herself. Not before, but afterwards, Golde dies of distress.

The literary historical reality that "Hodel," which contains Tevye's fantasy, was written in 1904, whereas "Khave" and "Shprintse" were composed in 1906 and 1907, respectively, probably reveals something about Sholem-Aleykhem's own unconscious thoughts and/or conscious plans. But the text as an independent entity yields its own implications: Tevye, that powerful father who encourages his daughters to form an identity with him, has succeeded beyond what he could possibly have desired because, in fact, they have read and responded to his unconscious messages. Tevye's daughters take after him not only in intellect, wit, and stubbornness: they fulfill destructive and self-destructive wishes of which he is unaware. Indeed, it may be argued that Tevye disposes of his three favorite daughters: Hodel through exile, Khave through conversion, Shprintse through suicide.[22]

Tevye has no conscious desire to lose his children. He sees their desertions as tragedies in his life, as tests of his faith. He also sympathizes with his daughters' sufferings as they attempt to resolve their dilemmas; and he knows that they are brave. For, all of them—Tevye as well, insofar as he can keep up—are caught between a traditional way of life and one that resonates with new political and social meaning. And yet, there remains something strange about Tevye's response to his fate, a tone not completely explainable as an effort to master anomic anguish. Rather, it is a fusion of his destructive and self-destructive impulses together battling against his life-affirming ones. This is how Tevye begins the tale of Shprintse's misfortune:

> I have had a terrible new experience with one of my daughters, Shprintse, something that exceeds all the miseries that I've had to stand up until now; and yet, despite that, never mind, one goes on living, as it is written: "Against your will you live"—though you could burst—may it befall the enemies of the Jews—singing the ditty: What good is my life, what good is my world, when I have no luck, when I have no money? . . . (p.143).

(The ditty, incidentally, fulfills in doggerel Tevye's prophetic fantasy in which the suicide's father is reduced to poverty. Moreover, with these exclamations, Tevye manages to undercut his own ostensible pursuit of optimism.)

Tevye's use of the line from the Sayings of the Fathers, i.e., "Against your will you live," is particularly significant in the context of Shprintse. Tevye cites this quotation on several occasions (in connection with Khave), and he always translates the original Hebrew as "A person doesn't take his own life."[23] In this case, however, the words serve not only as his attempt to cheer and comfort himself but also as a veiled criticism of his daughter and thus an indication of his continued anger at her. It is ironic that, by acting in accordance with Tevye's suicidal and homicidal hints to her, Shprintse nonetheless incurs his anger—as well as his intense sorrow, of course—because she has disobeyed one of his conscious precepts.

Tevye's conflict-laden feelings about himself and his daughters are inextricably complex. This is nowhere better revealed than in one of his comments, uttered after most of his heartbreaking experiences have already occurred:

> Listen, my Golde was one clever woman, may she rest in peace, if for no other reason than that she looked around her in time, said goodbye to this foolish world, and went to her

> eternal home. Because, I'm sure you would say this yourself, rather than incur the sorrow of raising children from your daughters, as Tevye has, isn't it a thousand times better to be in the ground and bake bagels? . . . But as it is written: "Against your will you live"—a person doesn't take himself . . . (p.204).

Here everything comes together: the open wish for death with its opposing pull, the sentiment that the pain of fatherhood can make death seem pleasant, even the use of idiomatic expressions with their literal, rather than figurative, meanings. The explicit envy of Golde also reinforces the notion that part of Tevye's character involves unresolved feelings concerning his role as a man.

Tevye is a lovable figure—and a believable one—because Sholem-Aleykhem has managed to combine in him the complex emotions and resultant struggles that exist in all of us. Tevye's story is that of a man whose world is changing all around him, so that he no longer has the stability he presumably once enjoyed. Still, it is clear that Tevye's difficulties stem as much from his internal world as from the swirl of events around him. He manages because he has found a balance, albeit an uncomfortable one, between his competing impulses. It is Tevye's tragedy that he could not fully accept this mixture in himself, and the tragedy of his daughters that he had to transmit his conflict to them.

Thus, in the end the suicide of Shprintse is more than the lonely decision of a desperate young woman, although it is that as well. Seen in the context of her family life, it is the conviction that role is all-important, that behaving in such a way that one's femaleness brings shame to the family is worse than bringing shame for an act that is not related to gender. Better a forbidden death than an improper love, with or without pregnancy. In this way, Shprintse's act allows her to do more than fulfill her father's unconscious wish for her. In a strange way, Shprintse also remains true to the way her family is supposed to live. Although she removes herself from Tevye, she paradoxically unites herself with and affirms him. By choosing not to humiliate her father—who would have been hard-pressed to find a husband for a penniless pregnant daughter—she proves ultimately responsive to his deep and powerful hunger for self-respect.

Sheyndl

Sheyndl, the complex heroine of Rokhl Faygnberg's *Af fremde vegn* ["*On Alien Paths*"],[24] (1925), is an unusual example of Yiddish literary suicide: the female creation of a female author. More than an interesting detail, this framework is essential to the novel as a whole. Faygnberg's work recounts the introduction of modern developing society to an Eastern European backwater, highlighting the tensions thereby engendered. Yet, unlike other works with a similar theme, *Af fremde vegn* proceeds via the author's concentration on women, whose concerns about their changing world are explored with candor, sensitivity and—so it seems at times—desperate clarity. The life of Sheyndl, daughter of Leyzer the miller, is portrayed with a fullness lacking in, for example, the world of Esther, Manye, or even Shprintse. The reader is privy to a multiplicity of factors that influence the way Sheyndl grows, the type of person she becomes; moreover, although these influences are related to her suicide, they are not the direct cause of her final decision.

Perhaps more clearly than in any other work, and this is as much a factor of length as anything else, Sheyndl's character formation resembles that of a real human being in that it derives from a combination of constitutional (and thereby internal), familial, and social factors; these, functioning in unison, provide the skeleton around which her thoughts and actions are shaped.

From early on in life, Sheyndl was different from other girls in the village of Radnikove. The major tension line of *Af fremde vegn* traces the thwarted love between Sheyndl and Borekh, her relative as well as childhood sweetheart. In part, this romance is nipped in the bud because Dvoyre, Borekh's gracious and clever mother, perceives that Borekh could become deeply involved with Sheyndl even though she is of a humbler station than he:

> She [Sheyndl] seemed more dangerous to her [Dvoyre] than any other village girl in several respects. First of all, she was

> the prettiest in the entire neighborhood. She was also remarkable for a particular stillness and dignity. Moreover, she was from the same family and, in addition, the daughter of a refined Jew; all of this could obliterate for Borekh the distinction between this type of beautiful girl and a bride (p.45).

Rather than risk allowing the youthful infatuation and friendship to blossom into a more mature and lasting bond, Dvoyre exploits her motherly awareness of her son's foibles. She invites the young daughter of a friend to visit, with the express purpose of encouraging Borekh's interest. The ploy succeeds, and within a short period of time, Borekh and Mine are married.

But Sheyndl's feelings are not easily subdued, for she is not only quiet and dignified by nature: she is absorbed by an inner life that, from the beginning of the novel, centers around Borekh. Dvoyre has no way of knowing that Sheyndl does not need the reinforcement of direct contact with Borekh in order to relive, time and again, the memory of their encounters. Although Sheyndl does not blame Borekh for his defection—she had been aware of the social distinction between them even if he had not—she is unable to move on, even when Mine is about to bear the couple's first child. Her greatest comfort is to lose herself in thoughts of him.

Thus, when Borekh decides that he is, after all, disgruntled with his wife and still attached to Sheyndl, there is fertile ground for his attentions, even though Sheyndl resists them bravely at first. And, once she succumbs to his seduction, she is obsessed by Borekh for the rest of her young life. At first, and in fact for much of their love, she is happy, living with the dream that he will divorce Mine and marry her—after his children have grown up a little:

> At this time, Sheyndl was strongly self-absorbed. She was so intoxicated with love that she forgot everything and everyone. Her whole life was now one person. She had one thought, one feeling, and one great, endless joy. Because of this one person, her father, her mother, [her sister] Khane were created . . . and she herself had been created just for him (p.148).

Although Borekh cannot make much time for her and is distracted and rushed when they do meet, she is delighted with every gesture, demanding nothing, treating each encounter as a precious gift. Unable to settle down when they are apart, she goes to his house or office, fleeing in consternation when she hears his son's cry from within the house; she rushes to meet every train when he is out of town, so longing is she for his return.

Later, when she is studying to be a midwife—a training program she is sent to pursue by Borekh, who is beginning to feel twinges of guilt about what will become of her if she never marries—Sheyndl's obsession becomes translated into behavior observable to others, rather than an entirely secret realm to be enjoyed only by herself. She tells her fellow students that she is engaged; when Borekh is in town, she celebrates the occasion as if it were a holiday, not attending classes, but rather putting on her best dress and entertaining lavishly.

Even towards the end of *Af fremde vegn,* when Sheyndl is no longer filled with joy and is, instead, beset by the miserable anxiety that she will lose Borekh, her obsessional thinking continues as before:

> . . . she lay down calmly on the sofa to figure out what she had to do. Thus she could lie around an entire day, unless an unexpected guest or a representative in a well-upholstered wagon woke her from her ideas . . . she was busy only with herself, with the Sheyndl who thought about Borekh and for whom that was her entire life (p.259).

In the end, Sheyndl drives herself into a state of maddened agony over the failure of her wishes to be realized. She becomes ever more agitated, less and less able to maintain rational contact with those around her.

Yet, Sheyndl's final isolation is hinted at much earlier and is the more striking because it occurs just at the time when she was experiencing "the truly good years" of her life (p.180). During the period of her student days, when Borekh had done a good deal of traveling, he had written to her frequently, plying her with letters, cards, and telegrams. Sometimes she would receive several telegrams in the morning while she was still in bed; they were always of the same sort:

> A greeting at midnight, a greeting at one o'clock, a greeting at two. Her heart was so brimming with joy and love that she had had to read them to her roommates. Afterwards she would rip the telegrams into tiny pieces, scatter them in her hair and walk around the house that way for hours, smiling and silent (p.181).

Sheyndl's emotional state during her hours of parading with the telegrams in her hair is dramatic: smiling and silent, she moves as if in a trance. Certainly, she is in a world of her own, inaccessible to others, that she has occupied at least since meeting Borekh. His presence is not required for her state to occur; in fact, it may be that, as a fantasy object, he is only necessary as a catalyst. At any rate, this early example is a harbinger of her subsequent reactions when, having family and others at her fingertips, she nonetheless chooses to spend her hours in dreamy solitude.

Sheyndl's existence may be described in a somewhat different way, and it is here that the connection between constitution and family upbringing emerges. Whereas Sheyndl may have been more susceptible than others—her siblings, for instance—to the lure of a fantasy existence and the pull of concentrating on one person only, her choice of outlets for her particular needs is based on the lessons she had learned as a member of her own family unit.

Leyzer the miller, Sheyndl's father, had come as a young scholar from the city to Radnikove, where he had enjoyed a fine reputation as a teacher and taken his meals at the home of Roshe-Leye, a widow with nine children who also ran the mill. He had garnered the respect of this family as well, and Roshe-Leye had even managed to get him exempted from conscription when that proved a problem. However, unbeknownst to him, Roshe-Leye had cherished an ulterior motive: to marry off Leyzer to her daughter Ite, twelve years his senior and considered an old maid. This union had indeed occurred, although Leyzer himself passed through the event almost without awareness, and, furthermore, helpless to escape because of his fear of the women and the additional incentive of gaining ownership of the house and half the mill.

Ashamed of his bride's family, Leyzer had failed to invite his own kin to the wedding; thereafter, he had even avoided his relatives when he visited the city. The years had not made Leyzer more appreciative of his home life. Finally, disgusted once too often by the sight of his spouse, he had fled. However, Leyzer was a man who loved being pampered, despite the costs involved. Thus, when the weather had begun to turn cold, Leyzer dreamed that Ite was seriously ill due to his abandonment. When he awoke, he returned to her and, of course, to the warmth of the house.

Ite had indeed tolerated Leyzer's absence poorly, pouring out her misery by cursing and physically hurting her two daughters, just as she had abused her younger siblings before her marriage, when she had also felt isolated and unloved. On the day of Leyzer's return, she had given birth to a stillborn son.

This, then, was Sheyndl's childhood: the eldest daughter of a father convinced that he was living beneath his station and a mother who was unhappy with herself and who attacked the little girl because of it. The home was outwardly stable, but inwardly insecure: Leyzer remained supercilious and Ite, together with her mother, were constantly wary lest Leyzer take it into his mind to run away again.

The precariousness of this environment was exacerbated by a further difficulty, that is, Leyzer's refusal to take pleasure in the four daughters with whom he was eventually blessed:

> Above all, people admired Sheyndl with her blossoming-charming grace and little Gitele, who bore a resemblance to her.
>
> But to Leyzer this was a meager honor. He felt insulted that God had denied him a son and he was not at all satisfied with his daughters . . . (pp.17–18).

Sheyndl's position was thus a problematic one, since, although outsiders praised her exotic beauty, she was cherished by neither of her parents; indeed, she was deprecated by her father and berated by her mother. It is small wonder that she would attempt to change her status.

An early example of this effort concerns the nineteen-year-old Sheyndl's reaction to an incident in which two older, non-Jewish men kiss her hand. She is delighted at the attention and offended when her parents and her grandmother react with contempt. Responding heatedly, she retorts that everyone kisses the hand of Borekh's wife. Leyzer, true to his bias, is incensed that Sheyndl would dare to compare herself to an educated city girl, whereupon the following exchange occurs:

> "Well, why didn't you educate me? Why do you keep your children in the village?"
>
> For Leyzer this was something new. It was the first time he had heard a daughter of his complain that he had not provided her with better guidance. But it didn't occur to him to think about it. He had his ready answer for it:
>
> "Oh, if you had a different mother?" (p.20).

Sheyndl has attempted to kill two birds with one stone, to differentiate herself from her mother while at the same time aligning herself with her father's taste, albeit angrily. The attempt fails completely, however. Her father disregards her, while her mother sees the challenge as a defection, throwing whatever objects she can lay her hands on and chastizing Leyzer for being so self-absorbed and haughty about his descent:

> Like her mother! Seems to me they all resemble his dirty city "stock." That's fine with me. After all, I'm not knowledgeable and I harvested such a respectable person (p.20).

Leyzer's concern with his social standing and self-respect forms a cornerstone of his personality as a father, and Sheyndl is affected by this. Although she had been raised by her mother to believe that the family's poverty was due to her father's trips to town and to his city "stock," she was proud of this quality in him; in fact, one of the least pleasant aspects of going to town with him was the occasional visit to a home where she observed that "her clever father became . . . sort of a foolish little Jew" (p.175), a transformation she hated to witness.

Sheyndl finally does manage to achieve positive regard from her father. This occurs when she has the opportunity to prove that she takes after him. Sheyndl has received an indirect invitation of marriage from Meyer Vilenkin, a village boy who has made good as a butcher in America. Meyer promises that he will provide everything for her, so that she need not even have a dowry or clothing. Sheyndl refuses, saying she will not marry a butcher.

The reaction of the adult family members to the twenty-year-old Sheyndl's determination is mixed. For Roshe-Leye the problem is that Leyzer is too indulgent a father, too willing to allow his daughter her say. Bluntly, she warns Sheyndl that she will become an old maid. Ite is not unhappy that Sheyndl does not want Meyer, but she worries that, by age twenty, the chances of a young woman marrying may already be few. Leyzer's reaction, in contrast, is one of great pride, combined with a sense of discovery. It is as if he had never known his daughter before:

> He was overjoyed now. In the fact that Sheyndl was refusing such happiness because she did not want to marry a butcher, he saw a sign of his noble lineage. He himself had erred. God had not given him a son and his daughters had gone in the direction of their mother's backwoods community. But now a miracle had occurred. Somewhere a drop of oil had lingered around them and now it had swum to the surface. The silken rope that he, Leyzer, had ripped asunder, was weaving itself again. It had attached itself to his boorish village girl and she would continue to braid the chain of his dignified family (p.71).

The irony of Sheyndl's victory is that, more than anything, her decision had not been based directly on her wish to become Leyzer's favorite daughter, although this is exactly what happens, but rather on her attachment to Borekh, which obsesses her even before they declare their love. Yet, this is not a contradiction, for Borekh, unlike any other young man with whom Sheyndl is acquainted, stands above the standards of the village, both socially and intellectually. In this, he does indeed resemble her father. Thus, Sheyndl's tie to Borekh is also a tie to Leyzer.[25]

Sheyndl's rejection of Ite's ways and admiration for Leyzer's is instrumental in leading to a peculiar conspiracy between father and daughter. That is, because he has decided that Sheyndl is his favorite, in fact his only true child, Leyzer views her actions with an especially liberal eye. Not only does he humor her in her refusal to accept any of the matches proposed to her, but he actively supports her in other instances as well.

Leyzer is not entirely approving of Sheyndl's behavior, however. At times, exasperated that she spurns every match, he questions her about the possibility that she is in love with someone else—maybe even Benye, a family acquaintance. On other occasions, worry is articulated as threat:

> Daughter, I'm warning you that I am going to make a match for Khane: everything that has been prepared for you, the dowry and the trousseau, I'll give to her, and you'll be left on the shelf. And don't think this is a little game. Now you are in demand, later you'll have to do the asking. At that point, daughter, things will be bad. I'm warning you. You still have time (pp.146–7).

Yet, while she is questioned and admonished, Sheyndl receives more positive messages as well. For one thing, far from depriving her of her dowry and clothing, Leyzer indulges her, taking her to town and buying her fancy attire, precisely because she is a young woman actively sought after as a prize match. It is at this point—that is, before she journeys to the heady atmosphere of her student world—that Sheyndl begins comporting herself like the fashionable women of Borekh's society.

Indeed, Leyzer defends Sheyndl against his third daughter, Khane, when the latter protests that Sheyndl is not assuming a fair share of responsibility in the family store. Leyzer explains to the completely unsympathetic and unconvinced Khane that Sheyndl does not want to touch any of the merchandise ". . . because, since she has to meet with prospective husbands, she wants to have refined hands" (p.147).

Leyzer's major step in reinforcing Sheyndl's abandonment of the life set out for her is his decision to let her pursue a career. Borekh has begun to worry, lest Sheyndl wind up unmarried with no means of caring for herself; therefore, he determines that she should train as a midwife. Sheyndl broaches the subject to Leyzer by saying that Borekh is going to lend her the money for the project. Leyzer, the *paterfamilias,* is offended by this, but he allows himself to be mollified by Borekh. The latter assures him that, contrary to his fears, Sheyndl will be able to find a husband after a year of courses, although she will be over twenty-five.

Leyzer nonetheless remains concerned about having given his permission to Sheyndl, especially when, upon their arrival in the city—she with the clothes and equipment she will need for a year's stay—his harsh and bitter aunt warns that the move is a foolish one; Sheyndl would do far better to find herself a husband. Leyzer is pleased with his daughter's mature response:

> Of course I will get married. I'll take a good groom, too, but first I want to be able to support myself (p.173).

The next day, Leyzer's courage fails him again as he takes Sheyndl to the home of Hillel Goldman, whose educated, self-supporting daughters have remained spinsters. However, Sheyndl insists that she is going to study, no matter what Leyzer's wishes are. He capitulates immediately and cheers up considerably as he observes how people admire Sheyndl's beauty:

> His offended father-feeling was now gratified. In that moment [when the innkeeper's wife had praised Sheyndl] the matter became clear to him. Precisely she, the beautiful child of his aristocratic roots, need not be a housewife by the stove. She also did not have to be a shopkeeper but rather a refined woman with a respectable living in hand, like all young women of high class city parents (p.176).

Leyzer goes on to convince himself that Sheyndl's goal, and his own acquiescence, represent modern mainstream thinking.

Sheyndl does indeed proceed with her courses, and Leyzer continues to protect her. At one point, his third daughter, Khane, complains that she is afraid to show her face in the streets of Zabolotov, where Borekh and she both work, because of the ugly rumors circulating about Sheyndl. Annoyed at what he decides is untrue, Leyzer nonetheless goes to visit Sheyndl in order to find out for himself. Sheyndl ". . . lied with an easy heart, as she always did when she talked to him about Borekh." (p.188). Leyzer scolds her for having visited Borekh twice at his inn—ostensibly to ask his aid in circumventing certain academic requirements—but is disarmed and calmed by her lightheartedness in the face of his earnest question.

In fact, however, Leyzer is not really fooled by Sheyndl's guise. It is just that, having recognized her as his sort, he wants to enjoy their connection:

> Leyzer experienced so much satisfaction because of his Sheyndl. That was how she braided the silken rope of his noble roots. People were envious of him . . .
>
> He now knew everything. Leyzer now understood how his Sheyndl arrived at her courses. Borekh's favors and his frequent visits to him, Leyzer, in Radnikove were also clear to him by now. And her Hebrew lessons, and the chess playing, and the bicycle and the mandolin, and her clothes. He knew everything (p.217).

Moreover, Leyzer is enthusiastic about the aristocratic Borekh, even envisioning him as a son-in-law. Rather than admit that his favorite young man may be trifling with his daughter, he assures himself that the attachment is more serious, that Borekh will surely divorce Mine and marry Sheyndl. He recognizes that he should side with Mine and her children, yet his reason and his wishes are in sharp conflict with one another. The compromise result is a comfortable passivity, wherein he abdicates any responsibility for what he sees:

> And Leyzer kept quiet. He ought to have done something—run, yelled, cried—but he swallowed it . . . he relied on Borekh . . . Borekh could accomplish anything (p.218).

Leyzer's belief that Borekh can do whatever he sets out to achieve is, in fact, part of his deep desire that Sheyndl redeem his own lost sense of self-worth. The connection is two-fold.

First, he judges his daughters by the men they love. Thus, he thinks condescendingly of his daughter Basye's marital choice and admires Sheyndl for refusing Meyer the butcher:

> If she had one drop of blood from her father's dignified roots, she wouldn't want a boor for a husband. He had Sheyndl as proof (p.88).

Similarly, he must now view Borekh positively if he is to maintain Sheyndl as his vehicle of rehabilitation. Secondly, not unlike Sheyndl, Leyzer inchoately recognizes a bond between Borekh and himself. His early sense that he had much in common with the rebellious young scholar had not diminished over time, and Borekh's courtesy calls—in fact, paid largely for Sheyndl's sake—had continued to please him. It is as if he himself were suddenly being given a chance to divorce his wife and start anew, in a marriage befitting his intellect and station.[26]

In a strange way, then, Leyzer identifies with both Sheyndl and Borekh. It is small wonder that he does his best to ignore his knowledge of Sheyndl's liaison. At first he steadfastly refuses to believe any of the rumors circulating about his daughter; he also argues that Sheyndl's inappropriately ornate wardrobe and style of dressing are not indicative of any failure on her own part, but rather constitute evidence of Ite's inefficient mothering. Ite complains:

> In everything you say she has a point. As if she ought to waste herself wearing her silk clothes in the middle of the week. People are just laughing up their sleeves!

Leyzer responds mildly: "Oh well, you remembered too late to guide her . . ." (p.210). Later, when his own eyes can no longer deceive him, he decides that the romance deserves to flourish. Still, there are limits even to Leyzer's dream of dignity. Ironically, it is in a moment of childlike wishing to please that Sheyndl reveals the one thing her father cannot accept—the sexual nature of her love.

While much in the early and middle parts of *Af fremde vegn* confirms Leyzer's involvement with his daughter, it is abundantly clear by the end of the novel that this influence is by no means one-sided. Indeed, the more Sheyndl disintegrates, the more obviously she needs her father and his approval.

Despite her obsession with Borekh and her singlemindedness about him, Sheyndl is not as insouciant with respect to her father as might at first appear. Even before she goes off to her courses, during which time she will lie to Leyzer with an easy heart, she is distressed by her own deceit, realizing that her father feels undercut as family provider. Although there are indications that she will once again get her way—she has not been refused and Leyzer has agreed to speak to Borekh about his financial involvement with her schooling—Sheyndl is far from triumphant. In one of the novel's starkest moments, Leyzer turns homeward after their talk:

> Behind him Sheyndl walked in silence, pensive and unhappy, like the surrounding forest with its mute half-naked trees and rotten, withered grass./By the time they got home, it was pitch dark (p.152).

After her return from studying, Sheyndl is more confident of her status with Borekh. She has accepted his designation of her as his queen, while Mine remains his servant. Although somewhere deep within herself she is pained to tears, her outward demeanor reflects her exultation. She brushes off her grandmother's anger as well as her sister Khane's delight in repeating the latest gossip about her. She is amused by her mother's angry response to this idle chatter.

When it comes to her father, in contrast, Sheyndl's conscience pricks her. The undercurrent of responsibility that causes her to experience anguish over the demeaning of Mine is active as well in her dealings with Leyzer:

> Only in connection with her father did she feel a certain duty. She was, of course, far from the notion of telling him the truth, but answering one of his looks with a hidden smile was beyond her as well (p.208).

Even as Leyzer steadfastly refuses to believe the rumors about her, forbidding Ite and Roshe-Leye to so much as mention them, Sheyndl is frightened of him. It is almost as if her guilt is magnified because of her father's determination to trust her: ". . . she, Sheyndl, trembled before his gaze. Particularly when he paid attention to something of hers that had been bought with Borekh's money" (p.209).[27]

Finally, the uncomfortable status quo is ended, ironically enough, through a kind of misunderstanding. Khane has fallen in love with and married—over some opposition from Leyzer—Davidke, a socialist. Musing about the personalities of the men who are loved by his daughters, Leyzer decides that he can understand Davidke but not Borekh, for the young socialist had merely exchanged one god for another, whom he served as faithfully as Leyzer did his. Borekh, in contrast, had decided that he did not have to obey any authority higher than himself. And Leyzer's sad conclusion is that:

> If Borekh had managed to pluck from his neighbor's garden the most beautiful tree in its fullest bloom when he had no right to do so, he could also throw it away one fine day, leaving it to be trampled by anyone happening by (p.241).

Deeply distressed by his insight, Leyzer determines to talk seriously with Sheyndl, who is twenty-eight years old by this time. Moreover, he resolves not to be charmed by her, as he had been in the past. In this state of mind he goes to visit her and asks her simply what significance Borekh has in her life. In response to a counter-question from her, Leyzer announces that he would like to see the young man as his son-in-law.

Sheyndl can scarcely believe her ears. She is delighted that her father would wish what she wishes for herself, yet even more important is the prospect that, by indulging her love, she can actually please him:

> Sheyndl's heart began to pound with happiness. She wanted to tell him the truth. He is such a good father, so refined. Basye and Khane had caused him so much sadness. Let him get his gratification from her. She'll tell him that he really will get Borekh as a son-in-law (p.244).

But the conversation does not continue as Sheyndl anticipates. When she explains that the wedding will occur as soon as Borekh makes some provision for Mine and the children, Leyzer reacts with skepticism. When, he inquires, is this likely to occur, since Borekh is such a spendthrift? Moreover, he cautions that all men who behave in this way are alike: today Sheyndl may be his beloved, tomorrow she might just as easily be spurned.

At this, Sheyndl's pride and anger are piqued, and she retorts that Borekh would sooner cast off Mine than her. Leyzer heatedly contradicts her opinion, reminding her that Mine is Borekh's wife and wives are not subjected to summary rejection. Hearing her father's harsh and critical words, Sheyndl's control snaps and she blurts out: "A wife! A wife! I am also a wife! Look, here you can even see his wedding ring. He has sanctified me . . . / She was frightened by her own voice" (p.245).

Although Sheyndl recognizes instantly that she has gone too far, she sees as well that it is too late to change the situation. Instead, she explains to her incredulous father that Borekh has indeed married her, just as in Biblical times Jews had more than one wife. Leyzer, outraged but still unclear about the significance of what Sheyndl is telling him, feverishly contemplates Borekh's perverse exploitation of Judaism.

Finally, the full truth dawns on Leyzer. Although Sheyndl asserts vaguely that she had wanted to be married "just because," Leyzer understands that at the heart of the matter is a sexual relationship:

> Just because?! Just because, you say?! . . . he stammered, barely able to breathe, but at that moment he tore himself from his seat and a sharp slap echoed through the room (p.246).

While Leyzer's explosive response appears to shock Sheyndl, it may have occurred to her unconscious beforehand. At the very outset of their encounter, Sheyndl had reacted to her father's interrogation by curling up "as if she were afraid lest the same hand would once again strike her" (p.243). Somewhere she had recognized that Leyzer would never condone the fact of her defilement. Her notion that he could be gratified by her affair is revealed as a pathetic fantasy, made possible by discounting—on a conscious level only, it appears—the limited nature of her father's support.

The result of this disastrous encounter between Leyzer and Sheyndl is, in the end, the latter's death by suicide. Although the link between the two events is not immediately obvious, for other elements as well determine Sheyndl's decision, her despair and desperation may be traced directly to her moment of exposure and shame before her father.

When Leyzer storms out of Sheyndl's apartment, he abandons his business and retires to a contemplative, scholarly existence. When Sheyndl tries to visit him, he throws her out. If this were not bad enough, Sheyndl receives another nasty blow to her self-esteem: Mine gives birth to a third child. Although at first Sheyndl continues to hope for better times, the mistrust planted in her by Leyzer slowly begins to take root and grow.

The change starts with Sheyndl's perception that, in fact, Borekh's real bond is not with her, but rather with his wife. For the first time, she experiences jealousy and senses that the role of Borekh's queen might not be glorious after all. In this frame of mind, she recalls her father's admonition that a man like Borekh could, at any moment, cast her off for another.

Significantly, while she begins to mistrust every woman with whom Borekh comes in contact, it is finally her youngest sister, Gitl (or Gitele), whom she chooses as her enemy. Gitele, who resembles the beautiful Sheyndl more and more each day, is of a similarly studious bent, and is still young enough to marry. Just as she had for years been obsessed with Borekh, Sheyndl now focuses on Gitl, destroying the trinkets that Borekh brings her, living with the dread that he will claim Gitl as soon as she finishes school, suspecting that the intrigue has already begun.

Finally, Sheyndl comes to a resolution of how to solve her problems: she will get married for convenience to Benye, her perennially-besotted admirer. Thereby she will be free to bear Borekh's children, which would be completely out of the question otherwise, and by this tactic bind him to her just as strongly as Mine had been able to do.

While Sheyndl's immediate conscious impulse is to find a way to assuage her feelings of jealousy and insecurity about Borekh, her motivation has much to do with her father, who has been on her mind since their estrangement. Sheyndl's sense of rejection by her father and her susceptibility to his opinion are clear from her attempt at reconciliation as well as from her acceptance of his formulation about Borekh. There are other indications as well that she is most of all in need of his renewed good opinion and that she knows there is only one path likely to achieve that goal. By deciding to marry—that is, to assume the role for which her family has been preparing her since birth—Sheyndl is making a desperate attempt to show her father that she is love-worthy after all. In this way, the link between familial pressure and social influence is forged in Sheyndl's life.

Indeed, when Sheyndl's uninhibited associations are examined, Leyzer's centrality emerges with clarity. While contemplating her course of action, Sheyndl goes through a period of great sadness, where she cries—not, as in previous crying scenes, to get her way, but rather out of sheer misery. And now, although she had shed a few tears when telling Borekh about her father's having hit her, she remembers that blow as a crucial part of her anguish, quite as if it were part of her problem with Borekh—which, in fact, it is, although not in the same way as her other impediments.

> Remaining alone, she spent hours walking around her apartment, wringing her hands, and from time to time she dissolved into quiet tears. She cried out of insult. Mine's child hurt her, [as did] her father's smack. She wept from jealousy of Gitele and out of pity for herself (p.253).

Later, when she is hatching her plan to marry, she recalls a childhood experience in which marriage and harmony with her father had been intertwined. At first, she is frightened by her own scheme:

> But then, considering the matter carefully, it appealed to her so much that, out of great joy, she sang some long-forgotten dance melody from a shtetl wedding she had been at as a child, together with her father (p.259).

Clearly, then, the thought of marrying evokes not only a happiness, but a specific connection with her father. Moreover, the resurfacing of this recollection just at the time when she is attempting to recover from the ignominy of her rejection is further evidence that her goal is linked to her father as well as to Borekh.

Sheyndl gets her way with Leyzer. Once she is married to Benye, her father begins to soften towards her, finally inviting the couple to his home for *Sukes.*[28] There, father and daughter resume their old relationship, or at least so it appears:

> On the first morning of *Sukes,* Gitele came to summon Sheyndl and Benye to Radnikove for dinner. And she went. She endured his [her father's] look of pity and exchanged kisses with him as she had back then, when she was still his best child (p.292).

Yet, things can never again be as they once were because Sheyndl has failed to understand one aspect of her action. In marrying Benye, she has done more than enter a new status for the sake of public appearances: she has changed in her own eyes. The implications of her new position turn out to be more than she is able to tolerate. She is no longer Leyzer's little girl.

The marriage that was to be a sham is actually all too real. This discovery is particularly distressing because in her milieu, the paucity of satisfied wives for Sheyndl to look to as models is striking and alarming. Both in terms of role and treatment by their husbands, these women lead lives of unhappiness, insecurity, and hopelessness.

Borekh's wife Mine is a case in point. She is married to the man for whom Sheyndl spends most of her time pining, yet her lot is not enviable. Borekh is unfaithful to her and she knows it; she lives in constant dread that he will abandon her and the children and run off with Sheyndl. At the same time, she puts immense energy into her housewifely duties and is ridiculed behind her back by Borekh and Sheyndl. Mine's position is perfectly clear: she is the servant, Sheyndl the privileged one. It is Sheyndl Borekh will take to the theater and accompany to Palestine, not Mine. As Sheyndl puts it:

> She will do everything, everything the way he likes it. But cooking the good suppers and raising the little boys—that she

> will leave to Mine. In no way would she trade places with her—even if people were to stone her for it (p.208).

Sheyndl has a clear vision of what being married to Borekh is like. On one level, of course, she does wish to marry him, trusting that her life with him would remain unconventional. Still, she is wary of being a wife. Her perceptions are not surprising, considering her upbringing. For it is not only Ite's boorishness that she rejects in deprecating her mother: it is an entire way of life. All her days, Ite is at the mercy of Leyzer's whims: if he wants to leave her, he does so; when he returns, she accepts him humbly. When he decides that he wants to retire to Radnikove after his rupture with Sheyndl, he simply goes, leaving Ite no choice but to assume his position at the store.

Even at the end, when Sheyndl has already taken her life, Leyzer behaves as the master of his wife. Having decided that he cannot cope with his wife any longer, he informs her that he intends to divorce her. Finally, Ite asserts herself, but her gesture is characteristically wretched: at her mother's urging, she begs to remain married to him, so as to partake of his final, heavenly reward. She requests the further honor of doing his laundry.

Sheyndl is, in her own way, as slavishly devoted to Borekh as Ite to Leyzer, yet her view of marriage is entirely different. To her, marriage should be the culmination of her adulterous dreams with Borekh, an endless experience of mandolin playing, chess games, bicycle riding and journeys to Palestine. And it is significant that Sheyndl gains the initial respect of her father for refusing to marry. She is caught between the notion that she should adopt a traditional role and the idea, unconsciously fostered by her father, that her high-class heritage entitles her to live beyond the usual constraints.

Of course, not everyone in Sheyndl's sphere is unsophisticated and uneducated. Borekh's mother, Dvoyre, is the prime example of an elegant, clever woman to whom Sheyndl could look for encouragement and inspiration. Yet, Sheyndl has ample opportunity to observe that even Dvoyre may have compromised too much—or, to look at it somewhat differently, may have been compromised too much. Throughout the novel,

Dvoyre is portrayed as a woman who, although no longer young, still manages, when entering her sixties, to remain "straight-backed and beautiful, with the charmingly feminine smile of days gone by" (p.195). So accomplished an inn hostess was she that "people used to leave behind bags of money on the table in order to return and kiss her hand because of her dignity and honesty" (p.37). As a young bride, she had even managed to tame her irascible father-in-law, who adored her for her "dignified city understanding and her delicately feminine charm" (p.35).

For precisely these same reasons, some of the local women, including her own mother-in-law and Roshe-Leye, disliked Dvoyre, finding her sophisticated manners and customs a blight on their friendlier, more relaxed and generous habits. Thus, Dvoyre represents, in some respects, the antithesis of Sheyndl's home environment. And because of this, the married existence she leads seems all the more humdrum and disappointing.

Dvoyre had been raised in a pedigreed urban milieu; as the daughter of a distinguished man, she had been married off into a rich village family when her father's position had declined. And, although she managed the family's affairs with grace and efficiency, thereby providing herself with some satisfaction, it is also evident that she had married beneath herself. Unlike her father-in-law, who had cherished her in an uncharacteristic fashion,

> Her husband [Kalmen] was less of an expert about her. Short, fat, with a hairy face like his father's, he was none too bright and had the heart of a child. Always intimidated by his father and the latter's strict upbringing, he was also frightened of his young and beautiful wife with her citified refinement in which everything was weighed and measured. He also became frightened when, shortly after the wedding, she became his schoolteacher, sitting him down to read little Polish and Hebrew books. But with time he got accustomed to her (p.36).

The marriage had produced three children: two accomplished sons who took after Dvoyre, and a dull-witted daughter who resembled Kalmen. Despite the intellectual failure of the daughter and Borekh's flights of fancy about his career, Dvoyre had managed to marry everyone off.

Yet Dvoyre herself does not feel fulfilled, even though she has achieved a level of which Ite could never have dreamed. Deep down, she knows she is missing something in life. True, she manages her conditions well, and she has sent her children out into the world with all the advantages of their upbringing. But now they no longer need her. This means that, according to convention, she is left with only the prospect of living out her remaining years at her husband's side, a thought that causes her to weep inside. At times, observing herself—an aging woman—in the mirror:

> Somewhere deep in her soul a sinful thought would awaken about her uselessly lost youth and modesty, which nobody had appreciated (p.195).

She remembers how attractive and high-born men used to return to the inn, just for a smile or even a single glance from her:

> And she, Dvoyre, had had Kalmen as a husband . . . She had seen to it that not even a speck of dust fell on him and it had never even occurred to him that the situation could be otherwise. He hadn't even known how beautiful she was. Maybe the whole thing had been stupid? Life was so short . . .
>
> A tear fell from her eye, a hot hidden tear for the youthful joys that she had never experienced (pp.195–96).

Dvoyre comforts herself with the notion that the younger generation of women will themselves grow older and that, unlike them, she has maintained her purity. Her reward is that she had obeyed God's will and learned how to serve Him.

Dvoyre cannot be a satisfactory model for Sheyndl: she is too old-fashioned and too self-righteous for that. She may be admirable in her own way, and she is certainly more attuned to watching out for herself than Freyde, Benye's mother, who has grown old before her time under the cruel regimen established by her husband Shakhne. Yet she renders her larger situation equally unpalatable by subjugating herself to a man who is not her equal, and by further denying her plight, instead casting aspersions on Sheyndl's generation.

It is in any case logical that Sheyndl would look to her own peers to get ideas about marriage, especially as she grows older and more and more of them, including two of her younger sisters, enter that state. If her arch-rival Mine is no example to emulate or envy, neither are her sisters, for they take after their mother's side and do not step outside her basic framework. Even—or especially—her well-educated relative Sonye is a disappointment, with her faded demeanor and willingness to go, sight unseen, to Meyer the butcher after Sheyndl has rejected his hand.

There is, however, one woman whom Sheyndl apparently does admire: Anna, the wife of Borekh's boss and mentor, Leon, whom she had seen when she visited Borekh in his fancy hotel room. Anna is unlike the other women with whom Sheyndl is acquainted: wealthier, more cultured, more elegantly attired, simply more polished. Yet all this does not prevent Anna from being a most unhappy person, something that Sheyndl does not know. Anna's problem is that after marrying Leon at a time when she felt neutral about him, she had fallen in love with him and consequently begun a life of suffering severely, since he is a philanderer. Her time is spent in complete absorption with ideas about how to entice him, including a secret delight with his decision to move to Zabolotov—since there, among the boorish natives, she will be the only intelligent and well-dressed woman.

Anna's position is, in a way, worse than that of the other wives in *Af fremde vegn.* For, like Ite, she is constantly insecure, lest her husband decide to abandon her. In her own way, she spends as much time devoting herself to his well-being as they do; at the same time, she does not derive the same enjoyment from her three children as, for instance, Dvoyre does from hers. Nor is she able to throw herself into the details of housekeeping in the style of Mine. Indeed, she most closely resembles Sheyndl herself: a woman whose only true interest is her man and how to keep him from straying.

The narrative exposition of Anna's plight deserves attention, because, unlike the situations of the other women in Sheyndl's life, Anna's situation appears to be hidden from her observation. Yet the narrator makes certain that the reader knows about Anna's unfortunate circumstances. There are several possible reasons for this. First, the escapades of Leon and his ilk are the *fremde vegn* [''alien paths''] after which the entire novel takes its name. Borekh, although he seems to struggle against the allure of this lifestyle, is actually closer to it than he wants to recognize. Anna, and Mine, too, for that matter, illustrate the miserable effect on women of the attempt to lead a hedonistic existence.

Second, the portrayal of modern marriages as untenable strengthens the message that marriage is not a viable way of life for a certain type of woman, no matter how ''enlightened'' the husband. Mine's case is obvious to Sheyndl; by revealing Anna's plight as even worse, in certain respects, the narrator indicates that the problem is a general one, lurking behind every façade of harmony. In this way, the narrator implies that Sheyndl's behavior is a response, not only to her particular circumstances, but to a *Zeitgeist*.

Finally, and in contrast to the previous idea, Sheyndl's resistance to marriage, and her response to it when she finally does embark upon it, show how different she is from others—even when she doesn't understand this—a contrast underscored by the revelation of Anna's controlled unhappiness; that is, Anna manages to exist within a hypocritical marriage. Sheyndl, once she has taken her vows, cannot.

Sheyndl's final period of suffering reveals with particular clarity the extent to which a person in her position, and with her temperament, fails to function within a traditional Jewish social structure. She is unable—even if she were willing—to accommodate herself to what is expected of a Jewish wife, because her interest in marriage is purely to hoodwink her social milieu while achieving her goals with Borekh. Once wed, however, she is incapable of executing her duplicitous scheme. Too independent or fearful of intimacy to endure the constraints of conventional marriage, she is yet too imbued with her father's values to flaunt those constraints. Lacking any way out of her predicament, trapped, she takes her life.

Sheyndl's marriage represents a defeat for her, the end of a life's dream. She has had to admit to herself that Borekh is less devoted to her than she to him. Her ploy of inspiring his jealousy so that he will choose her over Mine has misfired. Thus, part of her inability to continue relations with him is based on the anger she feels towards him. Yet Sheyndl's problem is not simply Borekh, nor is it merely the problem of what others will think. If this were so, she would not, on one hand, have needed to create the illusion of a Jewish marriage to yield her sexuality in the first place, nor, on the other hand, would she have been able to continue her affair despite the gossip of townspeople. Rather, her plight occurs because she believes she has to be a certain way by dint of being married, and that precludes extramarital affairs, even with the man whom she considers her true husband. The fact that she initially considers her second marriage as no more binding than the first is clear from one of her thoughts around the time of her wedding. Contemplating her ring, which is the same one given to her by Borekh to sanctify their union, Sheyndl thinks: "What fortune that ring had already had: this was the second time she had been sanctified with it and she was still married only temporarily" (p.271).

Once she and Benye are wed, Sheyndl's despair deepens catastrophically; she begins struggling with her new and confusing role even before the couple has returned from a lonely ceremony in the city. Benye, the loyal son as much as the loyal lover, dreads his father's anger and suffers because he has not married in the public, celebratory way that his parents would have expected and enjoyed; he is worried about the implications of his self-consciously undertaken phony marriage. A pious man, he fears God. In this context of wishing he could look upon himself as a married man in the usual sense, he tells Sheyndl that she should have bought him a *talis* ["prayer shawl"], the traditional wedding gift of a bride to her groom.

To Benye's surprise, Sheyndl replies that she has a talis for him. In fact, she had not remembered to purchase the talis. However, Borekh had given her two taleysim that he had brought from Palestine in order for her to have a dress made. Planning to have something sewn for herself, she had taken one on her wedding trip. As soon as Benye makes his request, she gives it to him, at first concentrating on the new link she has forged between Benye and Borekh. As with the ring, Borekh's sacrilegious gift to her becomes her gift to Benye, appropriate in form if not in spirit.

Sheyndl's attitude soon changes, however. Jokingly, she places the talis across Benye's shoulders, only to have him respond with horror at her improper—to him, impudent—use of a ritual object outside its proper religious context. Rather than defend her own position, Sheyndl yields immediately:

> He held her by both hands, trembling, and looked imploringly into her eyes. It made a powerful impression on Sheyndl. Once again she remembered that the *talis* was fated to be used in prayer, and directly afterwards she implanted firmly in her mind not to forget to write Borekh about it. At that moment, it occurred to her to ask him to give the other *talis* to her father, when circumstances improved. If it was thus fated, they should both be used for prayer (p.275).

Sheyndl's train of thought suggests that her inclusion of a talis in her packing may have been motivated by an unconscious wish to perform her wedding tasks correctly—hence, her desire to give the second one to her father. As far as she knows, Sheyndl would like to feel united with Borekh and contemptuous of the rules to which she has, with deliberate hypocrisy, subjected herself. Underneath this, however, is the need to yield to her father's conception of the way the world works, which means loyalty to her spouse. In her mind, Leyzer and Benye are now in one camp,[29] Borekh in another. This alliance is based singly on the fact of marriage, since Leyzer's own respect lies with Borekh, not with Benye and his undistinguished family.

Sheyndl is married, whether she likes it or not. One of her problems is that, although she had been motivated to marry because of her father, now that she is married, he is no longer her guide and protector. Rather, she now belongs to Benye. She tries to pretend that it is all a joke, but she cannot fool herself:

> It was simply laughable. That wild boar Benye, whom she led around like a faithful dog, was now her master. People wrote

> to her care of his family. His name was engraved on the golden spoons and if her mother lived to be gladdened by her, people would announce all over town that there was a *bris* at Benye's . . . a crazy world (p.278).

She comforts herself with the belief that she has managed to outwit everyone with respect to her marriage. But she soon learns that she has underestimated one person: her father-in-law, Shakhne.

Soon after their wedding, Sheyndl and Benye are invited to spend *shabes* with Shakhne, an invitation about which Benye is overjoyed and Sheyndl distressed. As there is no choice in the matter, she goes along and is catered to and admired.

At the end of their stay, however, Shakhne indicates that he wants to speak to her alone, and, with a quaking heart, Sheyndl follows him outdoors. There, standing in the light from a window—the only bright spot in the pitch-dark night—Shakhne addresses her in his firm manner:

> You should be aware, daughter, that you are now someone's wife. Whatever was in the past is in the past . . . may God forgive you . . . Under the marriage canopy all sins are forgiven. But remember now, woman!

Shakhne enjoins Sheyndl to be a good Jewish wife, indicating that only non-Jewish women are unfaithful. Sheyndl makes a feeble effort to insist that the lecture is unnecessary, but Shakhne interrupts her and demands that she look him straight in the eye. Sheyndl finds this impossible:

> Sheyndl looked down at the ground, into the darkness, at the misted-over window. She could not endure his gaze . . .
>
> 'Remember, woman! . . . You're a Jewish woman . . .' (p.284).

The encounter leaves Sheyndl in a state of great agitation from which she never recovers. Indeed, it may be argued that Shakhne's remarks haunt and torment her to death, with their combined impact of revealing that she has fooled no one more than herself and reminding her that she is now in a position that demands a certain morality of her. At any rate, after that confrontation, Sheyndl's obsessive thoughts now include Shakhne, as she vainly attempts to escape his authoritative power.

On the night of this important event, Sheyndl is unable to soothe herself. She quarrels with Benye, writes to Borekh, calls her old admirer Ashkenazi, then disinvites him when she realizes that she is an object of mockery among his friends. Finally, she achieves some measure of calm by burning the calling cards she had received, cards wishing her love and harmony with Benye, a satisfied life with Benye, unity and peacefulness with Benye. Only by destroying the public recognition of her new status can she attempt to counter, if not wipe out, the onerous meaning of Shakhne's words.

Sheyndl's relief is short-lived, however. Her symbolic act does not change the reality that she is indeed married to Benye. While on the surface she is adjusting well to her new status, underneath she is unstable, questioning the solidity of her identity. Safely alone in her room at night, she looks at herself in the full-length mirror of her beloved wardrobe and tries to be serene, to feel an improvement in her family relations, to construct a sense of well-being. At the same time, Shakhne is before her eyes like a shadow, and, when Borekh returns home from the trip he has undertaken during the time of her wedding, he finds her nervous and disturbed, unable to be alone with him.

On the night of their reunion, Sheyndl again stands before her mirror. This time, however, she has an imaginary conversation with Shakhne:

> I'm laughing at you, you old fool . . . you must certainly want a grandchild from your son . . . Yes, you old fool . . . I'll have a little boy and there'll be a *bris* at your Benye's . . .
>
> She winked playfully at herself in the mirror: 'Remember, woman! . . .' (p.291).

This scene reveals Sheyndl's plight: locked away from both her husband and her lover, she has an imaginary conversation in which she defies her father-in-law and leaves him powerless to retaliate. Yet, ironically, her dismissal of Shakhne is the fantasy; in reality she is unable to continue with Borekh. Thus, while laughing at the "old fool," she has already capitulated to him.

Borekh rapidly grasps what is ailing Sheyndl. He encourages her to obtain a divorce, assuring her that both Shakhne and her father would accept such a move.

Sheyndl, however, is unable to obey Borekh. Instead, she worries because she cannot manage her new life—one that includes both a temporary husband acquired for show and a beloved husband whose children she longs to bear and to whom she wishes to be bound forever. She marvels over the failure of her grand scheme, a failure that is entirely connected to her own inability to carry it through. And always, the spectre of Shakhne hovers around her, appearing from within her own image as she looks at herself in the mirror.

Sheyndl's position worsens instead of improving. She finally agrees to follow Borekh's advice and ask Benye for a divorce. She never does so, however. In part, this is due to her feelings about Borekh—her irritation with him for not taking her obsession about Shakhne seriously, coupled with enraged jealousy over his supposed attraction to her sister Gitl. More than that, however, she is simply too mired in her own quicksand for extrication to be a real possibility.

Instead of speaking of divorce with Benye, she shuts herself in her room and talks to Shakhne in the mirror, trying for one last time to convince herself that she can still have her fake marriage and her real love affair:

> Old fool! . . . You want to have a grandchild from your son . . . I laugh at you. Does a Jewish woman have to be a fool? He will never split up with me . . . never . . . never . . . (p.296).

Yet, even as she speaks, she is overcome with fury, imagining her sister's intrusion upon her happiness. In a fit of rage, she grabs the latest gift Borekh has brought for Gitl—a wristwatch—and hurls it against the mirror. Then she notices that the mirror is split horizontally and that her image is divided through the neck.

Like its famous counterpart in *Snow White,* Sheyndl's mirror refuses to cooperate with her fantasies. Rather, it presents her as she does not wish to see herself, and this in several ways. First, it provides her with the unwelcome knowledge that her undeniable beauty, and even the love of others, cannot ease her pain. Moreover, through the image of Shakhne, it reveals to her that she is a married woman, with all the responsibilities entailed in that role. Finally, when the reflection combines Shakhne's characteristics with her own, i.e., when she becomes the fool, Sheyndl is forced to recognize that the obligations she feels are an outgrowth of her own sense of what marriage constitutes. Thus, to some extent it may be true that she refuses to obtain a divorce from Benye because she still hopes to take advantage of him for the sake of her affair. Yet, as long as she is married, and because she is married, she herself cannot continue the liaison with Borekh.

The image of the mirror in this novel, and the role it plays in Sheyndl's disintegration, could be found as an example in the pages of Heinz Kohut's work, although Faygnberg's novel precedes his ideas by a generation.[30] According to Kohut, the child develops along bipolar lines. At one pole is a child's idealizing image of the parent, which is responsible for the ideals and values that will be incorporated. At the other pole is the mirroring image of the parent, that is, the aspect of the child's growing character that is formed by the parent's reinforcement—or lack thereof—of the child's natural grandiose sense of self. Kohut theorizes that if the mirroring function is not well executed, resulting in the child's developing a healthy narcissism, i.e., a realistic concept of self—one that is satisfied but not overblown—then narcissistic deficit will occur. The child will not achieve a balance but will, instead, maintain a split between grandiosity and emptiness.

Sheyndl's original primary caretaker, Ite, did not nurture her in an optimal way, one in which she felt a core of self-respect. Her second chance, with her father, was also doomed to failure through his early rejection. Later, as long as she is admired for her beauty and superficially appreciated by her father because she confirms his illusions about himself, she is able to function as if she has a solid center, denying her experience of rejection. Then, spurned by her father and beginning to fragment, she seeks stability in marriage. But when confronted both with her limitations and with her imperfection, she falls apart entirely.

It is the growing awareness of herself that leads to the culminating, ironic, prophetic, literally shattering image in the mirror: that of Sheyndl cut in two. The image is ironic, because it represents her realization that she cannot be two people, that she is incapable of splitting herself in two, with part of her available for all to see and part of her held secret; that is, the very unification of Sheyndl's position causes her fragmentation. Her fury at this discovery signals the beginning of her end. Certainly, the jealousy of Gitl motivates Sheyndl's action as well, but this rivalry is not a reality. As an element of Sheyndl's fantasy, it underscores her frustration at having so little control over Borekh, in part because she has so little over herself. The image of Sheyndl in two, injured at the neck, is prophetic because, just hours after her collapse, Sheyndl hangs herself.

Sheyndl's act could, on the surface, appear to be a response to Borekh's torture of her. Yet there are factors that suggest a different interpretation, namely that she is crushed by marriage, by the fact of her own torture of Benye. First, it is not the notion of Borekh's inevitable infidelity that causes Sheyndl to destroy everything in sight and finally herself as well; rather, it is the memory of his ridicule concerning her morals and her fear of transgressing with him. Her desperation is based chiefly on the need to have her beliefs respected, even when they contradict her desire to remain with him.

More telling, finally, is her choice of hanging material: a piece of talis that Borekh had chosen for her as material for a dress and that she had given Benye as a wedding gift. Here, the cause of her capitulation emerges with the special clarity of symbolic action. The deliberate merging together of Borekh's gift with the religious object that first made her aware of her obligations says much about Sheyndl's experience. Till the end, she is unable to leave Borekh; she remains forever tied to him—finally, almost literally so. At the same time, however, she is bound—again, almost literally—to the world of Shakhne, Benye, and her father. The two claims on her life can never be reconciled. Had she possessed a different disposition, she might have been able to relinquish her obsessions and choose one path or the other; had she been raised to see herself as ordinary, she might have made an acceptable match. This was not in her character, however, and her final action was her only way of achieving freedom.

After Sheyndl's death, Borekh decides that she had been one of the rare souls of the world who can truly love—as opposed to vulgar lusting—but who must die for their unusual capacity. Traditional chastity is the only way of overcoming the problem of lust, he concludes. Yet, he is, in his own way, as trapped as Sheyndl had been. At the end of the novel, it appears he is embarking on another "alien path": after the beautiful and independent Gitl. Sheyndl's sacrifice of herself to her shameless and selfish lover becomes more tragic in this light. Still, in Faygnberg's world of hopelessly unexamined souls helplessly repeating their mistakes, her decision assumes power because at least she has made a choice. After striving a lifetime to achieve an existence of love, acceptance, and a measure of liberty, she had realized inchoatively that, in fact, she had accomplished none of it.

In a milieu where family, lover, and society frustrate every attempt at health and independence, suicide may seem the only way out.

Merl

Khaim Grade, in his 1961 novel, *Di agune* [*"The Deserted Wife"*],[31] investigates the clash between compassion and law. As he states in his Forward:

> The relationship between the house of religious study and the street, and the battle between rabbis over a woman whose husband did not return from the First World War . . . this is the theme of the novel 'Di Agune,' illustrated on the canvas of the old, established Jewish life style in Vilne (p.6).

Religious and social issues notwithstanding, the novel's very title suggests that there is an individual and psychological theme as well: the exploration of desertion, rejection, and loneliness. *Di agune* is filled with abandonments, some physical—eventuated by insanity and consequent incarceration—and some emotional, the outcome of fear and weakness. A central victim is Merl, the young widow who cannot prove that her husband is dead. In an atmosphere of harshness and denial, Merl tries her best to survive but eventually capitulates to suicide. As in the most revealing cases of suicide studied here, Merl's decision is influenced by complex interactions with others as well as by her own inner mechanisms.

What is it that prompts Merl to embark on the journey that leads to her death? From the very beginning of *Di agune,* it is clear that her passion is not primarily sexual. She has been alone for fifteen years, since the age of twenty, and has felt no need for a husband. Neither does she seek extramarital love. Yet, Merl does marry again, motivated by a mixture of rebellion and submission that has guided her previously and that, ultimately, contributes to her suicide.

As a very young woman, Merl had been a flirtatious extrovert, "with a black twinkle in her eyes, and all the boys around wanted to kiss her" (p.6). Yet, when it had come to marrying, she had chosen the sickly carpenter Itsik, a socialist who was a poor provider, whose teeth began to fall out as soon as they were married, and whose constantly depressed demeanor frustrated her. An important element in Merl's original thinking had been her determination to reject the attentions of Moyshke Tsirulnik, a wealthy merchant whose leering ugliness, supercilious manner, and elitist values had disgusted her.

Later, when Merl makes her seemingly impulsive decision to marry Kalmen Maytes, Moyshke is once again in the picture. His behavior, a combination of deprecation and servility, so enrages her that she is driven to consult the one authority who might grant an agune's request for permission to remarry. As it happens, Moyshke once again plays a pivotal role in Merl's life, because it is to spite him that she becomes involved in the circumstances that ultimately defeat her.

On the occasion of Merl's first visit to the brilliant but controversial rabbi, Dovid Zelver, she inadvertently stumbles upon him in a position of helplessness. Just when she is unburdening her heart to him, much as in the dramatic Biblical scene between Hannah and Eli, Reb Dovid's older son rushes in to announce that little Mottele is once again having difficulty breathing. The rabbi, who until a moment before had been the one in charge—albeit weakly—is suddenly transformed into the supplicant. At first, he reacts in a confused manner, as if this event had not occurred frequently enough in the past. Then, however, he requests that Merl fetch the barber surgeon, while he runs home to tend to his wife and ailing child. Thus Merl becomes immediately involved in the problematic home life of the man from whom she had been seeking aid.

From the very outset, Reb Dovid assumes a prominent role in Merl's mind and heart. He is both an authority figure—someone she needs—and someone who needs her. More than that, even during their initial encounter, she had experienced a peculiar intimacy with him, feeling that their souls were linked, almost as if they had attained some sort of merger.[32] Merl had been standing in the darkened House of Study, listening to Reb Dovid's heart-rending cries for God's help:

> Merl felt as if a scream was tearing itself from her throat as well, as a wind transmits a fire from one burning ruin to another. But she bit her lips and contained herself. But the rabbi in the corner cried out even louder and tore with it the lament from her oppressed heart, which she had kept stifled within herself for so many years (p.45).

From this point on, Reb Dovid plays a central part in Merl's thoughts and even her behavior. At the beginning, she merely longs to help him and aid in supporting him, both financially and emotionally. In this, her response to the rabbi is similar to her behavior with her family and with Itsik, and this may be the root of her attachment to him. Despite Itsik's reputation as a mediocre breadwinner, Merl had happily undertaken to marry him. Later, after his disappearance, she had turned her attention to supporting her widowed mother and her two sisters, although one of them was already married. Merl had lived in that situation until shortly before the events around which the novel's action is based. Then her younger sister had married a hard-drinking idler, thereby compounding Merl's responsibilities. To annoy her, this new relative had become friendly with Moyshke, introducing him once again into the household. Unable to tolerate her surroundings any longer, Merl had moved away.

Merl's loneliness leaves her open to the fantasy of finding a new, more fulfilling family than the one she has left behind. Imagining that devoting herself to the Zelvers will ameliorate her isolation, she abandons her wedding plans:

> What craziness had entered her head—marrying! She should rather occupy herself with helping the rabbi and his family. She had great compassion for him, he was such a dignified man, and his wife wasn't bad either, merely bitter. Merl walked rapidly and became increasingly animated: her mother in the old-age home didn't need her help . . . she would help a refined family and she herself would not be so unhappy. She would have a home to visit (p.52).

Unfortunately for Merl, her wishful strategem is rudely destroyed by Eydl, the rabbi's frantic and disgruntled wife. Once she has learned of the agune's status and her role in further complicating Reb Dovid's already vexed professional existence, Eydl forbids Merl to enter the impoverished Zelver home again. Dovid's wife is too late, however, to prevent her husband's embroilment in Merl's plight; he soon emerges as the sole rabbinic authority willing to sanction her marriage to Kalmen. Feeling pressured by him as well as by her sisters and mother, Merl submits to their wishes.

Merl fully understands her decision to marry Kalmen only much later, when she has already separated from him:

> She had married Kalmen because of his honesty and kindness to her, and because she was lonely, because she wanted to spite Moyshke Tsirulnik and because the rabbi had told her to . . . (p.208).

Merl's internal relationship to Dovid continues after her marriage. While his outward manner may be anything but organized, he nonetheless gives Merl a sense of wholeness and purpose in life. She develops a day-to-day hunger for the sight of him. Without this connection, distant though it is, she is unsettled, scattered:

> Since her second meeting with the rabbi, when he had told her to get married, she could not sit down to the sewing machine in the morning until she had observed the diminuitive Polotsk *dayen* [associate rabbi] in his long kapote taking his son to kheyder. Today Merl had not seen the rabbi go by with his son and the whole day she had been drawn to the window (p.66).

Merl's superficially rebellious spirit is thus revealed as an overwhelming need for attachment to a powerful figure who will be like a parent to her, guiding, shaping her and providing her with emotional sustenance. Merl's craving for this sort of contact with Dovid is so great that it causes her to ignore the fact that his encouragement of her marriage stems more from the struggle he is waging with his colleagues than from any kindness towards her. This malleability born of need is nothing new, for Merl has had long experience with being similarly manipulated by her sisters.[33]

Even before Merl had begun to consider Kalmen as a prospective husband, Gute and Golde had adamantly advocated the match. They had contrasted him with their loutish mates, urging her to accept his proposal. At first, Merl had rejected the notion, since Kalmen was linked in her mind to death and aging.[34] Yet, when the time had come for her final decision, they had pestered her so mercilessly that she was swayed, as much to gain some peace as anything else.[35] At that point, their true motivation—if not altruism—had been unclear. Later, however, when Merl decides to divorce Kalmen, the two sisters reveal their selfish aims.

Merl first discovers that her younger sister Golde is interested in the divorce because she hopes to persuade Merl to marry Moyshke afterwards. Her motive is personal: she wishes to keep Moyshke on good terms with Shayke, her husband. Moyshke has encouraged Shayke to stop drinking and Golde is nervously pleased about the change in her fortunes.

Gute, the more modest and deeply pathetic of Merl's sisters, is also looking for aid from her younger sibling—as in the days preceding Merl's second marriage. Although it is Golde's idea that Merl should wed Moyshke, Gute does not fail to understand the benefits to her of the marriage:

> I don't need him to help me, my children contribute the household expenses . . . but if he brought over doctors to our mother and helped outfit my daughters, it wouldn't hurt (p.229).

Merl, for her part, is confused by the demands placed upon her. Although she feels trapped, she has the urge to comply, because, in her helping role, she can experience herself as significant and stable. In short, by nurturing others, she nurtures herself. As Merl's position becomes increasingly muddled, the underlying wish to be cared for, so carefully overlaid with mature or pseudo-mature coping, becomes ever more evident, finally erupting in a fantasy of maternal comfort.

At first, Merl's wish for emotional shelter is projected outwards as, continuing to ward off her own needs, she focuses on those of Reb Dovid. The scene is her apartment, where she is allowing herself to be approached by Moyshke—in large measure to aid Dovid, for Moyshke has been insinuating that Merl's permission to marry had been a special favor, evidence of an improper liaison. Once again, Merl humbles herself for the rabbi's sake. Emboldened by drink, Moyshke soon enough begins to push Merl towards the bed. Although she yields, she is greatly agitated, since she hates both the man and his manner. Her eyes wander around the room, in vain search for protection, until her gaze becomes glued to the window:

> Before [Moyshke] had come in she had stood by the window, thought of the rabbi and kissed the window pane: now she had the notion that the Polotsk *dayen* was standing outside and was looking up at her apartment, aware of everything that was happening (p.249).

Her response, however, does not reflect her malaise and her longing for Reb Dovid's support; rather she appeals to Moyshke on behalf of her would-be guardian: "Save the Polotsk rabbi, he is a very miserable man and the whole city is persecuting him, do something for him'' (p.249). Unable to face the enormity of her own panic and need, she maintains her well-honed pattern of deflection.

As the threat becomes more desperate, Merl recognizes a dreadful reality: her intense sexual passion for Moyshke and her wish to be punished for it, to be ravished but prevented from experiencing desire. The image of Reb Dovid once again comes into her mind:

> Her body was not her own, it was an alien body cut off from someone else and affixed to her neck. She would leave behind her body and she herself would flee, flee to the rabbi . . . and again she had the idea that the Polotsk *dayen* was standing outside, looking up to her window, aware of what was going on in the apartment (p.250).

Merl's thinking here reveals important aspects of her defensive structure and reasoning process. When projection fails, and she can no longer cast her wishes out of herself and onto someone else, she turns to splitting, here articulated in the image of Merl separated from her own body.[36] She now recognizes inchoatively that she needs help, but she cannot fully admit to this. Rather, she confronts only the fact that part of her—some part she can neither see nor actually feel—must run away in order to survive. Functionally, this response is similar to Merl's projection, since it allows her to repudiate the intolerable. In the case of projection she denies her wish by putting it elsewhere; here, she allows only a portion of herself to imagine being with Dovid, saved by him.

Merl's fantasy suggests that, in her experience, erotic impulses must be kept separate from strivings for emotional fulfillment. In fact, throughout the novel, she never attempts to integrate the two aspects of her adult existence: instead, she always ties sexuality to caretaking and denies herself sexual pleasure.[37]

Predictably, matters between Merl and Moyshke reach appalling proportions. Moyshke first callously informs Merl that Reb Dovid's son Mottele has died. This child had acted as a mystical link between Merl and the rabbi, inspiring both to believe that the boy's ultimate fate could somehow be affected by their actions. Cruelly indicating that Merl may be Reb

Dovid's lover but the dead child does not belong to her, Moyshke goes on to crow that the rabbi's wife had referred to Merl as a lewd bitch. In fury and despair, Merl smashes her would-be suitor's head with the whiskey bottle from which they have been drinking and flees to the forest near her family's property.

There, sitting in the cold, she hears a wagon passing, and she imagines being carried off by the peasant driver. In typical fashion, Merl's longing for salvation merges into the idea that she will reward the peasant by taking care of his family:

> How good it would be if the peasant took her along in his wagon, hid her in straw and took her to his village. She would sew clothes for his wife and children, help with the housework and be thankful for a morsel of dry bread and a cot to sleep on (p.255).

The content of this fantasy is a clear combination of the two major issues in Merl's mind: her weary wish for protection and her belief that she is worthy of punishment—not for having attacked Moyshke, but for having encumbered and endangered the rabbi's existence. This mixture of self-preservative and self-destructive tendencies culminates in Merl's next mental images, more dream than waking fantasy, in which she overhears a conversation between her mother and Itsik. Both are concerned about her: her mother scolds Itsik for having left Merl for so long, and Itsik, explaining that he has a wooden leg, speaks lovingly about his young and vivacious wife. The recent past, with all its pain and ugliness, evaporates temporarily as Merl basks in the warmth of two beloved figures in her life.

The dream does not remain sweet, of course. Suddenly, Merl's mother reports that she has remarried and is suffering, whereupon Itsik is inflamed with anger, interpreting this news as evidence of infidelity. He threatens to split open her skull, and this intrusion of waking reality forces Merl into full consciousness. Realizing her hopeless plight, she determines to take her own life.

Merl decides to commit suicide when she understands that the healing care of a loving mother or husband will be denied her. For, only her sense of connection to a strong and lively adult gives her a reason to live. Earlier, when she had visited her feeble mother, the latter had suddenly asked after Merl's husband Itsik. The event had caused Merl to entertain "a wild thought, that her mother would, before her death, begin to blabber 'Mama,' as a child does." As she had left the old-age home, Merl had continued her musing:

> . . . who would miss Keyle and her daughters if they had never been born? They were as important for the world as a heap of rocks in a field that is to be cultivated (p.206).

Merl's fantasy expresses the association she makes between her mother's regression and her own death. It thus reflects her deep wish to merge with her mother: if her mother lives, so does she—hence the importance of caring for her—but it also implies that Merl cannot survive if her mother is not available to affirm her existence.

The urge for union with Dovid manifests itself in different conscious images, but the underlying concept is the same: her being and his being are linked at the point of life and death. Some time before she actually kills herself, Merl had contemplated suicide as a way of saving the rabbi from Moyshke's shameful insinuations against him. Knowing that the agune was capable of such a monumental transgression, the Jewish community would forgive Reb Dovid his behavior, as it pitied Reb Levi Hurvitz—Reb Dovid's adversary—because he had to cope with an insane daughter, Tsirl. Already at that moment, Merl had equated herself with the difficult child of a respected rabbinic family. Moreover, she had viewed her life as bound to Dovid's, since, as a way of enhancing his life, she could destroy her own.[38]

At the end of her life, Merl does admit to herself that her reaction to Dovid has a sexual component. Before then, she had realized an attraction but had shielded herself from naming it:

> The rabbi! She knew that her love for the Polotsk *dayen* was sheer lunacy. Did she love him as a woman loves a man? She did not know. She only knew that she idolized him (p.208).[39]

But on the night preceding her fateful meeting with Moyshke, Merl's awareness expands. Considering her marriages and her sexual dissatisfaction with them, she lies naked and thinks of Dovid. This is the only time, aside from her disgusted excitement with Moyshke, that there is any hint of sexuality in Merl's view of herself—and she cannot tolerate it. Overcome with embarrassment, she tries to ignore her body and its gratifying sensations altogether. The effort is in vain. Furthermore, these unwelcome feelings bring associations of death and insanity. She muses about Tsirl: "Probably the rabbi's daughter was also deeply enamored of her own body." (p.237). Thus, the expression of sexuality is tantamount to disaster.

During the final hours of her life, when Merl is in the forest, watching her life pass by as if before her eyes, she has one more sexual fantasy about Dovid:

> If they are already saying about her that she was the rabbi's lover, she should really have been that. She knew that he would rather die than touch her (p.254).

Her final thoughts, however, turn not to adult sexuality but to a deeper bond, to Mottele, as her identification with Dovid's child becomes manifest:

> She did not want to live and must not live! The rabbi had hoped that by freeing her, God would have mercy on his child. But she had not been sufficiently worthy in God's eyes for Him to show compassion to the rabbi's child because of her. The child had died and she would die too (p.258).

Now her sense that she is lost without Dovid's life-giving protection comes together with her longing to be his child: if she cannot have that safety and vibrance, then she may as well be dead. Besides, she reasons, if the rabbi could not sustain his own flesh and blood, how dare she expect more?

It is in this hopeless mood that Merl concludes her existence, not out of guilt for having remarried, not for having harmed Moyshke, nor because she cannot bear the love she feels for Dovid, but rather, like a homeless waif, because there is no one to shelter her from the elemental powers of her life.

Shortly before her final dream, she observes a squirrel from her hiding place, near the house where she had grown up. Imagining at first that the squirrel must be cold, she then comments: "I am even poorer and lonelier than she, she is at home here" (p.255).

In essence, Merl dies of abandonment, but not because she is physically alone—any more than she had been during the uneventful months prior to meeting Kalmen. Rather, her inner isolation has become undeniable to her and she is overwhelmed by the force of her needs. In this, she resembles Tsirl, who like herself, has been destroyed by the rabbinic world. These two women are the only ones who appear with any depth in *Di agune.* Merl identifies with Tsirl as a helpless, yet blameworthy burden. Moreover, Grade's final and climactic juxtaposition of the two paves the way for understanding more about the connection between sexuality and deprivation, love and dependence.

While Merl's relationship to her father is shrouded in mystery, except for the fact that she is loyal enough to say kadesh for him at the cemetery, Tsirl's existence in the novel is defined virtually completely by her relationship to her father, the stern yet morose Reb Levi Hurvitz.

Initially, Tsirl's illness seems purely hereditary, the unfortunate result of her mother's insanity. As in clinical instances, the line between Tsirl's loss of a nurturing mother as cause for her own infirmity, versus a hereditary reason for the same, cannot be definitively drawn. And, since there are no scenes depicting the relationship between the two—which might shed light on Tsirl's vulnerability to her mother—there is no way of narrowing the area of uncertainty.

The contact between Reb Levi and his daughter, in contrast, is clear and indicative: a rough and critical parent, he simultaneously fears his daughter and her sexuality. Tsirl's habit of presenting herself, naked, before her father and other respectable gentlemen thus possesses dynamic logic, whatever secret significance it may contain as well.

Reb Levi, whose manner with everyone is commanding yet distant, cannot refrain from scolding his only child, despite his most fervent efforts. One such instance occurs at the end of shabes, while the two are celebrating *havdole* [the ceremony marking the conclusion of shabes]. Although pleased that she is sufficiently lucid to observe the ritual with him, Reb Levi is nonetheless incensed by the fact that Tsirl has washed her hair on shabes. He feels compelled to tell her so, even though he immediately reprimands himself for this indiscretion. Reb Levi goes on to chide his daughter for questioning God's will in the matter of her illness, and Tsirl finally retaliates. With the gay abandon of a little girl, she says:

> You think that I became ill when I was already an adult. In fact, I became ill when I was still a little girl. When grandpa died, you woke me up and took me to him . . . I wanted to cry. I thought that now grandpa would never stroke me again. You were always so strict. You either didn't speak to me at all or yelled at me. So I stood next to grandpa and thought that now no one would ever stroke me again (p.111).

Tsirl forces her father to recall the awful events of that night. A woman dressed as a bride had appeared at her grandfather's house and demanded to be buried with him. Abandoned by her groom, she had seen no other choice for herself. Tsirl had screamed in outrage at the thought of someone else being with her grandfather, while her father had labeled the unfortunate petitioner a madwoman. The would-be bride had threatened that if Tsirl prevented her from attaining her wish, she herself would never live to marry. Terrified, Tsirl had run away, only to suffer her father's anger because she was frightened. Thereafter, she had lived with the uneasy fantasy that the miserable woman would manage to dig up her grandfather's grave and receive the caresses for which she herself was starving. Tsirl confesses, furthermore, that she had seen evidence of the bride's curse in her father's refusal to let her mix with other young people—lest her piety be compromised, according to him.

Reb Levi, stroking her hair, "as if to compensate for her childhood years without tenderness" (p.112), admits that her youthful perception had been correct: after her grandfather, there was no one left to give her the affection she had so enjoyed with him. Her mother was already institutionalized and he, Reb Levi, had been young and still embittered about his fate (in fact, this bitterness has never left him and contributes to his unhappy relationships with others, including his daughter).

Tsirl's situation, as she herself manages to understand, is one of severe deprivation. This did not begin with the death of her grandfather; he had served as a vital nourisher in an otherwise barren environment. Yet, his influence was only strong enough to hold disaster at bay as long as he lived. So desperate was Tsirl's need for love, and so bereft was she without her grandfather, that the prospect of having to share his attention with anyone else had threatened her beyond control.

On the night of her greatest loss in life, the miserable bride's menacing words, combined with her father's anger over her frightened reaction, had convinced little Tsirl that her longing was unacceptable. Her father's subsequent oppressive attempts to squelch her strivings for companionship had then had fertile ground on which to grow: her belief that she was cursed, that she would remain in isolation, unmarried and unloved, that she was the unlucky new vessel of the disappointed bride's frenzy. As much in horrified identification as out of hopelessness and terror, then, Tsirl had begun her pattern of mad activity, alternating with fury at the fate that had pressed itself upon her. Within this context, her heritage from her mother need not be pathognomic.

It is too late when Reb Levi pats his daughter's hand after her outburst. Even worse, he soon reveals that he has not really understood an important influence on her life, that is, that his anxiety about Tsirl's sexual morality had not stemmed from any observed tendencies on her part, nor even from the dangerous influence of her mother. Rather, they had been a projection of his own guilty desires, and his struggle to suppress them: "He had felt that he had to be more pious and stricter than his brothers-in-law because he could stumble more easily than his brothers-in-law, particularly since he had remained without a wife for many years" (p.113).

As it turns out, Reb Levi's own confusion is reflected in Tsirl, whose nakedness is eventually revealed as anything but the attempt to be sexually arousing. The occasion is a discussion about Tsirl's cousin, who had been permitted a freer youth and is now married with three children. Tsirl makes a comment—"Isn't she ashamed?" (p.113)—meaning that, with three children, her cousin's sexual activity is an open matter. Reb Levi is incapable of recognizing that Tsirl is extremely oversensitive to what might be considered lewd behavior. Quite out of keeping with traditional Jewish values, where marital relations and subsequent childbearing are praised and expected, Tsirl has constructed a view that forbids even this. Thus, she invokes modesty even where the society does not.

Soon after their conversation, Reb Levi is occupied with a meeting devoted to Reb Dovid's decision about the agune. In the midst of this, Tsirl appears, naked, and is swiftly shut into her room by her father. From there she calls out that her nemesis, the bride, has been reunited with her missing groom and therefore "she is no longer an agune" (p.120). Clearly, the thought of an abandoned wife has inflamed Tsirl's memory—and her fantasy as well, since the woman who had been such a devastating object of her terrors was unmarried and therefore not an agune. Tsirl's association is significant, because it underscores the motivation for her behavior. Far from representing the need to be sexually provocative, it is a helpless plea for attention and affirmation, couched in the only form she knows of to reach her preoccupied father.

Predictably, Reb Levi misconstrues the meaning of this ploy. In a final example of his dire failure to display—or perhaps even to feel—love for his child, Reb Levi disavows her, declaring that she must be a bastard, since no daughter of his would want to run into the street naked. Tsirl's response is both wild and to the point: "The bride with the flowers in her hair is your daughter, the agune is your daughter, and I am your daughter" (p.121).

Tsirl thus accuses her father of being responsible for the pain of women: the abandoned bride whom he had chased away and labeled mad; Merl, whose barren future he understood because of his own loneliness yet treated without compassion; and Tsirl herself, the unloved, unstroked, unclaimed daughter. Hidden amidst all this is an accusation of Reb Levi in terms of his wife as well—if he could make so many other women distraught, if he could exacerbate a weak condition in them, then why should his wife have been any different? Indeed, Reb Levi's brother-in-law articulates this very thought during the wretched aftermath of Merl's suicide: ". . . he had to think once again the same thing that everyone thought, that if one had as crazy an anger within as Reb Levi, it was no wonder that the members of his household went completely mad" (p.287).

The connection that Tsirl forms between Merl and herself is later, after the agune's death, carried on by Reb Levi himself. In the first horror of the news, and in the midst of his own agony about the death of Mottele, Dovid calls Reb Levi a murderer in the matter of Merl's suicide. Thereafter, Reb Levi must withstand the fury of the townspeople who, easily swayed in any case, respond to the news of Merl's death with a call for revenge. The ugly events prove too much, and Reb Levi begins to hallucinate his daughter's presence. Knowing full well that she is institutionalized, he nevertheless finds her appearing at unexpected moments, the first of these on the day of Merl's funeral. On one occasion she actually scolds him gently for having gotten involved with the agune.

Reb Levi both dreads and longs for these visitations: Tsirl is, after all, his only close connection, far more so than his wife, whom "he had never loved very deeply" (p.311). At the same time, he fears her rage, imagining that she will one day come and strangle him—thereby disposing of him with much the same method as Merl has used on herself. One night, the dual "persecutors," Merl and Tsirl, finally merge in Reb Levi's mind, and he decides he can no longer abide the tormented existence he has been experiencing. Convinced now that he, too, has taken leave of his senses, he determines to quit his rabbinic position.

The moment occurs as the rabbi is considering how the sound of young couples laughing together, although it had once incensed him, would now be most appealing. As he closes his eyes, he sees two naked female arms scrambling up the walls, hugging the ledge in order not to fall. There is no head, just the arms, knocking at the window and scratching the panes to get attention. The figure says to him: "Let me come in and warm myself. I'm cold in the cemetery, very cold." Reb Levi recognizes the apparition: it is the agune. At that very moment, Tsirl appears in Reb Levi's mind. Standing in her room, she admonishes him once again, "I told you, father, not to get involved with the agune" (p.312).

In his fantasy, then, Merl reminds Reb Levi that he has caused her unending suffering, and Tsirl teaches him that she had understood certain matters better than he.

The reality is just the opposite, however, for it is Tsirl whom he has relentlessly harmed and Merl who has perceived the essence of humane Jewish existence that had somehow eluded him. Reb Levi has learned nothing. Furthermore, his attempt to atone for the rigidity and harshness of his previous actions does the women he has hurt no good whatsoever. Rather, it conforms to his view of what is best and most comfortable for him—as always.

The merger of Merl and Tsirl, or at least their immediate juxtaposition and confusion in Reb Levi's mind, does more than indicate how they have come to grief. The literary situation here sheds light on the artistic creation of Merl and reveals the spot where inchoate, probably unconscious, psychological insight meets literary device, although, at a deep level, the latter may also be unconscious. Grade does not tell the reader about Merl's childhood or her relationships with early loved ones. In contrast, this is essentially all he exposes of Tsirl. When these two characters are placed side by side, the reader is prompted to ask questions concerning their creation and to draw speculative conclusions, as one might do about the parents of two siblings.

Just as siblings are formed from the same genetic pool, may be similar to one another in looks and personality, and yet are unique individuals whose identity resonates with others in a particular way, so it is with characters. At first, or in the end, the formation of one artistic mind—and in that sense all part of the same consciousness—they are nonetheless, in the best cases, individual in conception, fitted with qualities that are suggestive beyond all the author's intentions. By his images, narrative construction and fantasies, the author provides the reader's raw material, much as a person presents traits that are both consciously and unconsciously perceived by others.

Merl and Tsirl have much in common: both fail to receive enough love to keep them on an even keel; both have been denied the opportunity of growing unfettered into sexual maturity; because of their deficits, both ultimately find themselves in positions where a tenable existence within the Jewish community is impossible; both succumb to the vicissitudes of their lives. The beauty of *Di agune* is that Grade, rather than accusing either of these unfortunate women, sees insanity and suicide alike as natural, albeit tragic, responses to individual and social failures.

CHAPTER FOUR

Like Father, Like Daughter

The writing of Borekh Glazman is as strange and perverse as anything to be found in Yiddish literature. Glazman's world is not a benign place: passions erupt as individuals can no longer control their impulses, needs, aggressions, and desires; stability, fragile to begin with, is ever on the verge of slipping—or dropping away completely. Thus it is not surprising that some of the most intriguing yet peculiar suicides in Yiddish *belles lettres* occur in the pages of Glazman.

Yet, even within this oeuvre, where the unexpected may seem ordinary, *Di mishpokhe pikuda* [*"The Pikuda Family"*][1] stands out, with its discussion of a bizarre suicide set against the backdrop of coarse sexuality, cruelty, and alienation. Moreover, *Di mishpokhe pikuda* provides an especially interesting example of fictional suicide because it probes the effects of early deprivation on both a male and a female. While subjected to similar suffering initially, these two engage in very different—albeit analogously maladaptive—behavior later on. Specifically, the male is withdrawn and inert, the female tempestuous and unyielding.

In a sense, the title of this novella is misleading, since the work, although it does introduce a family, focuses almost entirely on the father, Zakhari, and his eldest daughter, Raye. Their personalities, idiosyncracies and, to some extent, their interactions—with each other and with third parties—form the basis of plot and conflict development. Indeed, the entire composition is divided into a brief untitled prologue and three main sections: "The Father," "The Daughter," and "In the Faraway Land." These headings underscore the centrality of the relationship between Zakhari and Raye, at the same time revealing the extent to which father and daughter (and, for that matter, all the characters in the novella) remain isolated from one another, negating in that way, too, the concept of family as an integrated unit.

Zakhari is, from first to last, a depressed and hopeless man, apparently devoid of any humor, light-heartedness, or energy. The first sentence of the section devoted to him explains:

> Zakhari Pikuda was a silent Jew, and melancholy. He used to walk around silently absorbed, as if some time ago he had lost some valuable object and could never forget it (p.9).

Zakhari spends the bulk of his time wandering the rooms of his ever-emptier hotel, inspecting for dirt and, when successful in finding an offensive spot, summoning his wife to clean it up. In the midst of these tours, he stops in order to wash his hands compulsively, using perfumed soap. His one source of some pleasure is an occasional foray into the local Turkish baths, mainly because there he is lulled into a drowsiness from which he has no desire ever to awaken.

Zakhari is not alone in his family as far as sadness and depression are concerned. He is the sole survivor among four siblings, two of whom are documented as suicides, and the third as a suspicious death. His sister had taken her own life because her husband had said an "impolite word" (p.18) to her. At the time, she had merely looked at him hatefully. Some time later, however, when he was absent from the house on business, she had decided: "I have nothing against him, but this is the time" (p.18). After poisoning her only child, she had taken a hot bath and slit the most important veins in her limbs.[2]

Zakhari's elder brother, Naum, had died a similarly violent death. Returning from a ball with his "pretty, tall, somewhat spoiled" wife, Naum had railed against her for flirting. The wife, in an almost comical self-defense reminiscent of Sholem-Aleykhem's *Dos tepl,* had denied the accusation, asserted her right to flirt, and announced that she didn't care whether the man in question liked Jews or not. At this, Naum had ventured no reply; the next day his wife had found him still fully dressed, his throat slit with a shaving knife.

As for Zakhari's other brother, there is evidence that this death, too, was a suicide. Moysey had died far away, in a non-Jewish community, and his wife had needed to persuade the local police that her husband's death had been natural, caused by heart disease. Moreover, she had been forced to bribe the burial society to award him a proper Jewish burial.[3]

Zakhari's wife, Beyle, believes that her sister- and brothers-in-law had died because they were members of a family the collective character of which was truculent, stubborn, proud, and silent:

> Because of an insult, or because of something simply trivial, they would easily reach the point of blood—their own blood, usually (p.19).

A glance at the obvious Pikuda suicides, however, yields a picture quite unlike the one Beyle constructs. Both had taken their lives at a point where they felt alone, abandoned. Zakhari's sister had clearly experienced the "impolite word," the cause of her silence, with unusual intensity. Perhaps she had heard condescension in her husband's comment. Whatever her reason, she reacts by shutting him out; yet she stays alive as long as he is around. As soon as he leaves, however, she kills herself, all the time averring that she is not angry with him. The evidence suggests that, on the contrary, she feels a great deal of anger towards her husband, the source of which is not his rudeness or vulgarity per se but its special meaning for her, i.e., that she was not worth respecting, not deserving of loving companionship. Unable to endure the pain that recognizing her wrath and its underlying blow to her self-esteem would entail, she turns her misery against herself and her child.

Similarly, Naum is enraged with his wife for flirting and, especially, for her indifference to his sensitivity about anti-Semitism. Yet there is a deeper wound: she has withdrawn her intimacy from him. Naum's suicide is certainly one of revenge, an angry statement of his desire to punish his wife. At the same time, the act implies his sense that she is too far away to be affected by any less dramatic overture, as her dismissive attitude and subsequent absence during his last night could only corroborate.

Even in the most dispirited of homes, the suicide of three out of four children—and eventually Zakhari joins them—is an unusual event. On the surface, at least, their early existence had not been particularly unusual: the family had moved from Lithuania to a burgeoning city in Southern Russia, in the area of the Don River. At first, the Jewish presence in this new location had been sparse and, in later years, Zakhari continues to remember the homey quality of life before the move, unable to feel comfortable in the place where he has spent most of his life, despite the growth of Jewish activity.

Zakhari had lost his father at a relatively early age, just at the time the city was expanding enough to build its first synagogue. The only reference to him suggests an overwhelming sense of sadness and defeat:

> Around that time the elder Pikuda—Borekh Pikuda—had already died, leaving behind a mound of sand on the unfamiliar ground as a sign of himself, making it his own. He hadn't lived to see it (p.13).

Zakhari's mother, Gnesye, is not portrayed in any great detail, yet there is enough information to reveal her as a cold, aloof woman. She is the one member of the family who is still traditional in her Jewish observance, yet she feels she cannot impart any of this to her grandchildren and she therefore barely tries, contenting herself with taking Raye to synagogue on holidays and teaching her the *moydane* ("the morning prayer"). There is more to the problem than a generation gap, however. Gnesye is unable to bring any warmth into the household, despite the performance of her rituals. She lights shabes candles, says the blessing, but:

> Besides the little candelabrum that burned at the edge of the table and braced itself not to fall down, there was no feeling in the house that shabes had arrived. Just an ordinary held-in, gnawing sadness spread through the dining room (pp.25–26).

Moreover, although the grandchildren crowd around her, fascinated by her exotic practices, she chooses to dwell on a reverie of her past, barely acknowledging their presence:

> She would be silent and answer their many questions with a quiet, distant smile. From her eyes remoteness shone cooly (p.24).

It is expected, then, that with the combination of a physically absent father and an emotionally absent mother, the Pikuda children would desperately crave human contact yet simultaneously fear impending loss.

Unfortunately for the victims, an upbringing of psychological deprivation can mean that the very resources necessary for repairing the damage have never been developed. Zakhari's marriage, for example, has an aura of distance and loneliness that combines aspects of his mother's behavior with predictable reactions to that behavior. The narrator describes Zakhari's passage into adulthood with the offhand comment—in a subordinate clause—that he had "gotten older and married, like all people" (p.14). The hint is that Zakhari had married not because he wanted to or felt interested in that role, but merely because he considered it his only option. Trapped in a way of life for which he is unequipped, he behaves, not surprisingly, in a manner inappropriate and disappointing to those who expect much more of him. As he was raised with chilly restraint, so he responds with chilly restraint to his new family.

Zakhari's miscasting as a husband does not pass unnoticed by his wife; Beyle feels about him that:

> Her husband had always remained a stranger to her, even in the most intimate moments of union, and thus she had had children with a stranger (p.28).

Their sexual relationship is not only alien to her, it is deadly:

> She had the feeling that she was lying in bed with a corpse, had had children with a corpse; he might, then, soon return to the place where, in the end, he had to go (p.22).

Beyle finds her husband a drain on her energy, and, faced with a failing hotel business, she and Gnesye decide to send him to the United States, ostensibly so that he may pave the way for them in the land of opportunity. Actually, they are motivated by the desire to be rid of him, since he embodies the stuff of ruin for them. Their reasons, however, are not entirely identical. Gnesye responds to her son as incompetent and, in fact, unmanly. For her part, Beyle is eager for Zakhari to leave because, not only is she fearful that he will commit suicide, but—entertaining the wish that he do so—she is frightened of herself:

> Now, before daybreak, Beyle became much afraid that her husband, too [i.e., as his siblings had], might commit suicide,—and then she felt, with even greater fear, that she was longing for that, that she looked forward to it . . . there had to be a way out: Oh, it was surely a great sin to think of it, but if "it" happened, it would then be in the past (p.23).

Beyle's reaction is that of a woman who has spent long and frustrating years with a withdrawn, morbidly self-absorbed[4] spouse.

Since Zakhari's childhood is not narrated as part of *Di mishpokhe pikuda,* it is impossible to know what was transmitted to him—or, for that matter, to his siblings. Judging only from his mother's estimate of him and her manifest lack of warmth, however, the speculation emerges that Zakhari and his siblings were never affirmed and encouraged to become self-confident and active individuals. Their suicides, and his own, may thus be identified, at least in part, as a response to that experience of rejection.

Perhaps the clearest suggestion of this familial blight occurs in a description of Zakhari's last night at home before embarking on his journey. Observing his mother fussing over her candelabrum in preparation for welcoming shabes, he realizes that she has become old. Nonetheless, he remains silent, and she is so absorbed in her task that she fails even to notice him. Zakhari leaves the house and walks to the marble *shul,* the symbol, for him, of identification with a community. Yet, since that connection has always eluded him, he does not enter the shul. Instead, he remains alone, bemoaning his fate and complaining about his earlier life. His words reveal something about why he has just walked out on his mother:

> What, then, have I wanted all my life? All my life some feeling cut me at the heart. It was doubly painful because I never knew what it was I lacked. I wanted something and knew unconsciously that I would never get it (p.32).

When Zakhari finally does return home, it is clear that he had been correct in despairing of closeness with his mother. As he might have anticipated, she is no more able to concentrate on him during this, his last night at home, than she has been on any previous occasion. Beyle's attitude only reinforces the impression of neglect, highlighting the extent to which Zakhari's marital relationship is a recreation of his unhappy situation with Gnesye:

> His old mother silently looked at the *Korbn minkhe*[5] and was absorbed in her inner shabes. Beyle quietly served him his meal. It was a workaday supper on Friday night (p.35).

Zakhari duly leaves home and makes his way to America. His mother and wife had been correct: he never sends for the rest of the family. They were also, apparently, in the right concerning his negative effect on the hotel business, for, once rid of him, they are soon flourishing again—although with a somewhat questionable clientele. In an environment that now resembles a brothel, Zakhari's daughter, Raye, passes her childhood and discovers the world around her.

In many respects, Raye is the opposite of Zakhari: where he is depressed, isolated, and passive, she is spunky, aggressive, and constantly active. In their relationship, Raye had early proven herself to be more than a match for her father. Not surprisingly, they had started out on the wrong foot with one another: he had not been noticeably pleased by her birth, and she had responded with insecurity in his presence. The nature of this interaction is epitomized by two occasions when Zakhari had struck his child.

In the first instance, Raye had fought back physically, biting, scratching, tearing at her attacker's hair. The second time—when she was not yet five—had prompted a different response. Raye had locked herself in a room with a glass door, making herself visible, audible, but not reachable. She had screamed, wept, and gesticulated wildly, until her father had run through the hotel in a desperate state of helplessness. Raye had refused to come out even to eat, insisting that she would not emerge from her self-imposed exile until her father had drowned himself. Zakhari's answer to this outburst of rage had been a combination of exasperation and detachment; he had "torn out his hair and thought with quiet coldness that in his house a strange, hostile creature was growing up—in his own house" (p.43).

In the end, Zakhari had left the house, but Raye had experienced no triumph. On the contrary, she had thrown herself face down on the floor of the room and had remained there for the rest of the day. Raye's victory had been empty, even though she had beaten her father. For, when he had walked out, he had ceased to be involved with her. Her retaliation for the violence done to her was the sole vindication she achieved. The deeper goal, that of a loving relationship with her father,[6] resulted in total failure on that day; rather than opening her father's heart to her and making him see that he must not abuse her in such a hateful way, she had managed only to convince him that he should protect himself against her:

> And from that time on, her father never so much as touched her again; he left her to grow alone and paid no more attention to her (p.44).

Only when he is about to die does Zakhari once again try to forge a link with his eldest child.

During the course of their dispute, Zakhari and Raye had each acted in a characteristic manner: he had torn out his hair but done nothing save run away, while she had moved with all her energy, hazarding whatever ploys lay within her limited repertoire. Raye's verve remains undiminished throughout the remainder of her story; moreover, two distinctive features of her behavior in those early instances emerge as essential aspects of her growing personality. These are her stubborness and her streak of aggression. Added to the latter is her preoccupation with adult sexuality, an aspect of her disposition that was not evident from her original outbursts at Zakhari but that nonetheless fits with their conflict. Not surprisingly, perhaps, these traits, so different from the ones that mark her father's essence, finally result in an uncanny resemblance between their separate lives.

Just as she had been willing—or had felt it necessary—to drive her father away in order to restore her self-control, Raye later allows her obstinacy and demands to prevent friendships. On one occasion, she comes home in tears because of an incident with some other children. They had all been playing together, and Raye had begun giving orders. When the others had not wanted to obey her, she had thrown a tantrum much like the one with her father. Then, stamping her feet in the sand, she had insisted that she be queen over the other children, who had thereupon retreated in fear. Once again, she had won her point but forfeited human contact: "The children had run away from her, but she remained queen anyway . . . alone with herself and the imaginary children around her, she was the queen" (p.54).

Even when Raye's aims are altruistic, she nonetheless manages to convey her desires so that others cannot understand them and therefore cannot respond to her favorably. Once, at the age of no more than five or six, she had been invited to a party. An instant success, she had played with and led the other children, delighting everyone with her beauty and spirited charm. She had been showered with gifts as a reward for her personality. Suddenly, she had run into the middle of the drawing room, dropped all her new toys onto the floor, where they had immediately broken, and insisted on being taken home: Beyle had had no choice but to comply. Only later—too late—was Raye able to reveal that she had behaved so perversely out of sympathy for one of her friends, a child from a poor family, who had not been included in the festivities.

Raye's habitual self-isolation is complicated by the fact that her loving feelings are inextricably bound to aggression, often manifested in violent behavior. As a small child, for instance, she had loved to amuse herself at the seashore by crushing pebbles with a stone. Her fantasies in connection with this game reveal the mingling in her of destructive and tender impulses:

> She throws herself at the pebbles, grabs them—small, gleaming birds—and begins, out of a great sense of love, to strangle them in her little hands, the cold pebbles trying to escape

> from her—and she strokes them, and cuddles them, tosses them onto the beach and dances a lonely-festive dance around them (p.45).

Raye's actions make evident her loneliness and her perception that, in order to possess anything, even a pebble, she must somehow prevent it from fleeing. Experience has taught her that others do not want contact with her; therefore, she expresses her desire for companionship, her rage and disappointment at its absence, and her need to control the reluctant object, by holding on until she has destroyed the very thing she wants. Raye's fantasy and her actual behavior are yet another example of how she works at cross purposes with herself. To some extent she knows this and therefore experiences some contrition, vowing that she will never again smash the beautiful pebbles. The wish to change her behavior, however, is not as strong as her need to repeat the cycle of domination and loss; the next day she is at it again.

There is another important aspect to Raye's continual fusion of love and violence, namely that, as a child, she had been alternately harshly treated and ignored by her father. Thus, attention had implied pain, and the alternative—disregard—although safer, had meant deprivation. As Raye grows older, the burgeoning of her sexual awareness is inevitably drawn into the already established patterns and ideas of her earlier years. That is, as she begins to be openly fascinated and excited by sexuality, she fits these feelings into a framework of anger, pain, and humiliation.

With the improvement of her mother's hotel business, Raye notes the appearance of a new type of guest. Now visitors do not stay as long as they used to; moreover, they arrive long after she has gone to sleep, and in the morning they remain behind closed doors. Intrigued by strange sounds, Raye haunts the corridors, searching for an opportunity to discover their secret.

One day, the eleven-year-old girl finally finds a door ajar and, hearing cooing sounds and heavy breathing within, opens the door further and peers inside. A nearly naked couple is lying on the bed, so involved in an embrace that Raye is unnoticed. As she perceives it, they begin "murderously to hit and bite one another, and each to incorporate the other's body." (p.57). Terrified, she wants to run away, but instead tiptoes even closer to the couple on the bed:

> And just then she saw how the battle on the white bed suddenly became so frighteningly grim that the two unknown people, the hotel guests, seemed to be drowning in convulsions of mutual strangulation, and soon the unknown figures lay still upon the bed, like bloody murder victims (p.58).

As the narrator explains, Raye's world had changed that day. Initially terrified by what she had observed, she had considered running to her mother for help. In the end, however, she had resisted confiding in her mother, and had persisted in her spying attempts, maintaining a particular loyalty to the place where her first knowledge had been gleaned. In the process of investigating adult sexuality, Raye becomes friends with Zhenye, who now occupies the girl's favorite room. She considers herself Zhenye's equal, loves to visit her, and feels angry when men come to call and she is displaced.

On one occasion, Raye hears Zhenye scream. Frantic with anxiety, Raye's response is to throw herself on the floor outside her friend's door, biting her lips, pinching her cheeks, and moaning in a dry voice. Only when her lips have reached the bleeding point does she experience some amelioration of her anguish.

Raye thus behaves in much the same way she had during the two physical encounters with her father. Her self-mutilating methods resemble the means of attack she had turned on him the first time he hit her. Indeed, Raye's fantasy while she is biting her own lips, i.e., that she wants to bite Zhenye's attacker, is no different than her reality had been years earlier. Simultaneously, however, and still in keeping with her original trauma, Raye must suffer pain in addition to applying it. This is her method of self-consolidation. Finally, the mixture of excitement and fear that so richly fills her fantasy recreates her earlier emotional state at the prospect of battling someone so much larger than she:

> She would be so frightened of him that she would not have the strength to escape. She would throw herself into fighting

> with him because he is such a strong person . . . She would get even with him again, that unknown strong male (p.62).

Raye's continuing relationship with her father, who has been absent for so long, does not mean that her mother is insignificant to her. There is no love lost between Raye and her mother. Beyle develops a gradual sense of respect for her daughter "as for a grown-up child, long married off, who lives somewhere in a faraway city and only comes to visit now and then" (p.64). At the same time, however, when Raye suggests that she would like to pull her weight at home by working on the outside and helping her mother as well, Beyle becomes enraged, reminding Raye that she is "such a nothing, such a little thing" (p.66). Thus, Beyle wants to consider her daughter as an adult insofar as she is reluctant to become deeply involved with her, but she cannot encourage her attempts at achieving equality. Seen by her mother as heartless, Raye defends herself against the hurt of Beyle's distance, treating her with detachment and trying to convey the impression that she, the daughter, is somehow stronger.

In fact, the disharmony between these two Pikuda women is not a new thing but, rather, a mutual rejection of long standing. As a child, Raye had loathed being embraced and had wiped away her mother's kisses—always in silence. Beyle's reaction was to contemplate Raye with a mixture of reverence and amazement. On another level, however, matters were different:

> That feeling [of reverence and amazement] sometimes merged into enmity, into a quiet enmity against her own blood. It was a blind enmity, and even in her most hidden thoughts she denied it. But the enmity was definitely within her (p.51).

However much Beyle may have succeeded in keeping her negative feelings from Raye, she was doomed to misunderstand her child, and this was inevitably noticed by the little girl. On the occasion of her agonized outburst about wanting to be queen, for example, Raye had run into the house, crying:

> "Mama, the children don't want to obey me! The children don't want to obey me!"/The mother was used to her caprices, so she just smiled and wiped her little nose (p.53).

The interchange had ended in a dual miscarriage. Beyle had not only neglected to respond verbally to Raye's suffering but, in doing so, had treated an issue of great importance to the child as if it were a trivial affair.

A picture of misery emerges: Raye is estranged from her father, who has in any case removed himself from the scene; perceived as a peculiar, unlovable creature by her mother, she is consequently misapprehended and rejected; she is unable to capture the interest of her grandmother, and too stubborn to endure friendship's attendant compromises. As the narrator explains, "Raye felt herself to be alone, without friends, a stranger in her home" (p.66).

Despite the great superficial differences between them, then, Raye bears a profound resemblance to her father. The similarity is neither mysterious nor coincidental, for Zakhari had chosen a wife in the image of his mother and had—albeit in a totally different manner—abandoned the family as his father had done before him. In this way, he had unconsciously recreated his own youthful living conditions for his daughter. Raye, like Zakhari, suffers emotional starvation, and the fear of further, renewed deprivation results in her defensive isolation. This lack cannot dim her general vigor and her sexuality, but it does prevent her from engaging her energy in the service of reaching others.

The final section of *Di mishpokhe pikuda* provides a resolution of sorts to the problem of disrupted, abortive relationships—indeed, to the work as a whole. This unraveling, however, clashes with the realistic detail that characterizes the bulk of the narrative. Only the introduction, with its purposely vague allusions to the subsequent story, gives any sort of preparation for a mystical climax, wherein Raye and Zakhari are united spiritually precisely as Zakhari is about to die of self-inflicted wounds. My own understanding of this conclusion is that Glazman was attempting to describe the wish for merger with a beloved but unattainable object, yet he did not have the psychological language to do so. Therefore, he depicted the fantasy as actually occurring. In this way, paradoxically, he causes the event to appear more abstract and illusory than if he had discussed it as an intrapsychic or intersubjective phenomenon. This scene finally reveals the similarities and differences between Raye and Zakhari, even as they share a last, ultimate, experience.

On the fateful day, Raye has been feeling increasingly forlorn and separated from the rest of her family. In her fantasies, she belongs somewhere else; specifically, she allows herself to entertain the hope of leaving Europe and immigrating to America. Gazing at the ocean from the hotel veranda—a favorite perspective of her father's as well—she muses about salvation, wishing for a friend with whom to flee. Her father comes to mind and it occurs to her that she misses him around the house, despite his glum demeanor. Recognizing that she has scarcely thought about him during his long absence, she feels some remorse about her failures as a daughter and wonders how he might be occupied that evening.

Raye falls asleep and awakes in a strange temper, full of fantasies of rescue yet at the same time weakened, partly by the very dreams that have sustained her. Just at this moment she is "visited" by Zakhari, a "diffuse-milky figure" enveloped in sheets. Pressing his "soft-compassionate face" close to her own, he says:

> Look, my daughter, I must die abroad. I cannot even see my wife and children before my death; I have lived abroad and died abroad (p.70).

Ever macabre, Zakhari brushes her cheek with cold lips. Raye, feeling this caress all over her body, runs home in a condition of extreme excitement and scrubs her face with cold water—as her father had been wont to wash compulsively and much as she had habitually wiped away her mother's touch. Afterwards, she enters an empty room of the hotel and collapses on the bed, exhausted. Three weeks later, news comes that Zakhari has died of heart disease. Of all the family members, only Raye does not cry—"perhaps . . . because she already knew . . ." (p.81).

In fact, Zakhari has not succumbed to heart disease at all; rather, he has slit his neck three times. The coverup of his suicide recalls the suspicion surrounding the demise of his faraway brother, while his method of self-destruction is the one previously chosen by his brother Naum. The larger Pikuda family resemblance is hereby emphasized: all four children of Gnesye and Borekh have taken their own lives.

Zakhari's fate in the United States scarcely differs from his previous experience of life: his is a world riddled with failure, disappointment, desolation and, as always, the certainty that he is an outsider wherever he goes. Near the end of his life, Zakhari has reached bottom. Earlier, he had stopped working, his heart incapable of adjusting to the suffocating air of the factories in which he had sought employment. While he regrets that he is not, therefore, in a position to send for his wife and children, he is simultaneously too depressed to care whether he finds new work or not. And anyhow, he reasons, why bring them to a place where he himself feels so alone? They would only suffer.

The thought of a quiet death becomes increasingly appealing to Zakhari. And then he realizes that he is free to destroy himself. Brightened by choice, he quits the small house where he had been boarding with distant relatives. Their response to his move is mild surprise, because he has always been a silent, distant man. Nonetheless, they recognize that something is dramatically wrong:

> If this person had always seemed like a silent shadow, now his face surely looked like the shadow of a corpse (p.74).

Zakhari's decision to spend his last days in a hotel is significant, for it is the environment best known to him and at the same time most evocative of his loneliness. Like Raye, who experiences home as if she were a guest there, Zakhari remembers feeling like a traveler:

> Oh, the hotel atmosphere was like water for a fish. After all, he had spent his entire life in a hotel. And in every place he feels like someone passing through, like a stranger (p.75).

It is here, rather than among family, that Zakhari will carry out his plan.

After remaining in the hotel room for three days, assessing his life, Zakhari becomes feverish, to which he responds by repeatedly washing and treating himself with hot baths.[7]

During his final hours, Zakhari behaves "as if he were preparing for his wedding night." (p.79). The connection between Raye and Zakhari is already approaching that of union. This union, however, is not sexual, but rather the more complete and fundamental fusion for which sexual intercourse is one substitute: that is, a total merger of one being with another, experienced truly only prior to birth but continued, in approximated and attenuated form, during infancy. "There is no such thing as a baby," the British psychoanalyst Winnicott comments, ". . . if you set out to describe a baby, you will find you are describing a *baby and someone.* A baby cannot exist alone but is essentially part of a relationship."[8]

For Zakhari, the actual moment of oneness occurs after he has slit his throat:

> . . . he opened his eyes wide and saw himself next to his daughter, his eldest and the first fruit of his loins. It was the first time that he had spoken to her in such a warmly friendly tone (p.80).

Such is Zakhari's state as he utters precisely the words that Raye, awakening from her troubled sleep, will hear.

In their final interaction, Zakhari and Raye reveal their deep involvement with one another. Each has thought of the other shortly before the end of Zakhari's life. Moreover, both fantasies constitute affirmations: for Raye it is the resurgent hope that her father will rescue her from her stifling existence, for Zakhari the realization that his daughter is a part of him. Raye finds the momentary parental bonding insufficient. She perceives clearly the separateness of her father. His face may be soft and his body milky, but he never becomes a mother for Raye to cleave to. She does not achieve fulfillment of her need for comfort and belonging, but, instead, an explanation of why it is that her father can never save her.

For his part, Zakhari is able to die with the feeling that he is at one with a part of himself. In fantasy with his daughter, Zakhari achieves the intimacy that had eluded him with his mother. During his lifetime, he had known better than to wish for satisfaction from the woman who had borne him; however, he had hoped in vain that his wife and children would help him overcome his misery. Instead, they had left him more deprived and depleted than before. At the very beginning of *Di mishpokhe pikuda,* the narrator explains the process of Zakhari's spreading isolation:

> His own wife seemed alien to him, as well as his children and others around him. He always had the feeling that he belonged somewhere else, and that his wife and children—they were not transformations of his life but, on the contrary, parts of himself that were becoming alien to him even during his lifetime. He was dying from them. The alienation was invading his very being and forcing everything else out of him. Soon he would become alien to himself (p.16).

The course of becoming alien to himself had been a slow one for Zakhari, but in the end it resulted in his decision that he might as well terminate a life that had ceased to have meaning. Zakhari's increasing feeling of aloneness suggests that his initial anger at Raye may have stemmed from his belief that she was getting the care and attention more rightly meant for him. If each new person who entered the family impoverished him internally, it is small wonder that he would especially resent the first intrusion.

At the point of death, Zakhari manages to claim power that he has not possessed before. For, he does not choose to slumber into death, as he had once dozed in the Turkish baths. Rather, he takes some steps to ensure the final satisfaction of his archaic wish—even though it is only by relinquishing his life that he can allow himself to do so. In the relatively safe environment of a hotel, which is familiar to him, he is able to summon up his daughter and keep her with him while he is dying. In this way, Zakhari finally provides for himself what he could not discover elsewhere—not with his mother, not with

Beyle—that is, the image of complete union—fusion—with another human being.[9]

There is no such thing as a baby. Where essential nurturing is absent, the wish for it is not abandoned. Instead, the search continues relentlessly, often forever.

Di mishpokhe pikuda ends as Zakhari's family arrives in America. Raye is overjoyed; she has finally escaped the confines of her old home. But what will happen to her in the new place? There are certain ominous signs: Raye's overriding sense of loneliness and strangeness, which she shares with her father and his siblings; her similarity to Zakhari, including their telepathic interaction, and the implication that he wants a reunion with her; finally—and perhaps most important of all—is the fact that Raye, like Zakhari, is unable to assume the role set up for her by her society, as epitomized by her mother. If her insistence upon walking in the sunshine and darkening her skin is a symbol of her willfulness, her overall behavior indicates an untameability that is quite unlike her father's nature but equally unacceptable. Again, Glazman's inchoate psychological sense may be in advance of his conscious understanding. Although in the end he makes no claims, he has prepared the reader to conclude that Raye, too, will likely come to grief, the possibilities offered by America notwithstanding.

CHAPTER FIVE

The Men

Shloymke

Zalmen Shneyur's novel *A toyt: shriftn fun a zelbst merder a tiref* [''*A Death: Writings of a Lunatic Suicide*''][1] is unusual—even among the works discussed here—in its painful concentration on the development and fulfillment of a suicidal plan. In diary form, this work recounts, with obsessive detail, the progression of twenty-year-old Shloymke from a position of functional, if withdrawn, activity to his self-inflicted death by shooting. Yet, although *A toyt* may be the most exhaustive investigation of suicide in Yiddish literature, Shloymke's history and his problems closely resemble those endured by other characters.

The young man's family situation is by now familiar: his mother had died while giving birth to him and he had spent his early years with his father and an old cook. The house was a dour, depressing place, and Shloymke a delicate child, preferring to spend time on his own rather than in contact with other children: ''Children of my own age I didn't like—and I didn't dislike. I reacted to them with a sickly cold-bloodedness, almost with disgust'' (p.19). Most of all, Shloymke found comfort in being ill, for then he could remain alone and quiet, lost in his own thoughts. He knew he was odd.

> . . . I was strange somehow, with my silence, with my truculence, with my fondness for remaining at home all alone. I was pale and I used to catch cold frequently. Then, lying with

> a swollen throat, wrapped with a woolen sock and warm salt, I used to think a great deal . . . (p.18).

The young child indeed remained largely isolated, pushing away potential playmates, not—like Raye in *Di mishpokhe pikuda*—by attempting to force them into submission, but rather by treating them with silence and condescension. His only relationship of any warmth was with his preoccupied father who, although he loved his son, failed to concentrate much time or energy on him. Their major interactions occurred at night, when the father would urge his wakeful son to go to sleep. Then, Shloymke—who slept in his dead mother's bed—remained awake, frightened of the dark, listening to his father's snoring.

Despite the limitations of this connection, it provided Shloymke with a sense that he was important and that he belonged somewhere. Then came the fateful day when his father announced his plans to remarry, promising that the new stepmother would cherish and care for her small charge, just as his real mother would have done had she only been granted the opportunity. In fact, things were to work out differently, disastrously so; not only was the new member of the family unresponsive to him, but Shloymke perceived that he had lost his father as well. Displaced from the bedroom into the dining room, he suffered even greater loneliness than before:

> From then on, my father's relationship to me changed a bit. When he used to return late at night and pass by my bed in the dark, he would ask me: "Shloymke, are you asleep?" "No!" But he no longer approached me, rearranging the blanket, as had been his custom. He merely uttered his "Sleep, sleep," more out of habit than love, and soon went into the bedroom (pp.25–26).

Shloymke's disappointment at this dual betrayal was bitter. At the same time, he felt paralysed by his stepmother's indifference to him, because it denied him any chance of expressing his negative reaction to her. Instead, he felt compelled to contain his hatred, and the effort caused him greater depression and misery than ever. Nonetheless, the child's longing for motherly love did not abate, and it finally inspired him to make one covert plea for affection. Imagining how wonderful it would be if his own mother—conjured as blue-eyed and calm—were to stroke his head as it lay in her lap, he had realized that his stepmother's touch would fulfill him as well. Yet when he tentatively approached her as she lay, fat and sweating on a sofa, she was so uncaring, or simply so exhausted by the weight of her own body, that she failed even to turn in his direction. The rejection had unleashed Shloymke's rage, causing him to deliver his sole expression of anger at a situation of gross neglect; accusing his father of tricking him, he had railed as well against the immediate object of his fury.

Unfortunately, but predictably, the stepmother did not respond effectively to the child's outburst. Much as Raye's mother, Beyle, had done, she misperceived the content and underestimated the passion of the youthful tirade:

> Shh—shh! What—is—it? Food?—Soon . . .
>
> And she stood up heavily, sighing, to give me something to eat. Due to laziness, neglect, and sweat, she had apparently not understood me at all . . . That was my first and last protest against the boredom, cold, and barrenness in our house, in my entire being . . . (p.33).

As Shloymke later reports, he had given up hope that day—hope of love, of acceptance and of understanding. His external circumstances did not improve either. First there was the death of his father, which, although he remained dry-eyed, ostensibly shielded from grief, nonetheless dramatically altered his external life. His aunts and uncles had first apprenticed him to a watchmaker, then to a tanner, both of which jobs proved to be unsuitable for him. Finally, as if in grim fulfillment of his earlier conviction that he was unacceptable, they banished him at age sixteen, buffered only by the small inheritance left behind by his father.

The critical attitude towards him on the part of his relatives was to continue over the subsequent years, mainly through the belittling, demanding, and chiding letters they sent. Moreover, Shloymke began to believe a fantasy that remained with him—and influenced him—until the death, namely that he was surrounded by demons bent on causing him harm:

> . . . I began to suspect that all people . . . even my father, my stepmother, my uncles and aunts, my friends in *kheyder* and the *rebbe* . . . were none of them real people . . . but rather demons . . . and I, I was the only true person in the world . . . all the demons tortured me, disguised themselves as rebbes and fathers and tortured me . . . God had sent me to them specially for this purpose . . . (pp.74–75).

This image of a unique position and function in the world served the boy as an explanation for his own isolation, protecting him from the realization that sheer human frailty was at fault. Unfortunately, it also made him vulnerable to the idea that he was destined to suffer, a thought that never left him. Thus Shloymke had started out in life. Subsequently, with little experience of comfortable, warm interaction, he continues to encounter great difficulty in establishing new relationships, responding to both men and women with distance, strain, and the conviction of life's futility.

Finally, seizing the chance to buy an acquaintance's revolver, Shloymke determines to do away with himself. His diary discussions of the events leading up to this final act reveal much about the etiology of his predicament. At first the decision seems to have been almost intellectual, since he had been fascinated by suicide fully a year before the purchase of his weapon. At that time, he had assiduously followed the newspaper accounts of suicide, titillated by the self-inflicted deaths of other young men. Only somewhat later does his true reason for withdrawing from life emerge: he has been bitterly disappointed by a woman.

Even after he has made up his mind to die, Shloymke nonetheless retains a superficially strange goal—the achievement of sexual intercourse. To this end, he makes plans to visit a brothel, although the prospect is difficult for him, precisely because he is such a novice with women. Yet, his pained reactions to women are intimately related to his ultimate renunciation; for, having believed that he would never form any close bonds with women, he had discovered an apparent exception.

Shloymke's initial negative reaction to women had been part of a general mistrust—people were demons whose raison d'etre was his misery:

> I began to suspect that all the tenderness and beauty of these creatures was created solely to torture and agitate me, the ugly and sad one. And in reality there was no hope of approaching them ever (p.88).

With time, matters had merely become exacerbated:

> Then there came a time when I began to fear all women, even ugly ones. I feared their gaze, their laughter, the way they turned to me. I tried to avoid them altogether: not going to them, not inviting them to me, not having any dealings with them—who knows how persistent this situation might have been—and what point it might have reached—if not for Henye. I had no fear of her. From her I learned how to behave with all other women (p.89).

Moody and emotional, Henye is somewhat coy from the start of her relationship with Shloymke, pretending unawareness of his existence at first. Still, the two become fast friends before long, Henye never relinquishing the upper hand, however. Shloymke gradually understands his love for her, recognizing at the same time that his capacity for emotional involvement remains diminished. Perhaps for this reason, he never lets his tenderness show. One night, as he and Henye are walking, their friendship suddenly assumes an ambiguously sexual aspect. Shloymke, noticing that her jacket is open at the breast and afraid that she might catch cold, points this out to her. Ever the flirt, Henye suggests that he close it himself—she does not want to chill her warm hands—and Shloymke diffidently complies. At that point, however, Henye abruptly halts the escalation by thanking her suitor and changing the subject.

There is one further charged encounter, when Henye requests that Shloymke write something in her autograph album. As is his wont with her, Shloymke inscribes an impersonal comment, yet he allows himself a veiled declaration of love for the young woman. Her laughter in response to this attempt at self-revelation, a combination of sadness and hilarity, disturbs Shloymke. Within a few days he discovers that Henye has eloped with a young socialist.

The result of this betrayal is cataclysmic for Shloymke, but he feels his injury only indirectly, as if someone else were suffering. By the time he is in the middle of his suicidal plans, however, he can admit that he has lost all hope of ever finding a partner in life. On his way to visit Henye for the first time since her marriage, he tries to bolster his spirits by telling himself that if he formally severs their tie, his incentive to go to the brothel will increase. Yet no sooner does he have these thoughts than others rush in to indicate his true state:

> But why, during this entire month, have I seen her as if through a fog and why do I long for her so much now? Someone is to be pitied . . . Who? Perhaps I? Whom will I have now and who will have me? (pp.91–92).

Shloymke's desolation at the prospect of never again experiencing the warmth of a beloved female's company is clear. So, too, is the connection between his loneliness and his decision to kill himself: although he had been actively fantasizing the possibility of his death for a year beforehand, it is during the month of his separation from Henye that he buys the revolver, the instrument of his self-destruction. She had provided him with a reason to live and, once he realizes that she is lost to him, he no longer wishes to exist.

Indeed, finally confronting her presence, Shloymke finds a spark of vitality kindled in him anew. Henye has begun to speak tenderly to him and to stroke his hair. Although he wants to stop her, he is unable to interrupt his own pleasure. Amazed, he perceives that he is, after all, far more involved with life than he had heretofore acknowledged, and he senses that he will never reject the world as long as Henye inhabits it, caressing and cajoling him. He even entertains the fantasy of abandoning his suicidal plan altogether, in exchange for her affection and care:

> I frightened myself with the sudden thought that all at once came over me and completely shocked me: soon I would snatch my revolver from my pocket, fling it at her feet—right there between the two tips of her shiny shoes, which smiled out from under her frock . . . after that I would quietly lower my head into that small, young lap . . . (p.98).

Indeed, Shloymke is about to reach into his pocket when Henye's husband enters the scene. Devastated, but anesthetized against the reality of his crushing rejection, Shloymke grows cold inside. Lest he ever again be tempted to imagine happiness via Henye, he insures her permanent enmity by denouncing her, claiming—before her astonished husband—that she had been kissing and embracing him only moments earlier. As a distancing device, the ploy works: the couple is aghast; but Shloymke is forced to realize that his deepest wish is to possess Henye for himself, to actually feel the touch he had apparently so callously invented as an insult. Within a day he is dead, a victim of his inability to tolerate the longing stirred by Henye's unreachable devotion.

Shloymke's extreme response to the final loss of Henye is more than the rash act of a lovesick young man. Rather, it represents his conviction—although he claims to have learned how to behave with all women—that Henye is his first and last chance to achieve a fruitful union. Aware that his relations with women are strained, he blames it on the fact that he is "too passionate and too weak." (p.88). Where he had once perceived his father as frail and nervous, denying these qualities in himself, he now admits his difficulties.

Similarly, although he avers that he can be straight-forward and casual with men, he is able to be neither with Mirkin, his sole male companion. Moreover, this relationship suggests that Shloymke's problems with both sexes stem from his hidden belief that he is not a normal man. Deeming his efforts with women a failure because he lacks sufficient control and strength to hold his own, he considers himself inadequate and inappropriate around males as well.

Mirkin, whose very name is a matronymic, epitomizes gentle but robust youth. Friendly, able to enjoy life to its fullest, he thus differs sharply and significantly from Shloymke, who envies his friend's good looks and cordial spirit. Despite his bluster, Mirkin is at heart soft, yielding, and willing to comfort, all of which Shloymke, in the tradition of Sholem-Aleykhem's Tevye, identifies as feminine qualities. To his dismay, Shloymke is drawn to Mirkin's compassion, overcome by the desire to complain and release his sadness—as he puts it, "Mirkin's femininity was transferred to me" (p.76).

For Shloymke, the realization of these reactions in himself in anxiety-provoking, although not because of their existence per se; after all, Mirkin is no less an attractive man for exhibiting the same characteristics. Rather, their presence makes him feel abjectly immature. His profound longing for solace thus serves both as a reminder and a corroboration that he still needs more nurturance than he considers proper. In one of the novel's more poignant scenes, Shloymke describes for Mirkin his internal experience of vulnerability and pain, his perception of a chasm between himself and his healthy friend:

> I lack what you have. I have only many nerves and a little piece of flesh that quivers, and seethes, and becomes elated and hurts—it is called a heart. And my brain is overly sharp, [with] ideas passing through me like lightning. But around this there is no outer skin . . . nothing that will protect it like armor so that no-one sees, no-one knows what is under it! . . . And have you ever in your life seen a fruit grow, ripen, and be sweet without an outer skin? (p.77).

Shloymke goes on to tell Mirkin about the misery he had suffered at the hands of his domineering relatives after his father's death. Yet, his self-portrayal as raw to external stimuli illustrates the extent to which any situation, let alone a trauma, would have rendered him exposed, open to harm. Having failed early to acquire a sense of inner well-being and safety—as attested to by his sickly and isolated childhood—he remains similarly debilitated in young adulthood.

Ironically, it is through the relationship with his revolver that Shloymke reveals the nature of his immeasurable, unfathomed need. Here, he expresses his constant and desperate wish for contact, for a feeling of being connected, as well as for some force or being that will help him regulate and understand the maze of turbulent emotions within him. He looks to the revolver for help with both these basic strivings.

From the outset of his association with the weapon, when he had been overcome with a passionate desire to possess it, and throughout his subsequent misadventures, Shloymke finds that the revolver provides him with companionship lacking elsewhere in his life. Initially, it most closely resembles a lover in his fantasies:

> . . . I close the door of my room, slowly take out my revolver, my beautiful, beloved revolver, lay it down in front of me on the table; afterwards, I carry it over to the pillow, where it feels softer and better . . . I regale myself with it, observing it from all sides. Lovingly, I stroke its smooth, polished back (p.5).

At other times, Shloymke thinks of the revolver as a child, lavishing on it the coddling he himself never received: "My little son . . . you must be good and hungry, right?" (p.106). And, towards the very end of Shloymke's life, when a series of images flashes through his mind, the revolver becomes an equal with his uncle, with Mirkin, with Henye's husband Yasha, as well as with the red lantern from the brothel he has just visited. As an object, then, the revolver substitutes for human closeness, at the same time as—by dint of its function—it symbolizes strength, mastery and the capacity for autonomous action.

Connected to, but not identical with, its use as an antidote to feelings of loneliness and impotence, the revolver also plays the role of mood regulator for Shloymke. When overwhelmed by the intensely uncomfortable sensations that prompt him to conceive of himself as having no skin, Shloymke is able to console himself through his association with the revolver. On one occasion, for instance, he receives a nasty shock. As part of his scheme to annihilate any reasons for living, he has been resigning from his tutoring jobs. At the last home, however, he is summarily fired by his pupil's mother, who gives him no opportunity to state his own purpose. Until that moment, Shloymke has been enjoying—for the first time in his young life—the pride of controlling his future, of deciding his fate. His dismissal destroys this pleasure, leaving him simultaneously downhearted and frustrated—until he remembers his revolver, that is:

> . . . at the very moment of insult and losing my nerve, my hand unwilling slid into my pocket and touched the revolver . . . instantly my anger evaporated and disappeared, like a light vapor in the sun. A cold smile spread across my face: what is there to be angry about? (p.58).

Thus, while the revolver's existence does not bring complete equilibrium to Shloymke, who, after all, continues arranging his suicide, it does at least permit him to recoup some of the presence of mind shaken by a woman who, as he sees it, had merely been toying with him in order to watch his distress.

The events of Shloymke's last weeks are filled with anxiety and anguish; in these situations, too, the revolver supplies aid and comfort, helping to quell the fear and sense of wildness that threaten to immobilize him or reduce him to utter panic. After leaving Henye, for example, he clutches the revolver and talks to it, instead of obeying his urge to run back to his beloved. Shortly thereafter, imagining that Henye's husband is coming to murder him in retaliation for his purported relations with her, he again grips his weapon, this time experiencing the contact as a compulsive need—". . . I had to press the revolver in my pocket; I *had* to" (p.105).

Similarly, once at the brothel, Shloymke treats his revolver as a talisman, holding it as a source of courage for the sexual consummation he is about to attempt with a frail-looking young prostitute. Finally, and perhaps most dramatically, the revolver helps prevent him from losing his sanity altogether in the wake of the prostitute's public announcement of his deflowering and the attendant humiliation this revelation causes him:

> If not for the revolver, my dear, beloved revolver, which delights and strengthens me constantly with its smoothness, its

> nickel smile, I would certainly have lost my mind, I would have torn at my clothes, run down the street and screamed from inner pain (pp.148–149).

The revolver, then, fulfills a variety of important purposes in Shloymke's life: it is a respite from loneliness; a stabilizer of depressive and anxious affects; a necessary container of explosive emotion when internal pressures prove too much to bear.

It might seem that the weapon soothes Shloymke in this way because it is also the instrument of his ultimate power over life, assuring a final victory over pain. This is not the whole story, however, for Shloymke's diary reveals that his revolver is not the first such companion for him. Moreover, his descriptions make clear the underlying inner gap that the boy, and later the man, struggles valiantly but unsuccessfully to fill.

During his systematic preparation to quit the world, Shloymke goes through his room, discarding old possessions, but not before contemplating them, recalling their significance. Among his childhood treasures, he rediscovers a piece of earth from the Holy Land, a prize traditionally coveted by Diaspora Jews, for whom the thought of being buried together with a fragment of the homeland was comforting. Shloymke had pursued this possession with a fervor resembling his passionate quest for the revolver. Moreover, he had employed it in comparable fashion as well—fondling it whenever he might have hoped to be treated with friendship and love but where no tenderness was forthcoming—subsequently escaping into his private world both at school and at home.

Indeed, as he reminisces about a mealtime interrogation by his stepmother and father into the nature and significance of his clay-like nugget, Shloymke recalls a combination of coldness, criticism, and neglect. His stepmother's words had been accusing, her manner distant. His father had scolded him for bringing his toy to the table, yet his comments were filtered through the barrier of his perpetual preoccupation. As a consequence, Shloymke had felt both guilty and wounded. In addition, his stepmother's dismay that he might be preparing for someone's death—by implication her own—had instilled horror in the already miserable child, even though, in fact, he had frequently associated his bit of earth with the eyes of a corpse he had once witnessed being cleansed for burial.

In retrospect, Shloymke recognizes not only that his childhood possession had heralded the revolver in a formal, tangible way, but also that both were connected for him with the thought of death:

> Now I understand that the pale little piece of earth was, for me as a child, a type of contemporary revolver, a revolver that had not yet materialized. The little piece of earth had awakened moods in me then that were quite similar to the moods elicited in me now by the revolver. Those were, however, chaotic, without any thought or goal (p.120).

While the attraction to death often represents a profound desire to be rid of pain—and it certainly contains this meaning in Shloymke's life—it may also signify the longing for reunion with a beloved person who is dead. Although the small child's comprehension of death as an abstract idea may be limited, the experience of loss or absence can be deeply felt even at a tender age. Thus it is that Shloymke's earliest attempts to evade his lonely and neglected surroundings had been bound up with fantasies of the mother he had never known, whose existence he invented according to his needs and wishes. The one concrete piece of information he had received from his father was her name, Nekhome.[2] From this he had spun his vision: "The name Nekhome aroused in me the image of a pair of good, blue eyes, a smooth, merciful forehead under a black wig, with a white parting" (p.23).

More than this, however, he had used his mother's name, and the memory of his father's voice conveying it to him, as a powerful means of managing his isolation. He had endeavored to suffuse himself internally with their presence, to absorb an intimacy denied him in actuality. Moreover, he had tied the words to physical caresses, almost as if he were constructing an entire milieu of love, an atmosphere consonant with his desires, albeit not with his experience:

> My childhood years were poor in impressions, in words and games, in hearing and seeing; therefore I acquired the habit

> of repeating words and half-words that I had heard and found appealing. After the discussion with my father, as I was playing with my little wooden soldier, I stroked its head, gave its small painted nose a gentle fillip and tried to imitate my father's voice:
>
> —Nu, nu, Nekhome, nu, you silly little thing, Nekhome . . . (p.23).

The fantasy of a good mother had stayed with Shloymke, all the more so since he was soon to be dreadfully disappointed. As it transpired, his father's revelation of the name Nekhome had been purposeful: the very same evening, he had announced his plans to remarry, promising that his new wife would surely nourish and care for Shloymke. Long into the night, Shloymke had lain in bed, whispering to himself: "Kugel with raisins . . . kugel with raisins . . . Nekhome . . . walks in the garden . . . Nekhome . . . Nekhome . . ." (p.24). Unfortunately, his father's words had proven untrue, and Shloymke, hopes crushed, had clung to the image of a protective and generous parent—Nekhome—more than ever.

Since he loved his dead mother—or, rather, his fantasy of her—most of all, Shloymke was easily prone to regard death as a source of warmth, acceptance, succor, and comfort. Moreover, inasmuch as his mother's name, his piece of soil from the Holy Land, and his revolver all represent an effort at mastering his immense sense of aloneness—albeit through the isolating medium of death—Shloymke's behavior during the weeks prior to his suicide assumes an historical and psychological continuity that is not initially apparent.

Shloymke's three important possessions are all transitional objects, as elucidated by the British psychoanalyst, D.W. Winnicott. A transitional object, such as a teddy bear or the corner of a blanket, is the infant's first representation of the space between self and other. In this intermediate area, a perception of separateness exists that is nonetheless invested with the infant's own subjectivity.

Winnicott views this first possession—or an intangible equivalent, such as a melody or a word—as the basis for creativity and the capacity for symbolization; yet he also remarks that in the child whose early parenting has been deficient, transitional phenomena may not fulfill their purpose of preparing the infant to recognize and accept its healthy autonomy. Instead, the transitional possession's meaning may be truncated, and the child may give it up prematurely, before it can reach its natural, unmourned, demise; or, alternatively, the infant may never feel secure enough with a nurturing yet non-intrusive parent for this stage to result in the fluctuating balance between independence and intimacy that characterizes pliant adult relationships.[3]

Indeed, Shloymke's fantasies preceding his suicide reveal him as forever the lonely child, longing for—and finally achieving—merger with an outside source that he simultaneously experiences internally. Throughout *A toyt,* Shloymke is aware—more so than any other character—that his misery is a direct result of the treatment he had received as a child. What is more, he recognizes that his suicidal strivings stem from the same source:

> . . . already then, in my childhood, that kernel, *that thought,* planted itself in me. The atmosphere in our home, my stepmother's attitude towards me, my father, whose business stood between myself and him like an iron wall, these and only these caused that cold thing to be born in me, that thing which has fallen and sunken to the bottom of my soul, so that now no one can drag it out from there (p.36).

By the time Shloymke reaches chronological adulthood, he is no longer able—if he ever had been—to accept the efforts of those in his circle when they seek to console him and attend to his condition. His situation is thus truly impossible: like a starving man who refuses to eat, he rejects his friends and acquaintances. Although he anticipates that Mirkin will run away during their final evening together, and despite the rueful expectation that his friend will remain unaffected by his suicide, Shloymke nonetheless deprecates Mirkin for his loyalty and eventually throws him out: ". . . he brings me beer and gets ready to listen to what he doesn't like hearing . . . what a sucker!" (p.72).

Later, he entertains the fantasy that Henye will mourn his death, yet he does everything to ensure that she will have as little warm regard for him as possible. He even longs for his landlady to notice him: "Here a boy lies, without galoshes, without an overcoat, with a revolver in his pocket, with . . . with a headache, and she wants cutlets!" (p.118). Nonetheless, when the housekeeper tries to serve him and clean his room, his behavior is gruff and hostile.

Shloymke's plight rests in the fact that the ministrations offered him by well-meaning people are both too late and fundamentally inappropriate. He lacks, not the concern of contemporaries for himself as an adult, but rather the deep involvement of a parent, for whom his well-being is a matter of life and death significance. A hint of this desire emerges in Shloymke's attraction to Henye's "good black eyes, mother eyes" (p.89).

Henye appropriately neglects to absorb herself in this overriding fashion. Her abandonment devastates Shloymke, since—perhaps because of his fantasied impressions—he had loved and trusted her more than any woman, save Nekhome. When she casually betrays him, the disappointment resonates with familiarity: his mother, stepmother, and father all had proved unreliable, uncaring, emotionally absent. Under these circumstances, Shloymke's renunciation of life and the possibility of a fulfilling future underscores his hopelessness, his conviction that he will never be loved enough. In one of his final realizations, he admits to feeling cheated, "like an insulted child who has been promised something good and not gotten it . . ." (p.160). Although he has merely run out of matches, he faces this inconvenience with all his overflowing hurt.

Shloymke's response to his revolver, even before he buys it, indicates his longing. Watching, for the first time, as it is loaded by its owner, he worries:

> . . . my heart began to pound. Just as if he were operating on a child of mine right before my eyes.
>
> I became frightened, lest there be some misfortune and he ruin something, lest he lose a screw (p.16).

At the very end of his life, Shloymke has a strange experience: he discovers a deep ambivalence about killing himself, a split in which part of his consciousness is baiting the other. His fantasies during this tense dialogue with himself once again include a child and an operation. This time, however, the image is less benign:

> All this was heckling on the part of the mean, proud, bitter "I" who cursed and stimulated little weak and frightened *me* all night with the revolver—he saw the weapon and suddenly became so soft, so devoted, he joked so mildly, like a bad father with a child who will soon be operated upon (p.163).

Here, Shloymke's dream of a loving parent collapses, leaving him with his true belief: that no one, not even his father, wanted to be kind to him, to protect him from harm and suffering. Like the young child who had preferred to lie around, ill, than interact with others, Shloymke at age twenty still lacks the vitality to overcome his misery. Indeed, his bleakness overpowers any life-preserving impulses he may still harbor.

In the end, Shloymke does manage to reestablish faith in his connection to humanity; he sees that he is not the totally isolated person he has feared and known himself to be. As with Felye, Manye, Moritz/*zun,* and Zakhari, he finds resolution only because of, and through, self-destruction. Unlike them, however, Shloymke's satisfaction stems directly from the suicidal act itself:

> At the very instant, when I shoot myself, tens of people in all corners of the world will shoot themselves . . . Ha—one triumphant shot into eternity, one thought . . . thousands, and tens of thousands of miles away from me, many such people like I, many, will fall dead along with me . . . girls with white breasts that no one has touched yet . . . I feel their breath, I see them. I am not lonely, I am not lonely (p.165).

As the beautiful image fades, and Shloymke once again realizes where he is, he experiences a moment of disappointment. Now, however, he has the choice of imagining that his vision of union might in fact be true. For him, it is a viable alternative to agony, and he pulls the trigger of his beloved revolver.

In *A toyt,* Shneyur has created an unusually believable, and therefore disturbing, suicidal figure. Shloymke displays the constriction of Sheyndl and Felye, the trapped quality of Moritz/*zun,* the passive depression and listlessness of Zakhari. At the same time, however, he comprehends the origins of his malaise more deeply than they do, although he remains helpless to turn his life around. This fullness of understanding, combined with paralysis in terms of change, lies at the core of the work, rendering Shloymke at once clearly understandable and maddeningly opaque. The practical, clinical, lesson of the novel is sobering; it is a reminder that empathy, logic, explanation, sympathy, and even skill may sometimes not suffice to save a life.

Fliglman

H. D. Nomberg's Fliglman is a man who fits nowhere. Traditionally, this malaise has been viewed as a result of the social foment that unsettled turn-of-the-century Eastern European Jewish life. If a man abandons his heritage, this argument suggests, then he must expect to feel rootless, lost, even paralysed. According to this view, Fliglman's feeble suicide attempt is merely another sign of his impotence.

Perhaps Nomberg consciously sought to portray and criticize an historical phenomenon in his famous *Fliglman.*[4] Yet the work is psychologically far richer than this formulation: Fliglman, his relationships, his thoughts, even his memories, give a vivid if frightening picture of a man suffering from a narcissistic deficit so severe that he is unable to feel vigorous or meaningful. Nomberg's story depicts Fliglman's disintegration as his defenses crumble, first slowly and then with alarming rapidity.

Intellectual matters are virtually the sole means by which Fliglman contrives a semblance of social contact with others. At the very outset of *Fliglman,* the protagonist is still able to value his mental powers in order to think well of himself:

> Not infrequently . . . he thinks that many great men have lived in the world: Buddha, Spinoza, Kant, and many more, and he, the son of the Kuniver *shames,* knows their philosophical systems clearly and can repeat everything of theirs

> he has read, word by word . . . he thinks further, with pleasure, that basically all these philosophers had not been overly clever . . . (p.11).

Fliglman clings to his overblown self-image with others as well as in his own reveries. To his one acquaintance of any substance, Levantkovski, he boasts of his sensitivity to poetic themes while at the same time deriding Levantkovski's poor taste and obtuseness.

Fliglman's version of courting, as well, is marked by the tendency to discourse disastrously on subjects of his own choosing. Visiting the dentist who has become the center of his fantasies, for instance, he bores her with his talk:

> He always talked with her about books, writers and philosophers. She sat quietly and listened, listened to everything, but in the middle she would interrupt:
>
> —You want tea? (p.23).

Even later, when his sense of self is fragmenting, he nonetheless attempts to contain himself by resorting to beloved philosophical ideas. Refusing to recognize or acknowledge his growing despair, he tells Levantkovski that he has become a pessimist and that ". . . pessimism is, after all, the last word in philosophy" (p.24). At the end, moreover, as he is losing whatever vestige of self-control still remains to him, he reacts with special panic and agitation to the "illogic" of a pupil who has made a grammatical error in translation. The scene has a comic tone, but the fun is undercut by the pathos of Fliglman's initial screaming fit and his subsequent, futile effort to mollify both the boy and his mother. Unable to apologize for behavior that has reduced the boy to tears and thus disrupted the household, he continues explaining the impossibility of his pupil's response. This attempt fails both to comfort the child and to accomplish his underlying aim, i.e., the reestablishment of his intellectualized equilibrium. That same night, he attempts to take his life.

Fliglman's breakdown and subsequent suicidal gesture are not surprising, considering the way he has lived his life previously. His relationships to others, and especially to women, indicate the extent of his inability to lead an existence that allows him vulnerability to, and trust of, others. Indeed, he is from the outset unable to view others as individuals separate from himself. Fliglman's only relatively consistent acquaintance is Levantkovski, a scatterbrained spendthrift with a harried wife and six children who are perpetually hungry because Levantkovski cannot stay away from books and tobacco. His name, which includes in it the word *levant,* is an apt hint: Levantkovski represents the old world to Fliglman—emotional, unsophisticated, materially unsuccessful. Fliglman's relationship with Levantkovski—as long as the former is still behaving in his well-defended manner—involves his lecturing Levantkovski, who considers himself (on the surface, at any rate) a kind of pupil, arguing his points weakly and enduring Fliglman's condescending pronouncements with good-natured patience.

Certainly, there is no mutual opening of souls characterizing true friendship.[5] Instead, Fliglman subsists on the admiration of Levantkovski and on the gratification he receives from the knowledge that Mrs. Levantkovski admires him because he gives money to the family. Again, however, he enjoys this margin of rapport from afar, rather than being able to elicit a more direct response. On one occasion, the desperate wife stops him on his way out and asks to borrow money:

> Fliglman lends and stays a while in the house because soon shouts between man and wife are heard from their home. Levantkovski wants fifty kopekes for tobacco, his wife doesn't want to give it; Levantkovski says that, if not for him, Fliglman wouldn't lend to her. The wife answers:
>
> —You are not worthy of speaking to him! (p.14).

Fliglman reacts to this scene, which has silenced the man of the house, with satisfaction. Yet this contact, meager and superficial though it may be, is significantly more active and involved than his interactions with others. There, the misery of his situation emerges, for his only function is to lend money. Ignored for months on end, he is approached when a loan is needed. Afterwards, praising his generosity, his acquaintances promptly forget him again.

The reason for their perplexing behavior is actually clear: Fliglman keeps himself as distant as possible while serving tea and financial support. As the narrator explains, Fliglman does not want to have his *weltanschauung* disturbed. This world view is never explicitly articulated, but clearly it refers to his barricade of philosophical thoughts, behind which hides his vulnerable and terrified self. This deep part of him is so susceptible to sudden emergence that he must banish it lest it burst out and disorient him completely. As it transpires, Fliglman knows himself all too well, albeit unconsciously so. Once he can no longer hold such powerful forces at bay, they threaten to undo him altogether.

Perhaps the most revealing sections of *Fliglman* concern the protagonist's efforts to achieve contact with women. The first occasion of this, entitled *About Fliglman's First Love*[6] underscores Fliglman's dangerous failure to recognize others as anything beyond extensions of himself. So hungry is he for emotional nourishment that he misreads cues and invents responses, only to be bitterly disappointed in the end. The narrative heading tells much about Fliglman's past, as well as about his recent dealings. He is thirty-four—and this is his first love. His previous existence, therefore, has been barren of intimacy with a woman. The significance of this is underscored by his present "love." A virtual construct of his imagination, modified only by the fact that the woman does indeed exist, Fliglman's romance never results in a single exchange of words with his would-be beloved, let alone any physical bond.

"Fliglman has a very high opinion of love" (p.15). Thus begins the chapter devoted to Fliglman's great adventure, and the sentence encapsulates his problem admirably. Fliglman doesn't feel, desire, or wish for love; he regards it from afar. And, although his subsequent actions are indeed filled with emotion for him, he remains as removed from his deeper longings as ever. Fliglman is convinced, so the narrator explains, that a person who doesn't have a natural tendency for love is even more worthless than an illiterate, and although he trusts his own tendency in this direction, he nonetheless realizes that he has been unsuccessful with women. This he explains as a failure of the opposite sex to accept him even though he is unable to lie or flatter. He longs for a female soul to perceive his own, yet he knows this soul will have to be very special.

Fliglman wants a great deal from his fantasied relationship: no less than to find himself affirmed as never before. It is perhaps for this reason that he keeps such rigid control over the amount of time, and the manner, of his attentions to the young woman who sits reading in the window of the building next door. As if to protect himself from falling in love too rapidly, he forces himself away from his vantage point at the window, or gazes instead at the moon. These measures hardly influence his efforts at self-control because Fliglman is actually creating the personality of his beloved—as well as the ostensible romance—out of his own fantasies. Having noticed her looking at him "and there was something in that look" (p.17), Fliglman remembers having once read a saying: glances and laughter reflect the soul. Thus he "discovers" that his neighbor cares for him:

> He approached his little mirror, studied his face, and found that his glance was exactly like hers. There could be no doubt that she liked him: "A soul feels a soul" (p.18).

For weeks thereafter, Fliglman alternates between surmising the woman's sadness and vulnerability, and feeling weak and overwhelmed himself. He considers his own helplessness in confronting her as indicative that all women are sly. Finally, he makes his move. There has been a rainstorm and, not uncharacteristically, Fliglman has decided that the woman seemed sad. Noticing that her expression is bold, he prepares himself to smile:

> "The right time," thought Fliglman and gave himself courage . . . he gave a shake of the head, and a sweet smile spread across his face—
>
> But the woman quickly stood up, a large red tongue appeared, and the blind was lowered rapidly . . . (p.20).

Once he overcomes his shock, Fliglman retreats even further into his world of self-protective intellectualizing, telling Levantkovski that constant vigilance is required to ward off the unhappiness of life.

It is two years before Fliglman is willing to attempt another foray into the world of women, this time with the dentist, to whom he is not particularly attracted. Yet, he so longs to be married that he allows himself hope, although the interaction is lackluster, the conversation stilted. Here, too, Fliglman finds himself ridiculed and, as he finally realizes, rejected. The dentist has left the room to bring refreshments, returning to find Fliglman contemplating himself in the mirror. When she laughs at him, exclaiming that men scold women for primping while they do so themselves, he responds:

> "Yes—" Fliglman drew out the words—"We want to be appealing, why not? And especially I—to you" (p.23).

Unfortunately, Fliglman utters these words without force, and the conversation collapses. When another man comes in and the woman perks up, Fliglman takes his leave, never to return.

Fliglman's reliance on mirrors as an aid to his romantic endeavors illuminates his psychological position. As with the mirror in *Af fremde vegn,* these instruments of reflection indicate the state of the protagonist's mental health and emotional maturity. Although he believes himself ready to love a woman and exert himself on her behalf, Fliglman is in fact only seeking someone to sustain him. His wish is to be liked, yet he is so certain that this will not be the case that he cannot reveal himself to the two women for whom he experiences mental, although not truly sensuous, attraction. Instead, he approaches them through the haze of his own image and—in the case of the first woman—via the additional barrier of two window panes.

Because of his overweening need for acceptance and love, Fliglman is oblivious to the reaction he creates in the objects of his affection. He can neither recognize the young dentist's boredom and condescension nor his neighbor's frivolity. For the same reason, he is prey to bitter longing born of unfulfilled wishes as well as to bouts of hatred. In his fantasy, each woman could give him what he so wretchedly wants; she simply refuses to do so. Fliglman suffers from a profound lack of self-esteem; his apparent conceit before the mirror is not—as the dentist assumes—a sign of great pleasure but rather the opposite, dramatically so.

Fliglman's sense of a foundation in his past is unsubstantial indeed. Enjoying his first flush of excitement over the woman in the window, he remembers the exaggerated good cheer he had felt many years before, in anticipation of Passover. When he contemplates the moonlight from his room at night, he recalls a sad khasidic melody, the only one he has ever been able to commit to memory. These fleeting associations have a calming effect on Fliglman, but they are scarcely sufficient to regulate his moods, let alone to provide him with a sense of well-being.

On the contrary, his most vivid memory is a grim suggestion of just how empty and miserable his past—or, at least, what he retains of it—has been:

> He remembered his father, a small, thin little Jew who coughed constantly. Some cold night or other came to mind. His father had crawled out of bed with a cough and he got very cold, left alone in the bed. He remembered his father's death: lying on the ground he looked so small that it seemed that he had curled up and gone to sleep. Fliglman's only older sister cried bitterly and wiped her nose with her apron. And coming home from the funeral they both fought over half an orange which was left on the window ledge . . . (p.22).

Several aspects of this memory are significant. First, there is no mention whatsoever of Fliglman's mother, implying that she was physically or emotionally absent, or that some other reason compels her exclusion from his consciousness. Second, already before his father's death, Fliglman had perceived him as frail, sickly, and therefore unreliable, reacting to his temporary absence with physical discomfort and loneliness. Thus, even before the final loss of his father, Fliglman had known the suffering of abandonment, of helpless isolation, as he lay in bed. Moreover, the juxtaposition of this earlier event with the father's death suggests that, even as a young boy, Fliglman had learned to fear the older man's irredeemable disappearance at any moment.

A third meaningful factor in this memory is Fliglman's failure to express sadness. Unlike his sister, who had wept in response to her pain, he had shown anger, albeit indirectly—that is, in a displaced manner. The siblings' scuffle over half an orange symbolizes their struggle to retain something of their father, the sole nurturing presence they have known. Only in the ferocity of this competition does Fliglman's intense unhappiness emerge.

Fliglman's childhood recollection sheds light as well on his adult predicament. Deprived of warmth and full parental nourishment from an early age on, with the insecurity that corresponds to that plight, he consequently had lacked the freedom to expose his vulnerability and hurt. He had been forced to hide them or channel them elsewhere, rather than risk the added humiliation of finding himself denied a sympathetic response.

It is hardly surprising, then, that Fliglman encounters difficulty in forming close connections with anyone, and particularly with a potential wife, to whom he could look for stability and trust. Fliglman has suffered a dual developmental crisis: first, the evident absence of an all-important primary bond to an accepting—or at least accessible—mother; and second, the tenuous hold on his father, with the eventual loss of that figure as well. Rather than crying out, moreover, Fliglman deflects his longing to be cherished, denying his needs in the process.

At the root of all this maneuvering so as not to confront his loneliness lies Fliglman's fear that he will discover a reason for his wretchedness: his own unloveability. Indeed, after recalling his battle for the orange, Fliglman considers the present: "His sister is the wife of a *melamed* [teacher of children in a kheyder] today and surely doesn't want to hear his name, because he is a religious rebel" (p.22). This frail connection to his only living relative helps account for Fliglman's insecurity concerning romance and friendship and explains why, in the face of current tension, he possesses little emotional resilience to aid him in weathering the storm.

While the story's culmination—Fliglman's attempted suicide—reveals him as a man simply unable to tolerate his misfortune any longer, his decline begins much earlier. Indeed, as early as the time of his "first love," Fliglman's patched-together outer self is already starting to dissolve. The first indication of fragmentation is his experience, while in bed one night, that he and the bed are spinning. In addition, he sees spots shuttling between his window and the one across from him.[7]

The bed's movement does not disconcert Fliglman. Rather, he accepts it as natural, at the same time imagining that he is facing in the direction of his inamorata. Thus, when he can fantasize a relationship, he feels safe and content.[8]

Fliglman's profound need for contact as a bulwark against disintegration is manifested in his response to being harshly rejected by his would-be lover. Once again lying in bed, Fliglman tells himself that he is contemptuous of, or even angry at, the offending young woman. Yet, his fantasies—or delusions, perhaps—indicate a radically different psychic reality. Just as before, he observes spots before his eyes, but now they do not form a link between his room and the window opposite. Instead, "they [run] without any order somehow, [move] every which way." Moreover, far from soothing or satisfying him, they leave Fliglman all too aware of the darkness engulfing him. Finally, although he once again imagines his bed changing directions, the phenomenon fails to cheer him since, far from bringing him closer to the prospect of love, ". . . the bed somehow [turns] and [twists] in empty space" (p.21).

Despite Fliglman's protestations that he has managed to escape from this debacle unscathed, he spends the next two years in a state of ever decreasing efficiency. He dreams of a wife with heightened longing—but cannot hazard any enthusiastic pursuit of a partner. Rather, the craving impairs his mental clarity, causing his nerves to be on edge, making reading difficult. "It sometimes happened that he suddenly forgot a familiar word. He was often dizzy, and his mind was somehow empty and confused" (pp.21–22).[9]

Fliglman's internal sense of himself is vague, and his contact with the outside world is similarly limited. His major opportunity for introspection and self-evaluation, truncated though the process may be, occurs once every two years, when he receives a new passport, issued from his birthplace. This evocation of the past does no more to comfort him than his recollections of childhood. Rather, he is reminded that, at age thirty-six, he has failed to reach his goal of marriage and fulfillment: "The thought that it was already too late to marry frightened him. He began to look for acquaintanceship. This, however, was very difficult for him to accomplish" (p.22).

Feeling tentative, defeated, weakened, and confused as he does, Fliglman is singularly incapable of forming a satisfying bond. Realizing that he cannot keep up the pretense of inner solidity and well-being, Fliglman continues to disintegrate, to lose even the circumscribed protection of his intellectualized façade. His nerves are even more rattled than before; he can barely bring himself to read; as a symbolic expression of his shrinking ability to function effectively, he buys a pair of galoshes one size too large. His new passport shows him to be thirty-eight years old.

In Fliglman's eyes, the world is full of rain, mud, and funerals, and this malaise assumes a somatic aspect as well: "Fliglman felt tired, his brain became thin more and more often, he kept getting dizzy and his back ached" (p.24). In order to achieve some measure of relief, he visits a doctor, but when the doctor examines him thoroughly and then inquires into his marital status, it is more than Fliglman can bear. Ashamed, he pretends that he is married and then berates himself for having lied.

Things go from bad to worse, as Fliglman becomes increasingly isolated, cutting himself off finally from even Levantkovski. On the occasion in question, Fliglman makes an ostensibly idle observation concerning Schopenhauer, only to find his usually attentive friend more absorbed in preparing a fat cigarette than in listening to him. Enraged, Fliglman lashes out verbally, accusing Levantkovski of being a fool; to his further agitation, Levantkovski reacts with amusement. Deeply offended, Fliglman makes an exit, attempting to retreat as well from realizing his desolation.

The process of fragmentation has progressed too far, however, for Fliglman to shrug off this latest blow with some comforting intellectualizations. Instead, he remains in a state of upset for several days, wandering around his room and repeating over and over again his negative judgment of Levantkovski. At night, when his guard is even further relaxed, his bed no longer merely spins; instead, it mercilessly plunges him into "deep abysses" (p.25).

Fliglman's environment conspires to exacerbate his misery and sense of loss. One of his neighbors dies, and he becomes dizzy listening to the mourners' laments. Yet when he lies down to rest, he is catapulted into a frightening world of his own making: a bad dream. Here, Fliglman finds himself carrying a long, stiff corpse, wrapped in a black blanket, which he holds in both hands as he walks, bent over, from outside the city to bury the body. Two beadles accompany him and, through their conversation with each other, he discovers that the corpse is his sister. He is very tired. At the threshhold of a store he slips, and the corpse falls out, hitting its head. From within the blanket he hears the sound of crying, like a child's whine. One beadle says: "Keep on carrying, Fliglman. She is dead; this is just a reflex; keep carrying!" The dream continues:

> He had kept carrying. The voice got more and more shaky, and he was tired, very tired. The beadles pushed him forward, slapped him on the shoulders and rushed him. Fliglman wanted to cry and was afraid that that would be a reflex, that he was dead . . . He began to feel very bad and woke up sighing from his sleep (p.26).

Fliglman's first reactions upon waking help illuminate the meaning of the dream itself. First, he notices the total darkness of his room. Outside, the sky—cloudy as it is—sheds a reflection on the room, yet this is worse than the darkness itself. Second, he hears the wailing of a cat. The animal's howls tug at his heart but he understands that he cannot know what is wrong. When the sounds do not abate, Fliglman wraps himself in his blanket.

This last act provides a direct waking link with Fliglman's dream, in which his dead sister is enveloped in a blanket. Yet his other associations are equally important clues to the dream. Nomberg here supplies the raw material for an essential aspect of clinical dream interpretation, although one often ignored in the zealous literary critical use of dream symbols as if they are unconnected to the dreamer. That is, he furnishes a means of assessing the dream's impact on Fliglman, including the mood and pervasive ideas that remain with him after he has awakened. From these it is clear that Fliglman considers the external world—illustrated by the cloudy sky outside his window—more frightening than the darkness within him, as concretized by his pitch-black room. Moreover, he recognizes that a creature, be it a cat or himself, may cry out in anguish and yet fail to communicate its pain to others, even if they are interested and sympathetic. These ideas, filled with sadness, fright, and resignation, are the residues of Fliglman's dream.

The dream itself reveals Fliglman's sense of internal emptiness, his experience of himself and his true existence as dead. At first the dead person is not he, but rather his sister, a person both intimately related to him yet hopelessly distant from him, someone with whom he had once fought over a token of his lost father but whom he now considers uninterested in ever hearing from him again. She signifies both what is deepest in Fliglman and what he perceives as external to his inner being.

Moreover, Fliglman's sister had been with him during the agony of losing their protector and nurturer, only to abandon him herself, thus reinforcing his experience of rejection and loss. This is Fliglman's nightmare burden: the weight of a past which, although no longer vibrant, still haunts him with its reminder of isolation and despair.

Fliglman's response to his dead sister is also a dream manifestation of the split between his inner and outer worlds. When he trips and drops her body, he capitulates to his immense emotional fatigue, thereby ceasing to behave in the manner dictated to him by duty and adulthood. As a result, he is able to perceive his sister's childlike whine—an outward manifestation of internal nothingness. At this moment, Fliglman sees the possibility of achieving a balance between his most profound, forbidden, inner experience of death and the permission to articulate it.

This is not to be, however, for the beadles, the embodiment of social obedience and outer conformity, do not permit such freedom. One beadle explains that the voice he has heard is inconsequential, merely a reflex; both beadles encourage Fliglman to be more active. Fliglman attempts to comply, trying to adopt the role of a mature and responsible man, based on the example—perhaps idealized—of his father, who himself had been a beadle. The endeavor is not a success, however, and now Fliglman wants to cry himself. Yet he fears this response, since it threatens to reveal to him that, like his sister, he is actually dead inside.

By the end of the dream, then, when Fliglman begins to feel sick and wakes up sighing, his own fate and that of his dead sister have merged: any expression of malaise will not only serve to indicate a lack of internal vibrance, but will, indeed, fail to be recognized as valid by the social milieu. If he exposes his emptiness, therefore, Fliglman can expect no understanding. At the same time, he will no longer be able to pretend that he is a rational, contented man, unsettled only because, for external reasons, he has not yet found a wife to suit his needs.

When Fliglman wakes up, he hides himself in his blanket, trying, as it were, to keep his truth "under wraps." At the same time, he recognizes that he can no more rely on the external world as a source of comfort and equilibrium than can the cat, with its undecipherable agony. At this point, Fliglman's deepest self-experience—that of a lifeless inner core—finally bursts forth from its hiding place in his unconscious.

From now on, Fliglman's disintegration is rapid. During his one attempt to function normally—with his unfortunate young pupil—Fliglman finds himself making explanation for his confusion by using the excuse that his sister has died. This lie, and others he tells in conjunction with it, amaze him even as he utters them. No longer capable of distinguishing clearly between his fantasies and actual events, he is similarly unable to maintain the sharp, if inefficient, boundary between his true internal state and the face he presents to himself and the rest of the world.

Leaving the scene of this upset, Fliglman repeats over and over to himself "I am sick, I am sick, sick, sick, sick . . ." (p.28), and he feels better for doing so. Rather than an example of traditionally perceived obsessional thinking, this repetition, with its salutary effect, is a means of filling, albeit only temporarily, the inner void Fliglman feels. By talking in this way, he manages to stave off his internal chaos, even as he soothes himself by acknowledging it.[10]

Fliglman's feeble attempts at self-regulation exhaust him, and he goes home to sleep again, although he is frightened of his own room. He awakens from his slumber in no better spirits than before and, terrified by the sight of a white towel, lets his legs carry him to Levantkovski.

Here, Fliglman's crisis intensifies. Like the cat unable to convey its plight, his attempts to make Levantkovski understand the gravity of his condition misfire dismally. Perhaps because his previous emotional disguises and defenses have blunted Levantkovski to the true nature of his personality; or perhaps because Levantkovski and his family are ready for bed; or even perhaps because, in order to have put up with Fliglman for so long, Levantkovski must have been thick-skinned; whatever the reason, Fliglman is misunderstood and sent away as drunk after sinking into a stupor. Even when he mutters that he is going to Vistula, Levantkovski does not catch on, telling him instead: "Go to sleep, it's cold . . ." (p.28).

Fliglman does indeed go to the Vistula, but he does not actually attempt suicide, although he wonders whether perhaps he has:

> Fliglman felt that his whole body was reeling and he assumed that he had thrown himself into the water, but the reeling continued for a long time, the clatter of wheels on a hard bridge was heard. Someone talked to him in what seemed like Russian, and he did not understand.
>
> He went to sleep in the police station, all night he felt that he was lying in water; above his eyes a blue stream stretched and stretched and he felt light, but he had a pain under his head. And it seemed to him that he had fallen on a stone (p.29).

Now, the elements of Fliglman's dream have united and taken a place in his waking life, as he suffers the consequence of his own "slipping." In the dream, his dead sister's head had struck a stone when he, failing his charge, had allowed her body to escape its enveloping blanket. Now Fliglman himself endures similar pain: he has abandoned the struggle to project a socially acceptable façade, to maintain himself in isolation. Fliglman's failure to commit suicide thus represents his deep conviction that, for all intents and purposes, he *is* dead.[11] His utter emptiness consumes him, so that he is unable to care for himself and must delegate a policing force—here, literally the police—to do so.

Within this framework, *Fliglman*'s ending is ironic, as its protagonist makes one last effort to forge a link between his inner and outer realms. Awakened by force after sleeping in the police station, Fliglman cannot recall what has transpired and is intimidated by the police officer's uniform. Then he hits upon an inspiration. Reaching into his vest pocket, he says—in the last sentences of this work: "I have the great honor to request most humbly . . . bury me. I have a passport, here it is!" (p.30). Here Fliglman's past and present, as well as his internal and external states, merge in a new way. His passport had formerly symbolized the failure to marry and fulfill the promise of his earlier life; it had also represented Fliglman at his most external—a composite of descriptions without dynamic substance. Now it becomes his last hope. No longer a reminder of social and emotional bankruptcy, it signifies that he is somebody, that he possesses an identity.

Herein lies the irony, however. For, Fliglman is unable to draw any self-cohesion from this document. Instead, he hopes to impress those who rely on such externals so that they will permit him what he really wants: to be buried, to succumb to his most powerful urges, to which, precisely because he feels so weak, he cannot yield on his own. There is a further irony, however. For Fliglman, the inner experience of deadness is ultimately the most vibrant and authentic of emotions. Far from being a passive request, then, this final plea becomes Fliglman's most active step and, in a strange way, his liveliest.

Kreynin

Gavriel-Uri Kreynin is one of a quartet of characters in Borekh Glazman's stark short story, *Okean* ["*Ocean*"].[12] As a suicidal character he is both typical—according to the findings of this study—and unusual. Kreynin is familiar because he is lonely—a bachelor in his late-thirties—and because, by the conclusion of this brief work, he has come face to face with his sense of inner emptiness.

At the same time, however, Kreynin is highly successful, a popular author who, although he has not amassed wealth, nonetheless enjoys acclaim and respect. Indeed, he commits suicide at the height of his external, professional glory. Thus, the unhappiness that leads to his death is clearly unrelated to his status in, and significance for, the world at large. Rather, it reveals how a man can be crushed by his inability to establish firm personal ties and indicates that, if severe enough, emotional poverty may be fatal.

Kreynin's death is striking in another way as well: quite unlike other male Yiddish literary suicides, he does not depart from his customary patterns of passivity and withdrawal when he kills himself. Instead, he simply goes to sleep at the edge of the ocean, to be engulfed by the incoming tide. He is thus even more fundamentally immobilized than Zakhari, who had, after all, summoned sufficient energy to slit his throat.

Okean details the interactions and, more importantly, the private thoughts and fantasies, of four adults who spend a blustery autumn evening together in New York's Far Rockaway. In addition to Kreynin, they include Dr. Vaysgal, a prosperous physician in his fifties, who dyes his hair black and spends half the year ministering to the wealthy in Miami Beach; Mrs. Lamdn, a former flame of Kreynin's who has spent her married life promoting her husband's medical career; and Dr. Lamdn, an affable host and old friend of Kreynin's.[13] Throughout their time together, waiting out a potentially dangerous storm, the three men and one woman play pinochle, drink tea, nibble snacks, and attempt to communicate with one another.

Their conversation, such as it is, never progresses beyond stilted intellectual prattle, however. Dr. Lamdn bravely attempts to interest the others in a literary discussion, but Kreynin, the expert, refuses to participate and the conversation falters. Dr. Vaysgal, breaking the awkward silence, inquires: "Do you believe, Mr. Kreynin, in the immortality of . . . of the human being, of the human being in general?" (p.213). Rather than explore this personal issue, the three men spar with one another; Lamdn and Kreynin treat Vaysgal with contempt, and he buttresses his argument with examples from medical research. The only person who seems genuinely interested in the subject is Mrs. Lamdn, but she, too, is preoccupied with her own concerns:

> Doctor . . . Doctor . . . please, Doctor, express yourself more clearly . . . What do you mean—does it really help? Has it really helped? What do you mean, how—does one transplant the sex glands of a younger person or even an animal in an older person? And has this experiment been done on women as well? Please, Doctor, express yourself more clearly . . . (p.215).

This is neither scientific curiosity nor politeness, for Mrs. Lamdn has a vital reason for obtaining the information: "She was quite a few years older than Dr. Lamdn" (p.215).

The absence of direct revelation and the flat exchanges between the four are not matched by their internal experience of one another and of themselves. Here, the dynamic and powerful reactions of Mrs. Lamdn, Kreynin, and Vaysgal emerge with the air of incipient explosiveness characteristic of Glazman. Mrs. Lamdn's musings are perhaps the most oriented to her relationships with the others. Having years before chosen her husband over Kreynin, she is caught in a perpetual conflict concerning her evaluation of his celebrated position. While glad that he has succeeded, since that establishes the wisdom of her earlier affections, she is simultaneously plagued by anger and regret for having decided on the less spectacular man.

Kreynin and Mrs. Lamdn continue to be involved with one another—at least in her fantasies—but the relationship is certainly neither neutral nor cordial. Kreynin visits irregularly, always after he has executed a literary coup, yet he comports himself as if reeling from a major defeat. Mrs. Lamdn sees through this, however, and has her own interpretation:

> She would smile cleverly. With her shining eyes, she had seen how his great success—his triumph—shouted out from his

> modesty. She saw clearly that he had come there to display his victory and that he wanted her to be in pain about it (p.209).

In retaliation against Kreynin's ostensible hostility, Mrs. Lamdn's strategy consists of elaborate and demonstrative expressions of love for her husband.

Kreynin, for his part, does not have this game in mind, at least during what proves to be his final meeting with the erstwhile object of his attentions. His focus is Vaysgal, and the absorption is reciprocated. Each man secretly admires and envies the achievements of the other, seeing in them his own limitations. Vaysgal had, in his youth, published several well-received stories and articles in Hebrew and had dreamed of becoming a major literary figure. The fantasy had collapsed, however, when, upon his arrival in America, he had deemed it necessary to concentrate entirely on setting up and building his medical practice. From there it had been only a matter of time until he had gotten caught up in the ambition for wealth. Now, having attained that goal, it is too late, so he believes, to resume writing: exhausted, he no longer flows with creative juice.

Kreynin's difficulty is precisely the reverse, since his fame has not been accompanied by commensurate riches. He is furious about this, and the rancor easily attaches itself to Vaysgal in particular. Thus, he responds to the physician's question about immortality with condescension, because to him it represents yet another aspect of a monied man's acquisitive tendencies: "Wealth, health, good fortune, success—and in addition a drop of immortality. Pretty good swine, these well-off people" (p.213). Kreynin credits Vaysgal's affluence for the joie de vivre he imagines the older man possesses and that he covets most of all.

In this way, then, the two dissatisfied men, and Mrs. Lamdn as well, hide their true reactions, resorting instead to boring and trivial chatter, which leads them further away from one another as the evening progresses. There is no opportunity for disclosures of the sort that might ease the tension each one feels—as, for example, the fact that, far from enjoying a carefree existence, Dr. Vaysgal is dying of a rare disease that necessitates his regular stays in Florida. More than this, however, there is no opening for Vaysgal and Kreynin to find what lies beneath the ambitious surface of their awareness: both men hunger for a warm and simple bond with another human being—an experience of union, no matter how fleeting.

Vaysgal, for all his outward show of debonair insouciance, realizes consciously that his admiration for Kreynin contains an element of need, a wish to merge with the attributes he imputes to the famous author. In this way he is able to imagine that he himself is filled with well-being:

> . . . Kreynin's success—which certainly brought him, in addition to external fame, a deep internal satisfaction—was a confirmation of Dr. Vaysgal that this was the only path that he, Dr. Vaysgal, should have followed. And although he silently envied him, he nonetheless wished him further growth—just as if he were growing within Kreynin (p.212).

The illusion lasts only a moment, unfortunately for the doctor, and he finds himself almost simultaneously faced with the self-perception he has been attempting to squelch:

> But he himself had not actually grown. Only one thing grew within him: the ever fuller conviction that his life had been a failure (p.212).

By endeavoring, through fantasy, to connect himself with Kreynin's achievements and supposed inner calm, Vaysgal seeks—although it is far too late—to absorb into himself qualities that will provide him with self-esteem and a belief in his own value.[14]

During his visit at the Lamdn's, Kreynin undergoes a process similar to Dr. Vaysgal's, as he pictures himself in the other's fortunate circumstances. Specifically, he covets Vaysgal's opportunity to travel—particularly his freedom to visit exotic and sensuous Cuba:

> Kreynin greatly resented the fact that he had never been there and that, with all his writerly success, he had no possibility

> of traveling there . . . and *he* could have woven such dreamworks from his impressions and the visions evoked by the place! A pity (p.206).

Quite unlike Vaysgal, however, Kreynin defends himself temporarily against any wish for affiliation with the doctor's power and prosperity by assuming a stance of arrogance, from which he does not emerge until after he has left the Lamdn's windswept bungalow:

> He comforted himself with just one thing, that it was all wasted on Dr. Vaysgal . . . he doesn't *see* anything anyway . . . Kreynin looked at him obliquely with scorn, condescension—almost with contempt. He—he, *Kreynin,* would remain, his name was becoming increasingly eternal. The Vaysgals would be erased, wiped away—dust flying by (p.206).

Kreynin's apparent superiority makes itself felt, and the others in the group react accordingly, convinced that they are undoubtedly in the presence of a great man. Thus, they excuse his behavior and explain to themselves that his grandeur is responsible for their feelings of oppression, both when he speaks and when he is silent.

Yet, that very night Kreynin kills himself, or, rather, allows himself to drown. The process of his collapse is abrupt but not mysterious. Put plainly, he suddenly realizes his complete isolation and, stripped of the pretense that he can survive on the adulation of anonymous admirers, he gives up his struggle to exist.

Kreynin's battle is not new. From the very outset, there is an aura of melancholy about the writer, whose generally downcast eyes reflect both sadness and severity. There is also his pattern of seeking out company when he has achieved a victory, apparently in order to portray such moments in a negative light. On this night, however, something else occurs within Kreynin, and it proves enough to destroy him.

Kreynin had decided to venture the long trip home, despite the autumn storm that has preoccupied the Lamdns and their guests and served as an ominous backdrop for their complicated, albeit secret, entanglements. Just missing his train, he knows he faces an hour's wait; since he is ashamed to return to his hosts, he begins pacing the deserted streets, mulling over his life. He considers the possibility of taking a trip somewhere, then at once reminds himself that he has absolutely no friends, only superficial acquaintances. Kreynin's next association is to Vaysgal, whom he now recalls as haughty and deprecating—in marked contrast to his previous perception of the doctor. He tells himself that Vaysgal is the success in life, that he, Kreynin, is merely a "back number" (p.219), a humble pauper.

In the midst of these gloomy, unhappy thoughts, Kreynin suddenly spots a stocky figure walking towards the ocean. He responds dramatically: "His heart throbbed towards the stranger. But the steps soon died out in the sand" (p.219). From here, Kreynin's capitulation is swift. Abandoning his train, which is about to arrive, he himself heads for the ocean. On the way, he discovers himself near the Lamdns' house and imagines the occupants gossiping about him. Mrs. Lamdn had done well to abandon him, he decides, which leads him to bemoan his own lonely fate: unmarried, childless, central to no one. As if to join the presumably happy couple, he leans against their lighted window. This attempt at attachment warms him for a while—until the light is abruptly extinguished. Plagued by fantasies of the couple's sexual intimacy, he admits to himself that he has never really known love.

Kreynin can concentrate on one thing only: that he has focused his entire existence on writing, to the exclusion of any real, personal ties. As a result, he has nothing, he is nothing—except a lonely, excluded, literary success. He continues walking:

> Depressed, empty, with a wrenching feeling of being alone in the world—one among millions of strangers—he set out again through the deserted streets, to the water's edge, to the ocean (p.221).

Kreynin's bodily sensations are in strange harmony with his notion that he is utterly insignificant to the universe; helplessly, he feels himself shrinking, becoming ". . . a mite, which the monstrously huge eye of the world can scarcely see through a magnifying glass of myriad strength . . . a nothing, a nothing'' (p.222).

Eventually, Kreynin reaches a moment of some peace, where he accepts his plight; yet it is also a point of complete resignation, a self-castigation of his entire misery as both trivial and unavoidable. He is trapped within his life. Therefore, he cannot be moved by the discovery that his pounding heart has led him to follow none other than Vaysgal to the water's edge. Having experienced a final, powerful, urge towards contact, he understands that this attempt must fail—just as clinging to a lighted window can never bring true warmth. *Okean* concludes with Vaysgal—the man condemned to die—turning back from the water's edge, intent on living. Kreynin, on the other hand, does not move from his spot:

> He was tired. He closed his eyes. And under his eyes, he felt that the ocean was moving further and further onto the dry land. Everything was under water. Kreynin, too, was *underneath* by now. Above him was ocean and night—and *rest.* The only possible, eternal, rest (p.224).

In the end, Kreynin gives up because he assumes that nothing in life could conceivably bring him satisfaction. Like Fliglman, Zakhari, and Shloymke, he perceives that he is alone, without the internal sense of hopeful possibility that inspires endurance despite even the most adverse circumstances.

Kreynin's early history is not revealed to even the most limited degree, yet a picture emerges of emptiness so powerful that it leaves him unable to form bonds of friendship and love. The potential for these emotions may be innate, but the experience of them is not. Glazman, without discussing the sources of his protagonist's tragedy, nonetheless makes abundantly clear his present-day incapacities. Just as it is in a clinical situation, information about the past is of great help in illuminating current behavior and thinking, but it is not necessary in determining that a crisis may be at hand. At the same time, however, immediate events never occur in a vacuum. Thus Kreynin's external existence, for all its success and acclaim, is finally irrelevant when his internal, historical impoverishment and weakness—whatever its cause—eventually overwhelm him.

Yasha

Yasha Mazur, the protagonist of Isaac Bashevis Singer's *Der kuntsnmakher fun lublin*[15] [''*The Magician of Lublin*''], would seem not to fit at all in the context of suicidal male passivity. To begin with, he does not commit suicide. Moreover, at the outset of the novel, he is not introduced as passive: he is married, has two mistresses, and is courting yet another woman, whom he believes he wishes to marry. He commutes between Lublin, Piask, and Warsaw. He is lively, sought after by friends and acquaintances, desired by women. He looks ten years younger than his actual age of forty and is still able to use his body as a finely tuned instrument for acrobatics, lockpicking and their sexual equivalents—he is both an athletic lover and a master seducer. In short, he appears to be active and virile, an individual who has managed to remain a functioning member of his society while avoiding many of its constraints. Indeed, from the outside he approximates the dual achievement of success in love and work that epitomizes the traditional Freudian criterion of mental health. His only apparent difficulty is that he lacks the money to secure and support Emilia, the lady of his dreams.

Yasha's progress within the space of the novel may be (and has been) seen as a religious/spiritual or social/historical journey[16] during which Yasha goes from a secular, modern world into an orthodox, reactionary one, culminating in his self-confinement as a penitent in a walled-up hut. Forsaking his women and his questionable metier, he withdraws into a life of purity and contemplation.

While these elements are undoubtedly present in the novel, the extent to which they are central is debatable. When the issue of Yasha's psychological state is explored, another view of the changes in him emerges. It then becomes apparent that his retreat to the penitential hut serves an underlying purpose and is therefore not an end in itself. For, Yasha has a hidden motivation: *Der kuntsnmakher fun lublin* traces the course of its protagonist's regression from an apparently mature male position to one of pre-oedipal helplessness.

Throughout the novel, Yasha's escapades and reactions, as well as the revelations that accumulate about him, suggest a determination, albeit unconscious, to return to a blissful, safe state of existence. Specifically, the journey is towards a time when the conflicts over oedipal rivalries and their renunciations had not yet marred Yasha's horizon, and a dyadic relationship with his mother was still the essential framework.

Although Yasha strives to regain a realm in which he is passive, he is unlike those men in Yiddish literature who choose suicide as their solution. He is not physically destroyed by the need to retreat from responsibility. Rather, the suicide committed in *Der kuntsnmakher fun lublin* is that of Magda, Yasha's faithful, exasperated, and finally outraged lover. Yet the two events, i.e., his passivity and her suicide, are not unconnected, although they may at first appear to be. Moreover, the signs of Yasha's disintegration, which have a critical effect on Magda's psyche, are present from the very first pages of the novel. Already at that point, Yasha's world is beginning to crumble; he is aware that his inner structure is going awry.

When he is first introduced, Yasha is at home in Lublin with his wife, Esther. Although he exhibits his usual carefree, playful demeanor to her, he is experiencing something entirely different inside: "He became increasingly confused and withdrawn. Within him, forces raged; passions reduced him to terror" (p.23). He muses about others and about himself: "Each person has his secrets. If the world had ever been informed of what went on inside of him, he, Yasha, would have long ago been committed to a madhouse"[17] (p.20).

Yasha realizes that he is losing his grip on the world he has so carefully constructed. He senses that previously he had geared much of his behavior towards staving off the depression that constantly threatened to overwhelm him. Now, however, he begins to submit to his negative impulses. He does not rehearse as he knows he must if he wishes to succeed; he is forced to acknowledge a premonition that he will not perform (p.109). Moreover, his actions acquire an explicitly self-destructive aspect: having determined—and failed—to carry out a burglary, he commits the further blunder of leaving behind some pages of his address book. He thus implicates Emilia and, as a result, decides that he must sever his ties with her. At the scene of the crime, he understands that this, his first such error, is not only a debacle per se, but also an indication of his psychological collapse:

> He knew, deep inside of him, that the misfortune would not be confined to this night alone. That enemy which for years had lurked in ambush within him, whom Yasha had had, each time, to repel with force and cunning, with charms and such incantations as each individual must learn for himself, had now gained the upper hand (pp.166–7).

At this moment, then, Yasha's worst fear about himself becomes a nightmarish reality. The madman within him and the "enemy" he experiences are one: a part of himself that he has kept outside his conscious awareness. And from now on, Yasha's life may be seen as a struggle to allow this forbidden aspect to emerge without destroying him emotionally—coupled with his fear that it will do just that.

If Yasha's emotional state had been unstable from the very outset of *Der kuntsnmakher fun lublin,* the burglary signals the point at which he begins letting go of his controls and ceases being able to cope with his conflicts. A symbolic representation of this process is Yasha's injury, which he suffers while escaping from his ill-fated adventure. Like the internal enemy that overwhelms him, takes over, and plunges him into turmoil, his wounded foot becomes increasingly unwieldy, disproportionately large, excruciatingly painful, and is immediately a major focus of attention. As this is occurring, Yasha becomes convinced that he is insane, and the notion is not entirely unpleasant to him. In fact, in some way he wishes for it; he sees madness in others as something enviable: a man sits, "His watery, crossed eyes rolled in exaltation, the ecstasy of one on the brink of madness" (pp.247–8). He passes a woman: "She had tousled hair and eyes which were aflame with the joy of madness . . ." (p.249).

Yasha's reaction to his foot as more than a part of his body that has been hurt—indeed, as no less than an emblem of something unbridled emerging from him—can be seen through a connection that he himself establishes: he creates an analogy between the uncontrolled ballooning of his foot and an anecdote he had overheard earlier that day. A woman had prepared some yeast dough, intending to bake a cake for her mother; deciding at the last minute to do her baking at her mother's home, she had taken the dough with her on the bus:

> It was warm on the omnibus and the dough began to rise. It crept out of the basket as if it were alive. She tried to stuff it back but dough is something that won't be pushed. When she squeezed from one side it billowed out the other. The cover flew off. The basket swelled, and bang! it burst. Anyway, I *think* it burst (p.201).

The links between the randomly perceived, seemingly meaningless, tale and Yasha's central conflict exist on more than one level. First, there is the superficial similarity that Yasha discovers between the bread dough and his foot: in both cases a grotesque swelling occurs, and the person confronted with it is completely unable to master it. The concept of a possible bursting lends another layer to the interpretation: that is, like the bread dough, which cannot be pushed down once it has begun to rise, so, too, Yasha's insides—be it in the metonym of his foot or the metaphor of his emotions as concrete—are threatening to push violently forward and cause him to explode.

If the fear of disintegration is the *form* of Yasha's anguish, articulated through the vehicle of the anecdote, the *content* of his problem is hinted at in several of the story's details. First, the adventure takes place during a journey, one undertaken at the last moment because the daughter's own facilities were considered by her to be inadequate. Second, the daughter is going back to her mother's house to do her baking. Third, she is going there to bake a yeast cake. Like the baking of bread, which may sometimes symbolize pregnancy and childbirth, the yeast cake is supposed to be put in the oven, emerging somewhat later, larger and complete. These details suggest several possibilities about Yasha: (1) that he is about to make a move because he feels in some way damaged or ineffective; (2) that he wants to go backwards, in the direction of his mother, who could provide what he lacks; (3) that his craving has something to do with the needs of infancy, and that these needs have not been met previously.

In fact, when these speculations are applied to Yasha's actions and thoughts, they correspond to a remarkable degree. The "enemy" that Yasha had fought for so long and to which he succumbs in *Der kuntsnmakher fun lublin* is his wish, intolerable to him, to be cared for by a woman as if her were a child. When the notion of his regression is accounted for, his behavior during the entire novel becomes clear.

From the very beginning, Yasha's relationships with women are complex in a particular way. They involve sexual activity, but, with the exception of the encounters with Emilia, they are almost completely lacking in eroticism. Significantly, Emilia and Yasha never consummate their desire; thus it remains largely in the realm of fantasy for him.

Underneath the veneer of adult sexuality lies something else, namely the wish to be passive and nurtured. While this craving would be present even if Yasha were emotionally mature, its overriding strength makes it conspicuous in him. Thus, when he is finally built into his penitential hut, he has achieved the recapturing of a previous time: "It was as if he had become again a foetus in his mother's womb . . . He was free of all needs" (p.265). In developmental terms, his major striving has not progressed fully to the oedipal, triadic phase, but has remained chiefly at a pre-oedipal, dyadic stage. There are, to be sure, some glimmerings of oedipal issues, as when Yasha, who is waiting for Magda to come to bed, muses on the fact that her brother could kill him. But the overwhelming emphasis is on the women themselves, and whether or not they will be there when he wants them.[18]

Even before Yasha acts on his unconscious impulses, the females in his life perceive the problem. His wife, Esther, considers him both son and husband to her (pp.13–14). Magda would love to bear Yasha a child, "But he robbed her even of that. He, himself, wanted to be the child" (p.127). Indeed, the strong-willed and manipulative Emilia, who attempts to inveigle Yasha into taking care of her and her daughter, treats him "as one would a mischievous child" (p.96), at the same time as she wishes him to father one for her.

Yasha's effort to be watched over and attended to is not directed solely at potential sexual objects. Magda's mother thinks of herself as both his mother and his mother-in-law. The impressario Wolsky scolds Magda after Yasha's injury, saying: "We two made an agreement that you would look after him. He is a child" (p.193). Moreover, while attempting to maintain an intensely complicated adult life of work and love, Yasha frequently thinks of himself as a child. Early on, he muses that "At times he felt as if he were still a boy, at other times he seemed a hundred years old" (p.28). He experiences "a childish urge to flee" (p.236) from the sight of the dead Magda, and "a childish shame" (p.240) over his failure in making the proper arrangements to prevent official notice of her suicide.

Similarly, although the novel's narrator makes mention of the fact that Esther is barren, Yasha himself discusses her childlessness as something she had stopped mentioning to him, evidently despairing of his support, much as Magda had talked of becoming pregnant "but he had not taken her seriously" (p.122). Yasha even goes so far as to connect his childishness with his choice of career: "He could have been the father of grown children by this time, yet he remained the schoolboy who had played with his father's locks and keys and trailed the magicians through the streets of Lublin" (p.77).[19]

At the height of his passion for Emilia, Yasha decides that, unlike his reaction to Esther and Magda, he will grant Emilia's wish for a child. But his unconscious need to be the child himself insures that her longing will never be satisfied. The very next night, Yasha does not go to Emilia as he had promised, and instead commits his maladroit crime. The concatenations of this action change the course of his life entirely. Thus, just when he is confronted with his inability to gratify the demands of the one woman who requires that he behave like an adult, he begins disintegrating, becoming more infantile.

It is no accident that, in their last visit together before Yasha flees his Warsaw life, Emilia reiterates her desire to have Yasha's children (p.210) and twice reminds him that neither of them are children (p.208,210). After Yasha reveals to Emilia that he is the culprit in the Zaruski break-in, she is angry but nevertheless willing to deal with him. But Yasha has already embarked on the course that will carry him back to a fetal-like hut and a diet of "bread with groats, potatoes in their skin, cold water . . . rice with hot milk" (pp.264,284). Bidding Emilia farewell, he is unable to respond to her request that he remain:

> "Where are you going? You haven't murdered anyone!"
>
> "Forgive me if you can."
>
> Emilia shouted something after him, but he slammed the door and, injured foot and all, began to race down the stairs (p.225).

Yasha's conflicts about his role as a man and as an adult are deeply complex. Hence, they are not confined to the overt manifestations of childishness and sexual blandness. Rather, they emerge as well in a pattern of inconsistence with respect to the central women in his life, wherein he reveals his dependence on them. He feels addicted to women, particularly to sexual contact with them, yet at the same time he hates them because of this very need and the constant fear that affection will not be forthcoming. Thus he responds to an encounter with Zeftel, a deserted wife with whom he has sporadic relations, with the sense that:

> It was all humiliating, the kissing, the offering of the present, the waiting while she fetched the coffee with chicory, but just as the thieves had to steal money—he had to steal love (p.52).

He considers women opportunistic and at the same time greedy: "Whenever he was kind to someone, she wanted to enslave him" (p.130). His dilemma is summed up in his realization that "He lusted after women, yet hated them as a drunkard hates alcohol" (p.117). Thus he feels his need as unhealthy, something that will trap him and be detrimental to him.[20]

While Yasha's reactions are not limited to those of distress and surprise, and although he is active in pursuing sexual pleasure until he gives up on it altogether, his powerful expressions of disappointment and loathing indicate his unhappiness at not achieving what he wants from sexual intercourse—that is, contented fusion—and his disgust with his partners for making demands on him rather than giving to him.

Yasha also expresses his unhappy dependence on women through projection; that is, rather than acknowledge the extent to which he needs them, he attributes the need to them. But his ability to maintain this attitude is incomplete and fragile. He vacillates between pity and hate. When, after his accident, he arrives at the apartment he shares with Magda, he receives no reply to his rap at the door. In an odd premonition of her death, he wonders: "Was she as angry as that? Had she killed herself?" (p.187). He is angry that Magda is not there for him, but to admit this would mean conceding that he craves her presence. Later, however, he reflects on this same absence in a different, more direct manner:

> She had not spent the night at home, he decided. But where had she been? Was she capable of this sort of revenge? Jealousy and disgust mingled in him (p.196).

Yasha reacts similarly when thinking of a planned rendez-vous with Emilia on the fateful night of his downfall. This time, however, the unrefined emotion surfaces first. Angry because she has frustrated his wish for sexual intercourse the previous night, he grumbles: "Since she is so virtuous, let her wait!" (p.151). But at that point he is still healthy and powerful; moreover, he has Zeftel as a buffer. By the next day, when he is hurt and frightened, he wants to feel that Emilia is pining for him so as to hide his own sense of vulnerability from himself: "He was nearly penniless—injured, how could he earn his living! What could he tell Emilia? She must be frantic at his not showing up the day before" (p.186).

Even at the close of the novel, safely ensconced in his hut, Yasha contemplates breaking out, running away. But he tells himself that he cannot do this to Esther because she depends on him so heavily:

> Who could tell? She might even become ill from sorrow. He had noted how her health was failing. Old age was creeping up on her. Magda, peace be with her soul, had shown him the sort of thing that could happen (p.272).

In reality, Esther is self-supporting, financially and socially. She is secure within her role, despite the irregularity of her marriage. It is Yasha's fantasy that she would die of grief because of him. She displays none of the passionate despair and pathetic gratitude that characterize Magda's behavior. Yasha's comment about Esther, like his "premonition" of Magda's suicide, may reveal yet another aspect of his attitude towards women: his murderous hatred which, as a reaction-formation,[21] he transforms into a worried solicitude regarding their health.

Yasha's varied responses to women thus possess a common internal logic. His underlying impulse is to find a basic nurturance which will allow him to be passive. But, because this desire is unacceptable to him, he tries to conceal it. At the same time, he displays hatred and rage towards the objects of his thwarted immature love because they do not fulfill his unexpressed wishes. Moreover, he lives in constant misery and tension because his eroticized facade is insufficient protection against the emergence of those strivings.

Still, insofar as he is able, or compelled, to communicate them, Yasha does manage to attain partial satisfaction of his deepest longings. Both Esther and Magda do their best to take care of him, although—in the case of Magda, his real companion—the task is performed grudgingly at times. At least on a conscious level, these two women act consistently in Yasha's interest rather than in their own.

For this reason, Magda's suicide may at first appear uncharacteristic. Why would a woman whose entire existence revolves around one man suddenly kill herself because he has revealed himself, not for the first time, to be a philanderer? Certainly there is an element of animosity in her act, a desire to punish Yasha and to engrave herself on his heart.[22] However, when her death and the circumstances surrounding it are viewed through the prism of their effect on Yasha, a new connotation suggests itself. The first perspective provides interesting insights into one woman's sense of her own wretchedness; the second is a study of the complexity with which men and women imbue their lives.

Despite her essentially tangential role, Magda stands out as unusual among the suicides in Yiddish literature for several reasons. First of all, she is not Jewish. This criterion is largely artifactual. It might seem that Magda's Christianity enables her to easily accept an aspect of her life that is inimical to traditional Jewishness, i.e., her liaison with Yasha. Yet this is not the case. Rather, she is considered, and considers herself, a woman of "unsavory reputation;" she is branded "whore of the Jews" (p.126, 127). All the same, it is not the illicit nature of her love that causes Magda to take her own life, as was in some measure the case, for example, of Esther in Bergelson's *Der toyber* or Sheyndl in *Af fremde vegn.* On the contrary, she kills herself just at the point when that illicit existence may be in jeopardy. In this, Magda differs significantly from most other, Jewish, characters.

A partial explanation for her behavior emerges from the examination of Magda's feelings concerning her position in Yasha's life. Most of all, she believes herself privileged to be with him, as if no more fulfilling prospect could ever appear on her horizon. Magda's dependence on Yasha for love is reinforced by her mother's attitude towards her. Elzbieta makes it very clear that she considers Yasha her daughter's only hope—as well as her own, since he supports the family.

Elzbieta lives in constant dread that Yasha will tire of Magda. In her mind, it is something of a wonder that the relationship has endured for the eight years that Magda has been Yasha's assistant. As she muses:

> Yasha was both lover and father to the girl. Who else would bother with such a dried-up snip, thin as a twig, and with a bosom so flat? (p.40).

Elzbieta coaches her daughter to help her maintain Yasha's interest. Yet, privately, in direct competition with Magda, she cherishes the notion that it is actually she who keeps Yasha involved with the family:

> He, the poor boy, had himself been orphaned at an early age and Elzbieta was like a mother to him. She secretly felt that Magda owed it to her that Yasha had remained with them these many years (p.41).

(To some extent, of course, this may be true, given Yasha's urges. And, in fact, Yasha does worry that, if he leaves Magda, the news of it would kill Elzbieta. Of this complication, however, Elzbieta is not consciously aware.)

Magda has been trained by her mother to disparage herself and to serve Yasha, to think of him as a prize and to focus her life around him—as her mother gears her own life to caring about Yasha and her son, Bolek. Beyond her indisputable affection and passion for her lover, Magda lives in the spirit of another one of her mother's thoughts:

> She knew that he had a wife in Lublin, and associated with that gang of rogues in Piask, but she would not permit herself to dwell upon this—to what avail? One had to take what one could get (p.39–40).

That is, she lives this way until something occurs to make her change.

Magda's is possibly the closest thing to an explicitly angry suicide that can be found in Yiddish literature and this is another factor that causes her to be unusual. Yasha and she have argued; she has called him a "dirty Jew" and announced that she is leaving him. "You bring out the devil in me!" she exclaims (p.199). The action she will take is foreshadowed by the contents of her shopping basket—a dead chicken with a bloody neck. After Magda has run off to the kitchen following her outburst, Yasha, "for some inexplicable reason," covers the chicken's neck with a beet. The scene is confusing, grotesque and melodramatic, yet peculiarly humorous. The image of the slaughtered chicken implies that Magda's death is sacrificial[23] and that it is up to Yasha to make amends for the wrong he has done.

However, Magda does not die merely as a helpless symbol of her lover's cruelty, absorbing his sins as she perishes. Her final act before hanging herself is to kill Yasha's monkey, crow, and parrot. In doing so, she renders him professionally helpless. For, even if he hadn't sustained an injury, Yasha cannot hope to perform without his assistant and his animals.

Yasha does not interpret Magda's message in this way. "Why had she done this? No doubt to prevent the creatures from crying out" (p.237). Notwithstanding the evident illogic of this reasoning, since the animals had been in another room, Yasha's thinking has a useful function. By denying the retaliation and brutality in Magda's action, he is spared the realization that she had wanted the animals dead. Moreover, by avoiding this possibility, Yasha need not examine what might have prompted her to take such a seemingly unnecessary step. An earlier fantasy sheds light on this second layer of meaning in Magda's suicide. Almost immediately before imagining that Magda may have killed herself (and it is imagination at that point, since she had not yet committed suicide), Yasha had been in despair about the sudden change in his fortunes: "What was a man worth if his entire existence depended upon a foot—even his love? Now was the time to kill himself" (p.186). This juxtaposition indicates, once again, that Yasha's thoughts about others often reflect some process occurring within himself. Here he projects his suicidal ideation onto her, attributing to her what he has thought about himself.

A new motivation for Magda's act suggests itself: it is her submission to Yasha's unspoken wishes. It thus conforms with the conventions of their relationship—she obeys him, while at the same time attempting to protect and sustain him. Inchoately, at least, she had understood his reluctance to begin the entertainment season, even though he himself was unaware of this. Instead, he had been plagued by a fearful premonition that he would not be able to go on. The intuition had been strong, but he did not know what form his failure to work would take: "Would he grow sick? Was he, God forbid, due to die? Or was it something else altogether?" (p.109–110). However, Yasha's foreboding, like his demons, can be seen as an expression of his own desires. He fears this eventuality precisely because he wants it so much, yet believes that the notion is unacceptable.

The reason for his impulse to cease performing (and, here, performance represents various sorts of functioning, not just the earning of a living) is given by Yasha himself, directly after he contemplates his worrisome future: "He had wound himself into too many entanglements. He had driven himself into a dilemma" (p.110). Indeed, by the time Yasha injures himself and his fantasy becomes reality, the process of disengagement has already begun.

Magda recognizes Yasha's qualms about the new season. During their last happy interlude, she questions him concerning his apathy:

> "When do we begin to rehearse? The opening is a week away." / "Yes. I know." / "The posters are everywhere. Your name is in gigantic letters." / "They can all go to hell" (p.127).

Although she cannot be consciously aware that on the very day before her suicide Yasha has imagined it, her subsequent behavior assumes a logic that is missing without the concept of suggestibility.

It is impossible to assign clear-cut motivational meaning to Magda's suicide because so little is provided of her inner life except as it refers to Yasha; in fact, her thoughts apparently function mainly as a way of shedding light on him and his conflicts. Yasha contemplates suicide as a way of escaping the burdens he can no longer shoulder, yet he does not actually come close to taking his own life. Even after Magda's death, when he is overwhelmed by shock and despair, his musings do not result in action: "If he could find an open gate and an open grave, he would lie down in it, conduct a proper Jewish funeral for himself." Moments later, however, he concludes: "Well, fate does not wish me to die yet!" (p.255). His aim is not to obliterate himself but rather to achieve relief from an overly complex life, albeit one entirely of his own making.

Magda provides Yasha with the outlet of becoming a penitent.[24] Clearly, he had already begun to run from all his entanglements when he fled from Emilia despite her willingness to continue her involvement with him. But it is Magda's death that helps him see his future. By that act, she does more than destroy his potential for work. In addition, she provides him with the impetus to seek a place where he will be safe, where he will not have to endure the possibility of another such loss.

In the epilogue of *Der kuntsnmakher fun lublin,* Yasha has become a man of God: he prays and studies constantly, he listens to those who come to him for advice and speak to him ". . . as if he were God" (p.273). He feels God's presence in every snowflake. It might appear that this is the true purpose of his struggles, the answer to the riddle of who he really is. Perhaps this is the way in which Magda has helped Yasha. Why shouldn't someone who, almost against his will, repeatedly finds himself in places of worship—and who unceasingly contemplates the nature of God and Jewishness no matter where he is—why shouldn't such a person emerge as a religious fanatic?

Yet, once again, just as with Yasha and his women, the seemingly most important is not necessarily most significant beneath the surface. Once again, his self-perception may differ considerably from the way he actually behaves. The hand of God may in fact be Yasha's own, inner, design. From the beginning of the novel until its conclusion, Yasha's concept of God is abstract, universal, and so vague as to raise questions about whether it is heretical. At first, consumed with passion for the non-Jewish Emilia and frantically attempting to find some way to attain her, he declares that it doesn't matter where one prays to God—even in a church. Once ensconced in his hut, he no longer attempts to equate synagogue and church, but his ideas remain comprehensive:

> Each flake that fell on the window sill was hexagonal, complete with stems and horns, with designs and appendages, formed by that hidden hand which is everywhere . . . What can one call this force, if not God? Yasha asked himself. And what difference does it make if it's called nature? (pp.281–82).

Yasha's religious identity is informed not by an image of God but rather by the structures of Jewish life and the strictures of its Law. On several occasions, he finds respite from external danger in the safety of the synagogue: first, when he and Magda are caught in a rainstorm; then, when he is running away from his crime; and, finally, when he has fled Emilia. Nonetheless, even at the moment of his greatest helplessness, Yasha experiences the external forms of Judaism as little more than a buffer against other, internal, issues. After his final encounter with Emilia, for instance, Yasha attempts to tell himself that, if only he had kept to the ways of orthodoxy, he would have been spared his sins:

> He most certainly would not have been involved in all these love affairs and other escapades if he had put on a fringed garment and had prayed thrice daily. A religion was like an army—to operate it required discipline. An abstract faith inevitably led to sin (p.232).

The thought is full of possibilities for future, more productive behavior and, unlike Yasha's ideas about God, it conforms with an accepted Jewish precept, i.e., that observance encourages—even leads to—faith.

Yet, Yasha's next idea is that he must quit the house of study. He does not retreat immediately; first he opens a holy book and finds corroboration of the insight that he should eschew his secular ways. Despite this confirmation, he follows the impulse to continue his familiar style of life—hailing a droshky, he rides home to Magda. True, he soon assumes the role of penitent. But what does this signify? The decision per se does not necessarily indicate anything about underlying motivation. For that, Yasha's subsequent reactions provide the most fruitful testimony.

Yasha's penitential existence, his inner experience of the hut, highlights the extent to which his religious conviction is superimposed upon another, more basic, foundation. Yasha upholds prayer and study as his only weapons against temptation. Moreover, when he had looked into the *Eternal Paths* in the study house, he had determined that discipline is the only possible protection against sin: "If a man did not look, he did not lust, and if he did not lust, he did not sin" (p.232). Yet, these safeguards are unsuccessful, for Yasha remains prey to the dangers within himself, and these are the most insidious of all:

> No hour passed without Yasha's being besieged by every sort of passion. No sooner did he forget himself for a moment than they gathered about him: empty fancies, daydreams, repulsive desires (p.272).

To the defenses Yasha mentions as his guards must be added another one: the very fact of enclosure itself. This provides him his surest aid. It would be possible to confront evil anywhere, were discipline, prayer and study sufficient. But Yasha chooses the additional control of confinement, one in which he rids himself of mature responsibility. This is the submerged aim of his religious conversion. The change in Yasha, then, is less one of renewed trust in God and Judaism than one of abdicated adulthood. Once the drive to be infantile and passive is considered the major goal of Yasha's behavior, the epilogue becomes an exploration of his success in recapturing his origins. He attempts this regression in a variety of ways, and these, in turn, schematically represent different stages in his development.

Most obvious is his withdrawal to his wife, a move that would seem stable and healthy, were it not for its circumstances. For, despite Esther's wishes, Yasha is unable to maintain his marriage. He denies her his sexuality and, for all intents and purposes, his companionship as well. Esther has not altered her basic behavior with Yasha, which even at first had entailed her pampering him, feeding him, and being dependent upon when he would allow himself to be approached. It is he who has changed, who can no longer sustain even the limited interaction they had formerly achieved.[25] Penitence thus permits Yasha to relinquish his position as a sexually active man.

By assuming the role of an orthodox Jew, furthermore, Yasha can once again join his father. Earlier in his life, he had used his choice of career as a means of remaining ambivalently close to his pious father. Identifying with the symbols of the latter's interests—locks and keys—he had at the same time selected a metier of questionable respectability in the eyes of such a man. Much later, a memory floats into his consciousness, wherein his dying father, as a parting message to his only son, had begged him to remain a Jew. Yasha, recalling the scene, asks himself: "How could I have forgotten this? How?" (p.177). How indeed? The pertinence and pungency of this question notwithstanding, another issue demands attention: why does the memory return to him just after he has committed his crime? Not much later, Yasha responds to his impressario Wolsky's avuncular and critical worry over his injury by commenting crossly: "You're neither my father nor my guardian." (p.191). Yasha's feelings about his father, then, evidently center on a sense that the latter had neither fully understood nor approved of him. Instead, he had considered him a disappointment. At the height of his confusion and shame regarding all the women in his life and his fantasies concerning them, Yasha reflects:

> What was it Father called me? A scoundrel. Lately, his father had appeared in his dreams every night. Just as Yasha closed his eyes, he would see his father. The older man would moralize, warn him, counsel him (p.77).[26]

In fact, Yasha's memory of his father is that, after the death of his mother when he was seven, followed by his father's failure to remarry, "the boy had had to raise himself" (p.27). In direct response to this emptiness, Yasha had begun his pattern of erratic schooling and compensatory fascination with tricks and performance. Now, by rejecting sexuality, rejecting his work, and adopting orthodoxy, Yasha is actively attempting to regain contact with his father at a developmental point before the damage was done and he had become someone worthy only of loving contempt.

The fact that Yasha had raised himself when his father did not remarry implies that the task of bringing up children was considered solely a female one.[27] Without the benefits of such attention, Yasha had had no opportunity to flourish internally, although he had managed to achieve a protective veneer of worldly success which served him well as long as it remained unshaken.

The loss of a mother, especially when there is no compensation for the loss of love, can be a devastating experience for a seven-year-old child. Yasha's conscious fantasy about his mother is not as regressive as his unconscious one, yet it too reveals how much he still craves her. At the same time as he imagines his father plying him with moral instruction, he thinks of his mother as sustaining him, even protecting him from death:

> A while back, his mother had even saved his life. He had heard her voice caution him, "Move back, Son, move back!" and minutes later a heavy chandelier fell where he had been standing. It would surely have crushed him had he not heeded his dead mother's warning (p.76).

Even before he begins his final disengagement from responsibility, Yasha associates from these thoughts about his parents to the awareness of his own arrested development, and his failure to assume the burden of fatherhood. It is no wonder, then, when things reach an impasse—for he remembers his mother just as he is attempting to resolve the contradictory claims on his existence—that Yasha makes the unconscious decision to go back to the safety of her care. Once he has capitulated, he can imagine his father equalling his mother in benevolence. Thus, he decides that his injury and failure in crime signify the intervention of heavenly powers, controlling him as a parent might an unruly child: "It was obvious that those in heaven did not intend to have him turn to crime, desert Esther, convert." And he goes on to mention both parents directly: "Maybe even his deceased parents had interceded in his behalf" (p.178).

By withdrawing from active life, Yasha manages to recreate—or to create his image of—a previous phase in which he had been watched over, cherished, and shielded from harm. He has attained a long-held goal, and one long defended against.

At the same time, however, Yasha is not completely transformed, and his previous behavior cannot be discounted. It is in this context that the issue of magic emerges as central. At the very beginning of *Der kuntsnmakher fun lublin* which is more properly translated using the word "Trickster" or "Stuntsman" rather than "Magician," Yasha muses on his reputation:

> Some maintained that he practiced black magic and owned a cap which made him invisible, capable of squeezing through

cracks in the wall; others said that he was merely a master of illusion (p.9).

By the conclusion of the novel, the concepts of magic and illusion are completely different than they appeared at first, when they applied to Yasha's professional abilities. In the end they assume a symbolic meaning whose essence rests within him. As professional tools, magic and illusion appear to be mutually exclusive; that is, the actual possession of special powers would obviate the need to pretend their existence. But in terms of Yasha the whole individual, where this is all played out psychodynamically, the two traits must occupy some common ground. Magic—that supernatural, mysterious energy that lies beyond reason—is a way of representing the unconscious workings of Yasha's psyche. Illusion, in contrast, has more to do with his vain attempts to control and hide the urges that continue to clamor for expression, no less active for being excluded from consciousness. Forced to follow the dictates of impulses he knows exist but cannot define, Yasha operates within the realm of magic. In contrast, his surface activities, his hypervitality—from a taxing romantic life to the renunciations of a penitent—are artificial and hence illusory, meant to conceal his deepest wishes from everyone, including himself. Yasha's basic rhythm of behavior does not change, although the balance between frank regression and pseudo-maturity has been reversed. For, even as a penitent, he retains his ability to encourage the admiration, adulation, and attention of a rapt audience. Even from within his hut, he remains a valued performer. In this way, he holds on to his earlier means of striving for a sense of inner cohesion and autonomy. He is still attempting the same method, still finding it inadequate.

In the end, then, *Der kuntsnmakher fun lublin* is not so much a novel about relationships and interactions as it is a work concerning one man's confrontation with himself. The result of Yasha's intimate struggle appears to be a battle won but a war lost. He has, indeed, managed to achieve partially the fulfillment of certain profoundly experienced needs. At the same time, however, this has resulted in a virtual cessation of active, adult functioning. Moreover, the solution is not satisfactory—Yasha is still plagued by unwelcome thoughts:

> No, peace of mind was not to be found in this world. There is no tomorrow without sorrow, as the philosophers say. But even more powerful than the temptations from without were those born within man himself, in his brain, his heart (p.272).

Yasha has failed to recognize his ultimate longings and anxieties. Unless he can do so and integrate what he learns into the more mature aspects of himself, his unconscious will remain dangerous, threatening magic, and his conscious self will seem deceptive and false. One of the final questions one may ask about Yasha is this: Will he ever emerge from his hut? Based on the assessment of how he got there and how that action—whatever its shortcomings—has served him subsequently, the prospects are dim.

CHAPTER SIX

After the Holocaust

Two main ideas—and, from them, two purposes—form the basis of this study. The first is my conviction that, in certain important ways, literary narratives resemble human ones; therefore, they may be investigated using the same basic principles employed in exploring a living soul through psychoanalysis. In the preceding chapters, I have sought to illustrate how this process operates. There are limitations in literary inquiry, just as in clinical work, stemming chiefly from lack of data and the pitfalls of subjective perception.

In a way, interpreting a story like *Okean* or *Shvayg, shvester* most closely resembles the therapeutic bond in its essence: two individuals meet as partners in the present, slowly developing a relationship through which beliefs, fantasies, and behaviors come to light. Whatever memories emerge as well are enriching and may prove pivotal, yet it is not through these alone that cure finally occurs. In my clinical work, I have discovered increasingly that historical information, although it often illuminates the current situation, is never sufficient. No piece of background is useful if it fails to enter the arena of the present. Only there can it be scrutinized and made available to re-evaluation.

Thus, while *Okean* and *Shvayg, shvester* undeniably lack the kind of evidence supplied in *A toyt* or *Di mishpokhe pikuda,* the mistrust, emptiness, and fragility manifested by Kreynin and Felye point clearly enough to some terrible internal debilitation. This is the immediate cause of suicide. Even in cases of limited information, then, the model of psychoanalysis as an inevitably incomplete but profoundly revealing form of observation applies to fiction as well.

My second aim in writing this book was to show that pre-World War II Yiddish authors—far from avoiding the subject of suicide or condemning the act—exposed its existence in Eastern European Jewish life with acceptance, understanding, and sympathy. Their characters are portrayed as sane, often reasonable men and women, whose need to kill themselves—while intricately related to social pressures—always had an underlying, inner explanation. This consistent focus on deep personal motivations undermined the popular perception of suicide within the Yiddish-speaking community where, at least according to newspaper accounts, most suicides resulted from financial difficulty or severe mental imbalance.

It is impossible to guess how Yiddish literary attitudes towards suicide might—or might not—have evolved were it not for the Holocaust. In this regard, Isaac Bashevis Singer's *Sonim, di geshikhte fun a libe* [''*Enemies: A Love Story*''][1] is an intriguing counterpart to Grade's *Di agune* and, especially, to his own *Der kuntsnmakher fun lublin;* for, while all three novels were composed after the Holocaust, only *Sonim* has a postwar setting of New York City in the years just after the catastrophe. I have singled out *Sonim* precisely because it treats the subject of suicide as a particular and explicit response to the Holocaust. It may be argued that the same ideas are at work in *Di agune* and *Der kuntsnmakher fun lublin* as well, but this cannot be assumed. The consideration of suicide as a valid, even commendable, act appears in Singer's short fiction as well, notably, but not exclusively, in the more recent stories set in the United States. These, however, approach the issue parenthetically—as fantasies or reveries—rather than thematically.[2] Moreover, the main characters of *Sonim* are survivors of death camps and hiding; Masha, who commits suicide, has endured hell in order to live. These are not mere details, but rather an important factor in the underlying framework of the work as a whole.

Direct confrontation of the issues surrounding the Holocaust—considerations such as the meaning of survival, for instance, or the nature of evil—automatically leads to a different type of work than emerges from a more distanced type of approach. Yet, this is not the most significant difference between *Sonim* and other works, since even a displaced version of these questions can be fruitful and thought-provoking. Instead, it is the basic perception of self and surroundings that is revealed as changed and that merits scrutiny.

In the aftermath of a cataclysm, it is not surprising that social stability, especially where it had been weakened by challenge, should finally falter and collapse. *Sonim* takes as a given the impossibility of marriage as the backbone of Jewish existence. Whereas in the past, couples had been forced to contend with the temptations common to increased mobility and those attendant upon the breakdown of traditional modesty and piety—a loosening of the rules—now they faced a world that had seen all rules of decency destroyed. Survivors had often lost their spouses; in any case, they had endured unimaginable bestiality. Frequently, they had lived in conditions so without privacy that they had been forced to witness the sexual relations of others. Small wonder if their notions changed.

In fact, of course, survivors did remarry, or marry for the first time, and they did raise families as in the past. Yet Singer touches upon a significant absurdity when he renders as believable the escapades of Herman Broder who, by the conclusion of the novel, is married to three women. Believing himself a widower, he had married the non-Jewish Yadwiga after the war in a civil ceremony. When his prewar wife Tamara turns up alive, he finds he does not want to divorce her. At the same time, she urges him to remain with Yadwiga, and so he finds himself an inadvertent bigamist. It is only a matter of further complication, rather than one of perversion, for him to marry his mistress and soul mate, Masha, in a religious ceremony.

Sheyndl, in *Af fremde vegn,* had considered herself wed to Borekh because he managed—to some extent anyway—to dupe her. There was no formal ceremony and the purpose of the "marriage" was to convince her that sexual relations between them were now permissible. She had needed that sanction in order to allow herself the intimacy she so desired. However, once she had acted, she was ruined; the innocent side of her behavior counted for nothing. The opposite is true of Masha: her sexual experiences enhance her in the eyes of Herman and the other men who find her attractive, even though they pretend otherwise.

Moreover, the withering of accepted values can be seen in

the attitudes of the women themselves. Whereas Borekh's wife Mine is aware of Sheyndl's hold on her husband, she certainly has no idea that Sheyndl considers herself married to him. In contrast, by the conclusion of *Sonim,* each woman knows that Herman has at least one other wife. Yadwiga, in fact, is the only one not to be aware of the whole story.

By their acquiescence to the state of affairs, the three women indicate that, despite their longing for marriage and the stability it formerly provided, they understand that marriage can no longer, even on the surface, bring any such assurance. Herman, for his part, worries less about betraying his vows than he does about being deported or having to pay extra taxes. It is a far cry from Borekh's concern over his "alien path" in life. The hypocrisy is gone, but so is the reliance on age-old morals. Were it not already clear, Singer's position becomes unmistakable through his portrayal of Woytus and Marianna, two parakeets who represent an ironic comment on the humans in the novel. They are faithful to one another, untroubled by outside influences, cheerful in the simplicity of their existence. When Yadwiga is pregnant, Marianna lays an egg. Yet the barb, although presented with subtlety, is indicative: Woytus and Marianna are named for Yadwiga's father and sister. Thus, even in the closest approximation of a previous, better era, chastity is besmirched.

There are some characters in *Sonim* who do not fit this pattern, most notably Tamara's uncle, Reb Abraham Nissen Yaroslaver and his wife, Sheva Haddas. They, too, had married after the war, but their way of responding to the catastrophe had been to keep their environment as close as possible to its prewar style and appearance, and to devote their lives to mourning. This may be one of Singer's answers to the complexities of the post-Holocaust situation; that is, the people who seem least affected are those who refuse to attempt an integration of past and present. The other characters who fit this category are Masha's mother, Shifrah Puah, and, in large measure, Tamara. Certainly, such a notion would correspond to Singer's idea, expressed in the author's introductory note to *Sonim,* that he "did not have the privilege of going through the Hitler holocaust." (unpaged)

With these words, Singer in effect seeks permission *not* to integrate. Yet the very existence of the novel shows that he cannot allow himself to pursue such a path.[3] And, once allowing himself to question, he must question everything.

To be sure, *Sonim* does not represent a metamorphosis on the part of the author. There are several aspects of the novel that ring a familiar bell. First of all, Herman bears a certain resemblance to Yasha in *Der kuntsnmakher fun lublin.* For one thing, he is strongly involved with three women, each of whom plays a different role in his life. For another, he beats a radical retreat at the close of the novel. While he is not a professional trickster, there is something of the stuntsman about him as he juggles wives and lies, hoping that no one will see his hand. There is even a similarity in the structures of the two novels: a relentless building up of tension culminating in a breaking point and followed by an epilogue in which the protagonist's immediate problems are solved. Most important, from the standpoint of this study, one of the women commits suicide, forcing the protagonist's critical change.

Even on closer inspection, the characters in the two novels are comparable in certain respects. For example, Herman, like Yasha, collects mother figures. Yadwiga, who had started as a servant girl in his mother's home before the war, and to whom he owes his life, continues to cook and clean for him as she had done in his old home in Tsivkev. She does more than this, however, now that she is his wife. In one of the novel's early scenes, for example, she comes to Herman while he is bathing:

> Yadwiga started to soap his back, his arms, his loins. He had frustrated her longing to bear children and so had taken the place of child for her. She fondled him, played with him (p.15).

There is an Elzbieta-type character in *Sonim* as well: Masha's mother, Shifrah Puah.[4] She is, to be sure, entirely different in her outlook on the world and her estimation of her daughter than Elzbieta. Yet she feels some maternal and possessive sentiment towards Herman, treating him as one of the family, even as she seeks to assert her own special influences:

> She behaved toward him like a mother-in-law. Even before he was dressed, she had started to make his omelet; she had bought strawberries especially for him. Herman felt catered to and at the same time embarrassed when he ate breakfast with Shifrah Puah. She insisted that he wash his hands from a pitcher, according to the Orthodox ritual. Now that Masha wasn't at home, she gave him his hat to wear when he recited the prayer over the handwashing and later for the benediction (p.49).

Herman also manages to inspire the motherly instincts of his first wife, Tamara. True, she cannot express herself directly in those terms, possibly because of her guilty sense of having survived both of her children. Nevertheless, the impulse is certainly there when she offers to be Herman's manager just at the point when he feels that he has nowhere to turn: "I'll tell you what to do and you do it. I'll find you a job, too. In your state, you're in no position to help yourself" (p.219). Although she has put it in business terms, the sheer nurturing is present as well. Tamara and Herman go out for breakfast, and she takes charge of even this matter, behaving toward him as a mother might with a pre-verbal infant whose needs she understands and can fulfill:

> Tamara didn't even ask what he wanted to order. She seated him at a table and brought him orange juice, a roll, an omelet, and coffee. She watched him eat for a moment, then went to get breakfast for herself (p.221).

The attention lavished upon Herman by the women in his life is not enough to assuage his sense that he is an immense disappointment to his father. Indeed, during the elder Broder's lifetime, Herman had neither gone into the line of work his father had wanted, nor had he chosen a wife of whom his father could approve. Yet, Herman's guilt does not need the actual presence of a chiding parent to be mobilized. When his complex arrangement seems to be getting out of hand, for instance, Herman muses:

> It seemed to him that he heard his father's voice saying, "Well, I ask you, what have you accomplished? You've made

> yourself and everyone else wretched. We're ashamed of you here in heaven'' (p.189).

Thus, it is tempting to view *Sonim* as a kind of latter-day *kuntsnmakher fun lublin,* in which a passive man seduces women to take care of him, all the time hoping for the infantile bliss of feeling merged with his mother, combined with the avoidance of any oedipal conflict that might muddy the waters. In that case, Masha's suicide would be, like Magda's, an act of care and protection despite the aura of anger and revenge. Still, when *Sonim* is viewed more closely, it is clear that, despite the superficial likeness of plot and character, even considering certain details, the differences are more pronounced than the similarities. Certainly there is a divergence between Yasha and Herman; moreover, the contrast between the two novels is nowhere more obvious than with respect to Masha's suicide.

Herman reveals himself to be far more capable of commitment than Yasha. While it is, of course, easier to avoid one wife when there are two additional ones on the scene, Herman seems more motivated to fulfill obligations than to run from them. Herman enjoys accommodating and tries his best to do so. Perhaps the clearest example of this is his marriage to Masha, undertaken chiefly because Masha, who is in the midst of an hysterical pregnancy, wants to please Shifrah Puah by legitimizing her issue. Although he recognizes the absurdity—not to mention the illegality—of the situation, he is driven by his inability to say no.

Herman's sense of responsibility emerges in other ways as well, even though the development occurs seemingly against his will. One factor involves his attitude towards children. For, despite his gravitation in the direction of mothering females, he is not as adamant in his avoidance of children as was Yasha. To begin with, he had had two children with Tamara, in spite of his ambivalence about being a father. Then, when Masha believes herself pregnant, he does not insist upon an abortion or, alternatively, desert her.[5]

Similarly, although he had taken pains not to gratify Yadwiga's wish for a child, when she does become pregnant and refuses to obtain an abortion, Herman puts up with the situation. (He does, in fact, abandon Yadwiga shortly before she is about to give birth, but this is not directly as a result of his own wishes. Rather, he is caught between his feeling that he should be around when she delivers, and his desire to be with Masha, who demands that he run away with her then or never.)

Herman is able, as well, to accept the care offered him without feeling compelled to turn away in order to receive it; that is, where Yasha had needed to ensnare himself and finally build himself into a hut in order to take from Esther that which he wanted and nothing more, Herman is merely grateful in the end to let Tamara run his life. He does not have to objectify his need:

> Herman could hardly believe it himself, but Tamara had found him a job . . . Herman no longer felt that he was in control of things, nor did he want to be. He had become a fatalist in practice as well as in theory. He was willing to let the Powers lead him, whether they were called Chance or Providence of Tamara (pp.223,224).

Masha is unlike any of Yasha's women in that she is just as helpless as Herman and therefore unable to indulge him in the same fashion as Yadwiga, Tamara, or even Shifrah Puah. It is he who must watch out for her, warning her when her smoking and drinking reach an alarming level, catering to her moods, fearing for her health. Far from being able to lean back and be childish with Masha, Herman has to support her.

One scene between them epitomizes the situation. Masha and Herman are planning to marry, and they do not yet know that her pregnancy is a fantasy. Masha quarrels with her mother and rushes off to cry, not before Herman has given her a handkerchief so that she can blow her nose. When she returns, she is drinking whiskey from a flask:

> She was half laughing, half crying, with the mischievousness of a spoiled child. It occurred to Herman that as her pregnancy progressed she was becoming inappropriately babyish. She was full of the little-girl mannerisms, giggly, even playfully naive. He remembered Schopenhauer's statement that the female never really becomes fully mature. The bearer of children remains a child herself (p.135).

And yet, when the time comes, and Masha utters an ultimatum, Herman is ready to throw away everything he has—Yadwiga, Tamara, his unborn child, his new job—for the sake of Masha. He thus reveals himself as very different indeed from Yasha, who, when faced with a similar demand from Emilia, runs away forever. It is true, to be sure, that by the epilogue of *Sonim,* Herman himself has disappeared, and it is not even known whether he is alive or dead. Yet here, too, the action has been based on Masha and her decision. Having heard her declare that she cannot go away with him and leave behind the body of her recently deceased mother, Herman replies that he will leave everyone. While his behavior is certainly irresponsible and insensitive, it is not that of a man whose primary effort goes to having a woman care for him as if he were a child.[6]

For this reason alone, Masha's suicide cannot be equated with Magda's, i.e., it cannot be viewed as the fulfillment of her lover's hidden wish. Herman does talk and think about suicide with some regularity, generally with the idea that taking his own life would be a fine and proper thing to do, given the state of the world and the impossibility of change. As he muses, "Those without courage to make an end to their existence have only one other way out: to deaden their consciousness, choke their memory, extinguish the last vestige of hope" (p.33). Talking to Tamara about his final decision to go away with Masha, he explains: "I can't live without Masha, and I don't have the guts to kill myself" (p.237). He also expresses his worry that Masha has committed suicide, notably on the occasion when Shifrah Puah calls to inform him that she is ill—with the collapse of her hysterical pregnancy, as it transpires.[7] In the end, however, Herman makes it clear that he is not interested in taking his own life and also that he wants to maintain his connection to Masha, to have her remain alive as well. The decision to die is her own.

The two contemplate a double suicide during their final encounter. The discussion is initiated by Herman who, when confronted with the prospect of having to arrange Shifrah Puah's burial without the aid of the American rabbi, Lampert, simply wants to give up. "Masha, I don't want to live," he states. She responds with a direct suggestion: "You once promised me we would die together. Let's do it now. I have enough sleeping pills for both of us.'' Yet, already at this point, Herman begins to waver, perhaps having realized that his initial fear of responsibility is not the same as an actual desire to be dead. Moments later, when Masha is searching for the pills, Herman observes: ''I always knew she was my Angel of Death'' (p.248).

Finally, he stalls by saying that he wants to know whether she has been faithful to him. She wants to know the same about him, and Herman admits to his sexual experience with Tamara. Masha counters: ''What you did with your wife, I did with my husband.''[8] This is sufficient for Herman, who promptly decides ''There isn't any point in dying now . . .'' (p.249). Masha surmises that he wants to leave her, but this is not the case. Herman merely wants to run away, preferably with the woman for whom he has forsaken everything. When she refuses to leave with him, he goes without her. He may suspect that she was taking the sleeping pills while supposedly readying herself to join him; however, this is by no means clear. In any case, he is not present at her death and therefore cannot ''benefit'' from it.

Masha's situation is thus unlike that of the other women who are driven to suicide. Her pious mother may consider her behavior immoral, yet she does not make Masha feel that she must run away, as Manye's mother had done in *Zindik blut;* nor does she refuse to have contact with her until she is in a traditionally legitimate position, as Sheyndl's father had done. In fact, although Shifrah Puah had dreamed of a marriage between her daughter and Herman, the way it occurs is anathema to her. Whereas she had treated Herman as a son-in-law before, now everything is changed:

> Shifrah Puah complained that Herman's idea of marriage was a mockery. She forbade him to call her ''mother-in-law.'' Only the most necessary words passed between them (p.163).

If Masha's need to die is not based on shame concerning her so-called immorality, and if it is clearly not due to the fear that no one will ever marry her, it is also not attributable to the need to sacrifice herself for someone else's sake, as Magda, and to some extent Tevye's daughter Shprintse, had done. During their last moments together, after she has already promised that she will go away with Herman, Masha changes her mind, telling him: "I can't leave my mother" (p.250). Although she is ostensibly talking only about the fact that she will not abandon Shifrah Puah, Masha actually means that she cannot live without her mother. This is the meaning of her death.

From the very beginning of *Sonim,* Masha is portrayed as existing symbiotically with her mother, a set-up based—according to Masha—on Shifrah Puah's inability to consider her daughter as separate. Thus, for instance, Shifrah Puah smells something burning and asks Masha about this. Masha responds, then explains her interpretation to Herman:

> Nothing's burning, Mama, nothing's burning. My mother has a peculiar habit—everything she does herself she blames on me. She burns everything she cooks, and as soon as I make something, she smells it burning. If she pours herself a glass of milk, she lets it run over, and she warns me to be careful.

In other words, by projecting her own thoughts onto her daughter, Shifrah Puah denies, at the very least, that Masha has a separate set of reactions than she herself does; at most, she indicates that Masha has no independent existence.

Masha has accepted her mother's reality to a great degree. Despite her apparent wanton self-centeredness, she is acutely aware of her mother's thoughts and actions. When Shifrah Puah is in another room, Masha listens with close attention, "always on the alert should help be needed" (p.45). Her attentiveness is more than that of a good daughter, however; it betrays the same kind of confusion that occurs in Shifrah Puah's treatment of her. Both women are survivors who have remained deeply attuned to their past. Rather than recalling each in her own way and at her own time, however, they appear to feed off one another for their response, even though Shifrah Puah is piously accepting and Masha rebellious:

> Masha would attack her mother for grieving so much for the dead victims, but when her mother was silent, Masha would take over. When she talked of German atrocities, she would run to the mezuzah on the door and spit on it (pp.44–45).

In this way, mother and daughter fan each other's energies even as they wear each other down.

In fact, Shifrah Puah and Masha virtually live for one another. As long as this agreement is upheld, both may live; once it is violated, both die. Shifrah Puah, from her own perspective, would rather be dead; in a clear expression of survivor's guilt, she believes she has no business remaining alive when so many righteous Jews have perished. She holds Masha responsible for this fact of her life; had it not been for her, Shifrah Puah would have been able to die and rest in peace. Moreover, the mother does not credit her child with altruism; on the contrary, she complains to Herman, angrily accusing Masha of keeping her alive for her own selfish purposes:

> I told her openly, "I don't want to live anymore. I've had enough." But she pulled me back to life with a fury. You can destroy a person with anger, but you can bring him back to life with it too. Why did you need me? It suited her fancy to have a mother, that's all (p.38).

Thus, Shifrah Puah feels that her purpose in life is to live for her daughter, not in order to provide her with care and love, but rather to exist as a kind of slave to Masha's whims until the latter has finished with her.

From her vantage point, not surprisingly, Masha sees things rather differently. She believes that she had done the correct thing to ransom her mother from death. She feels unappreciated by her mother's lack of gratitude, angry that, instead of praising her for her efforts, Shifrah Puah criticizes her. And, in direct contrast to her mother's interpretation of their relationship, Masha feels that it is she who is living for the sake of Shifrah Puah. In what might be taken as a fit of pique, Masha warns Herman during one of their innumerable desperate arguments:

> I'll lock myself up with the old and sick people. Since there is no nunnery for Jewish women, that will be my nunnery—until my mother dies. After that, I'll make an end to the whole comedy (p.208).

It is only her behavior at the end of the novel that reveals how serious Masha was after all.

The talk of ultimates that consumes mother and daughter periodically is an extreme version of a daily reality for them, namely that each one holds the other dearer than any living soul. This is easy to accept of Shifrah Puah, who has no other real ties, save those—like Herman—with whom she is connected through Masha. It is more striking in the case of Masha, yet nonetheless true.

On the most superficial level, Masha takes her mother into account before she decides upon any action for herself. When she and Herman are trying to plan a vacation together, for instance, Masha worries because she does not want to leave her mother alone lest something happen. At the same time, she feels unable to take Shifrah Puah along because that would only confirm the latter's belief that Masha's behavior with Herman is immoral. When she demands that Herman marry her in order to legitimize their child, Masha claims that her only motive is to satisfy her mother's wishes.[9] As she puts it:

> "Jewish law and all the other laws mean as much to me as last year's frost. I'm only doing it for my mother, only for her" (p.118).

In her ongoing relationship with Herman, too, Masha allows Shifrah Puah to play a major role. In order not to offend her mother on Friday nights, she leaves the apartment to telephone him. And, even though Shifrah Puah knows of the affair between Herman and Masha, the latter will not undress as long as her mother is awake, nor will she openly spend the night with Herman: "For appearance's sake, she had put bedding on the sofa in the living room" (p.44). Shifrah Puah's centrality is so much a given that even Herman takes it for granted; he accepts Masha's reason for wanting to marry him and defends their decision before the skeptical Tamara:

> "She's afraid of an abortion. When it comes to such things, a person can't be forced. She doesn't want the child to be illegitimate. Her mother is pious" (p.133).

Even when he is frantically thinking about how he might flee from the fact, terrifying to him, that Tamara has actually returned, he cannot allow himself to hope that Masha would go with him: "Run away? Where to? With whom? Masha couldn't leave her mother" (p.61).

Masha's connection to her mother—both the symbiosis and the concomitant overriding importance of the bond—reveals itself in other ways as well. On certain crucial occasions, for instance, when it might be expected that Masha would be absorbed in thoughts about Herman, her associations, or her reactions, gravitate instead to her mother. When she first announces to Herman that she believes herself to be pregnant, Masha begins to worry about the dangers of having an abortion:

> "A woman who worked in the cafeteria had one. She got blood poisoning and that was the end of her. What an ugly way to die! And what would my mother do if anything happened to me? I'm sure you would let her starve!" (p.112).

Masha thus links her lover and unborn child with her mother. Moreover, directly before she informs Herman of her news, Masha has a vision of her dead father. In this way she shows her sense of being a child just as she is called upon to behave as a mother herself. This, then, is the other side of the merger between Masha and Shifrah Puah: the daughter who cares for her mother solicitously, if at times neurotically, in return expects to be taken care of by her mother.

Similarly, on the occasion when Shifrah Puah and Masha have quarreled, and Herman has observed that his lover is becoming increasingly childish, she is unable to act the part of lover with him:

> Masha didn't come to him that night. She fell asleep right after supper, having taken a sleeping pill. Fully clothed, she lay on her bed in a drunken stupor (p.135).

What emerges slowly during the course of the novel is clear by the end of *Sonim*: Masha is still her mother's little girl, despite what else she has managed to achieve in terms of independent behavior. In this respect, she resembles Yasha; in both cases a highly sexualized demeanor serves to disguise a more primitive longing to be indulged and protected. Whatever surface of functioning she has accomplished falls away when Shifrah Puah is dying:

> . . . Masha let out a wail . . . It was a sound unlike her own voice—catlike and primitve. Her face became contorted, she tore her hair, stamped her feet, leaped at Herman as if to attack him. The neighbor held the phone to her breast, stunned . . . The neighbor dropped the receiver and grabbed Masha by the shoulders. She shook her, as one would to relieve a child who was choking (pp.241–42).

This intense reaction could easily occur in any individual who is experiencing the anguish of watching a beloved person near death. Yet, Masha's subsequent behavior underscores her inability to exist without her mother. Moreover, she finally admits to Herman that only with her mother can she feel secure. Earlier in the novel, in the context of their peculiar fantasy and lovemaking sessions, Masha had begged Herman to buy a cemetery plot for both of them. Now matters have changed entirely:

> "Herman, I can't leave my mother," Masha said quietly.
>
> "You have to leave her anyhow."
>
> "I want a grave next to hers. I don't want to lie among strangers."
>
> "You'll lie near me."
>
> "You're a stranger" (p.250).

This decision is in a way a capitulation, for Masha had attempted to choose Herman. The two had separated after a bitter quarrel. Masha and her mother had gone off. Then, after some weeks, Masha had called Herman with her ultimatum, saying that she had not been able to live without him and that her mother had been the only obstacle to her return. Later, when Herman had queried her about Shifrah Puah's reaction to her decision, Masha had recalled her mother's warnings to her and, rejecting them, claimed that even if Herman did desert her as Shifrah Puah predicted, she would tolerate it. Her apartment had been robbed in her absence and this was of more significance to her than anything else. It was an omen to make a new start. Then she had mused:

> "In the Bible it says, 'Naked I came out of my mother's womb and naked will I return there.' Why 'there'? We don't return to our mothers' wombs."
>
> "The earth is the mother."
>
> "Yes. But until we return to her, let's try to live" (p.238).

Masha had, then, tried to choose a more positive route, but she had not bargained on the death of her mother. Shifrah Puah, the other half of the symbiotic bond, had been unable to endure the lonely existence of life in a New Jersey convalescent home without Masha. Therefore, she returns to the Bronx to die. Upon hearing that her mother has returned, Masha's first response is wrath: she accuses Shifrah Puah of killing herself out of spite. Again, the two are savagely tugging at each other's lives.

Whether or not Masha's indictment is correct—or even whether she believes it herself after her initial outburst (later, she shouts that those trying to save Shifrah Puah are murderers)—is never clear, nor is it important ultimately. It is Masha's response that counts, and she treats the loss of her mother as the end of her own life. When she returns home from the hospital to which her mother had been rushed, Herman suspects that Shifrah Puah is dead, yet nonetheless asks how she is. Masha replies: "I have no mother" (p.245). Then, when all hope, however infantile or unconscious, of rejoining her mother is rendered impossible, Masha chooses to be united with her through death. Her attempt to free herself has failed.

It is significant that Masha does break away from her mother for a short period, only to collapse when Shifrah Puah herself gives up. Clearly, it is a driving force in Masha's life to sustain her mother. Indeed, as it transpires, she needs Shifrah Puah's life in order to maintain her own. It is here that the specific issue of the Holocaust overlays the general one of symbiosis. Early on in *Sonim,* the narrator explains: "The ghetto, the concentration camps, the displaced person camps, had unsettled the traditions of both mother and daughter" (p.44). What might have happened in different circumstances is unknowable. There are hints that a less than independent relationship between mother and daughter would have persisted in any case, at least to judge by Shifrah Puah's self-recriminations about neglecting her only child. Perhaps Masha would anyway have been a woman suffering from deficit, from an insufficiency of those emotional supplies that are necessary for reasonable stability. Yet this is mere speculation. Whatever the hypothetical basis of the symbiosis, the reality as it emerges in *Sonim* is that the two women are joined by their experiences of the Holocaust, a force of death that paradoxically enlivens them. The evidence is clear from the text itself.

To begin with, the memories of both mother and daughter become stronger and more encompassing with the passage of time: "Other refugees used to say that with time one forgets, but neither Shifrah Puah nor Masha would ever forget. On the contrary, the further removed they were from the Holocaust, the closer it seemed to become" (p.44); that is, the Holocaust was actively incorporated into their daily lives, making it an increasingly significant aspect of existence rather than the opposite. It is also a vivid component of the interaction between mother and daughter: as the subject develops in importance, it serves as an ongoing source of combative contact between Masha and Shifrah Puah.

There is a difference in the way that each woman employs the subject, however, and through this they complement one another. Shifrah Puah concentrates on the Holocaust in order to bemoan her continued reprieve from death; Masha, on the other hand, uses it to vitalize herself. Her sexual encounters with Herman are always accompanied by discussions and complicated fantasies connected with her past. With Masha, the Holocaust becomes a necessary ingredient in the enjoyment of sexuality:

> The kissing, the fondling, the passionate lovemaking was always accompanied by stories from the ghettos, the camps,

> her own wandering through the ruins of Poland. Through them all, men pursued her: in bunkers, in the forest, in the hospital where she had worked as a nurse (p.46).

Not only does the Holocaust enter into Masha's relationship with Herman, then, but it figures prominently in her concept of herself as a desirable woman. Masha's need for the Holocaust as a framework is so great that she considers the world awry if it appears that this is missing. On her vacation with Herman, she looks out at the scenery and remarks: "Where are the Nazis? What kind of a world is this without Nazis? A backward country, this America" (p.104).

Masha is joking, of course, but behind the humor is a grimly serious matter: Nazis, camps, ruins—these are Masha's reality, as much as New York City or the Adirondacks, perhaps more so. Waking or sleeping, her torturers are there.

If Masha needs the Holocaust in order to feel alive, it is because, in the past, she had considered herself dead: during the same vacation trip with Herman, she thinks about where she had been five years previously, then comments: " 'Still among the dead' " (p.108). Just as she herself had come to life again after catastrophe, so, too, had she brought her reluctant mother back to the living.

Masha needs her mother in order to feel alive: her mother provides her with her strongest link to the Holocaust and she needs the Holocaust in order to experience herself and others fully. Shifrah Puah, for her part, needs Masha's insistence that she live in order to do so. When Masha attempts to view herself as Herman's companion, her mother is no longer provided with the incentive to exist. Then, with Shifrah Puah's death, Masha loses her raison d'etre and her life force. She cannot manage on her own.

Singer's message is a very different one here from the one in *Der kuntsnmakher fun lublin. Sonim* describes a world in which the old rules and taboos are rendered absurd in the face of current events. Traditional morality is meaningless where standards of judging immorality have been thrust away by incomparable evil. In such an environment, the meanings of life and death are also called into question. Shifrah Puah can feel, in contradiction to the view which her orthodoxy would otherwise impel her, that she is sinful for remaining alive. Masha, who remembers that in the past she was dead, is capable of looking at her wind-blown appearance and saying: " 'If I can survive this, I'll never die . . .' " (p.195).

If the very essence of life and death has become twisted and open to reinterpretation, then the position of suicide must also be changed. Singer seems to be suggesting that, for some survivors at any rate, the only importance of life is to keep in mind the destroyed Eastern European Jewish community. When this is no longer possible, perhaps suicide is an honorable, rather than a punishable, act. Certainly, it can have nothing to do with morality, because morality has been murdered as well.

In his Author's Note, Singer states: "The characters are not only Nazi victims but victims of their own personalities and fates." While this is undoubtedly the case, it is also evident that, for the purposes of *Sonim,* at any rate, the environment at large is a Nazi victim. Therefore, the lives these characters once experienced must be carried on by surrogates, and they themselves maintained in memory. Thus it is that only the convert Yadwiga, echoed by the parakeets Woytus and Marianna, can give birth. She is aided by the ambiguous Tamara, who says of herself, " 'I'm not alive and I'm not dead' " (p.174). Together, they devote themselves to raising little Masha, who represents a vestige of the will to live that was ultimately not strong enough.

Yet, little Masha also implies that the original Masha, even if she has killed herself, has not ultimately disappeared. If life is tinged with death after the Holocaust, then death—and suicide—may not have the finality of a previous age either. The novel ends with Tamara's response to the news that, because of the Holocaust, deserted wives will be allowed to remarry. Although she thinks it not unlikely that Herman has committed suicide, she scoffs at the idea of remarrying during her lifetime, musing instead that she will consider a new marriage in the world to come, and then to Herman.[10] Suicide or no, he is the most valuable person she can imagine. There is little question that—in part, in any case—Singer supports Herman's belief that rejecting a world such as ours by committing suicide is praiseworthy.

Singer's view has important ramifications, for, as radical as the departures of pre-World War II authors may have been, they did link their new view with an age-old Jewish realization: the supreme significance of a warm, harmonious family and home. By never losing sight of this fundamental value and goal, they managed—albeit inchoatively and indirectly—to comprehend with clarity a truth that continues to be overlooked, even denied, although the tragic consequences are legion and ubiquitous.

Precisely for this reason, the suggestion raised by *Sonim* is a new and somber one. In an age where unbelievable barbarism has become not only conceivable but, indeed, trivialized as commonplace, even the strength and comfort of a stable core environment may be catastrophically insignificant.

Notes

Chapter One

1. Interested readers, however, can turn to some useful sources where this matter is discussed. For example, H.Z. Winnik and L. Miller, eds., "Aspects of Suicide in Modern Civilization: Proceedings of the Eighth International Congress on Suicide Prevention and Crisis Intervention," 1978, Jerusalem Academic Press; C.W. Reines, "Jewish Attitudes Toward Suicide," *Judaism* (Spring 1961, pp. 160–170); David Daube, "The Linguistics of Suicide," *Philosophy and Public Affairs 1(4)*:387–437, 1972. For a specific study of suicide in Israel, see M. Amir, "Suicide Among Minors in Israel," *Israel Annals of Psychiatry and Related Disciplines 11,3*:219–269, 1973. For a comprehensive, yet highly readable account of the history of suicide, particularly as it relates to art, see A. Alvarez, *The Savage God: A Study of Suicide,* (London: Weidenfeld and Nicolson), 1971.

2. Emile Durkheim, *Suicide: Study in Sociology,* translated by John A. Spaulding and George Simpson, edited with an introduction by George Simpson, New York: The Free Press, 1951; first Free Press paperback edition, 1966, pp. 155–156. In his 1897 work, Durkheim comments, while conceding that the rate of suicide amongst Jews had increased as the nineteenth century progressed, ". . . it must be remembered that Jews lived more exclusively than other professional groups in cities and are in intellectual occupations. On this account, they are more inclined to suicide than the members of other confessions for reasons other than their religion. If therefore the rate for Judaism is so low in spite of this aggravating circumstance, it may be assumed that, *other things being equal* [emphasis mine], their religion has the fewest suicides of all." Validity of Durkheim's formulations may be questioned since he attributes the low suicide rate to the idea that, all things being equal, Jews should commit suicide more than they actually do. His formulation is thus more relative than might first be assumed.

3. Two such studies, in Yiddish, are M.J. Gutman, *Der zelbstmord bay yidn un zayne sibes* ["Suicide Amongst Jews and Its Causes"], in *Shriftn far ekonomik un statistik,* Vol. 1 (Berlin: YIVO), 1928, pp. 117–21; hereafter cited as *Gutman.* Y. Leshtshinsky, *Zelbstmordn* ["Suicides"], in *Erev khurbn [The Eve of Destruction]* (Buenos Aires: Tsentral farband fun poylishe yidn in argentine), 1951, pp. 142–149; hereafter cited as *Leshtshinsky.* Although Leshtshinsky's essay appeared after World War II, it is dated February 18, 1936 and refers to events occurring at that approximate time—some, in fact, in March 1936.

4. *Undzer lebn,* May 12, 1907, p. 4.

5. *Shprintse* was printed in four installments in *Undzer lebn*: May 16 (p.2); May 17 (pp.2–3); May 21 (p.2); May 22 (p.2). Gordin's play, *Got, mentsh un tayvl,* was reviewed on July 2 (p.4); *Di kreytser-sonate* was reviewed on July 23 (p.3).

6. *Di groyse tsol zelbstmordn in varshe* ["The Large Number of Suicides in Warsaw"], *Haynt,* no. 283, December 10, 1926.

7. *Durkheim* advances the theory that one type of suicide results from anomie. That is, when individuals are no longer secure in knowing their role and position in life, they may suffer an intolerable disequilibrium between their sense of self and their milieu. Durkheim's book was published in 1897, the same year as both the first Zionist Congress and the first congress of the Bund, the Jewish socialist movement. Thus, theoretically in any case, the increased choices available to Jews could have disposed them to suicide—particularly if they could not use socialism or Zionism as a substitute for the stability of religion. Yet the findings of *Gutman* and *Leshtshinsky* lean more closely to the causes indicated in the newspapers and journals. *Gutman's* evidence leads him to postulate emotional disturbance as the likely cause for suicide, while *Leshtshinsky,* writing in the latter nineteen-thirties, leans more towards economic factors as causal. Nonetheless, he admits that, whereas a hungry, unemployed non-Jew is likely to abandon suicide if food or work comes along, this is not the case with Jews.

8. For a crusty elaboration on this criticism of the Lacanian critics, see William Phillips's introduction to *Literature and Psychoanalysis,* edited by him and Edith Kurzweil, Columbia University Press, 1983, particularly pages 10–13.

9. Here I am in agreement with Theodore Reik in his fascinating book, *Surprise and the Psychoanalyst: On the Conjecture and*

Comprehension of Unconscious Processes, (New York: E.P. Dutton and Co.), 1937, where he says:

> Analytic theory is not the heuristic instrument for which it is often taken and so used and abused; it is the final precipitate of intelligence received through psychological work with living objects . . . *Terminology tempts us to intellectual laziness so that we substitute something learnt by heart for something experienced, something acquired for something really our own* [emphasis Reik] (pp. 77–78).

10. The danger of this, of course, is that often literary creations, while seeming to reveal, may have as their function the attempt to conceal. This point is convincingly argued by Heinz Kohut in his paper "Beyond the Bounds of the Basic Rule: Some Recent Contributions to Applied Psychoanalysis," first published in the *Journal of the American Psychoanalytic Association* (1960), 8:567–586; reprinted in *The Search for the Self: Selective Writings of Heinz Kohut, 1950–1978,* vol. 1 (New York: International University Press, Inc.), 1978. Kohut here mentions and elaborates on Freud's idea that Goethe used his literary productivity in an attempt to conceal himself (p.281).

11. Indeed, although Freud did not devote much attention to suicide in his writing, he did discuss one instance of a suicide attempt; in that case study, he interpreted the young woman's suffering in terms of her homosexuality which, in turn, he attributed to a negative oedipal resolution. See "The Psychogenesis of a Case of Homosexuality in a Woman" (1920), *Standard Edition,* vol. 18, pp. 147–172.

12. Even Freud was, on a clinical level, not entirely bound to his model. For a clear exposition of this issue, see George S. Klein, "Freud's Two Theories of Sexuality," in *Psychoanalytic Theory: An Exploration of Essentials,* New York (International Universities Press), 1976, pp. 72–120.

13. This is, of course, an issue that has been addressed by critics who are interested in reader response. The concept is very useful in understanding the effect of literature on the reader; regrettably, it is occasionally carried to extremes, as, for example, in the recent article by Marshall W. Alcorn, Jr. and Mark Bracher in *PMLA,* where the authors suggest: "Recent developments in object relations theories suggest that the process of reading and discussing literature is similar in a number of crucial ways to the process of psychoanalysis, which

is specifically designed to mobilize and alter the internalized structure of the self." ("Literature, Psychoanalysis, and a Reformation of the Self: A Direction for Reader-Response Theory," *PMLA,* vol. 100, no. 3, May 1985, p.345.) The ability to understand something about one's self through a character should not be confused with what transpires in psychoanalysis. There, change occurs slowly over time, through interaction with an analyst who is trained to interpret transference and resistance material. Neither reading, no matter how fervently and intelligently undertaken, nor classroom discussion, can hope to achieve the same depth or permanence of change as the structural alteration possible by dint of the psychoanalytic dyad.

14. In fact, a recent theoretical work makes this connection explicit, yet from the opposite perspective. Hence, rather than claiming that the process of literary analysis parallels psychoanalytic inquiry, Atwood and Stolorow contend that their clinical method approximates the hermeneutic circle of textual study:

> The interplay between individual hypotheses and the analysis as a totality follows a 'hermeneutic circle,' in which the parts give rise to the whole and the whole provides a context for evaluation of the parts. The structures of meaning disclosed by this mode of investigation become manifest in invariant thematic configurations that are repeated in different sectors of the person's experiences. The elucidation of such invariants forms the counterpart in the interpretive science of psychoanalysis to the doctrine of replication of observations in the sciences of nature.

See George E. Atwood, Ph.D. and Robert D. Stolorow, Ph.D., *Structures of Subjectivity: Explorations in Psychoanalytic Phenomenology* (New Jersey: The Analytic Press), 1984, p.5.

15. This is particularly obvious in the works of authors such as I.B. Singer, who have read Freud and even incorporate his formulations, yet in whose work evidence of early emotional deficit abounds.

16. The understanding of a text as corroborative is discussed in a somewhat different context by Kohut in his paper, "Beyond the Bounds of the Basic Rule." Commenting there on several works of psychobiography, Kohut states: "The reader has access to the very material upon which the author's conclusions are based, and there is no need to disguise information or to omit data for reasons of discretion as is unavoidable in clinical reports; the author's procedure is

therefore open to examination and direct study. The 'wild' analysis of the amateur can be identified by the discriminating reader, whereas the skill, caution and tact of the experienced and gifted in our field can be studied in their interaction with the free-flow of imagination that will always remain indispensable to the psychoanalyst'' (*op. cit.,* p.303).

17. Roy Schafer, ''Narration in the Psychoanalytic Dialogue,'' in *The Analytic Attitude* (New York: Basic Books), 1983, p.218. Hereafter cited as *Schafer.*

18. *Schafer,* p.219.

19. Donald P. Spence, *Narrative Truth and Historical Truth: Meaning and Interpretation in Psychoanalysis,* (New York & London: W.W. Norton & Co.), 1982, pp.52–53.

20. Sigmund Freud, ''Recommendations to Physicians Practicing Psycho-Analysis'' (1912), Strachey, James (ed.), *The Standard Edition of the Complete Psychological Works of Sigmund Freud,* vol. 12, London (The Hogarth Press & The Institute of Psycho-Analysis), 1958, pp.115–116.

21. Reik, *op. cit.,* p.234.

22. Kohut, *op. cit.,* vol. 1, p.10.

Chapter Two

1. Y.L. Peretz, *Ale verk* (New York: Farlag Yiddish, 1920), vol. 4, pp. 235–241. All references to this work will be cited in the text. Unless otherwise indicated, all translations in these pages are my own.

2. Der Nister, *A tog-bikhl fun a farfirer,* in *Yidish: a zamlbukh,* vol. 2 (1910), pp. 45–57.

3. The narrator of this work is characteristically oblique in his discussion of sexual details. Der Nister makes the discussion of suicide circumspect as well: the narrator quotes his neighbor using the popular euphemism *zikh a mayse onton,* literally, ''to do an act on oneself,'' rather than a more explicit description.

4. This does not detract from her legitimacy as a character, merely from her availability for scrutiny. It is much like the clinical distinction between the patient, who can be known directly, if always incompletely, by the analyst, and the people mentioned by the

patient—friends, family, colleagues—who cannot be perceived other than through the prism of the patient's experience.

5. Edwin Shneidman, *Voices of Death* (New York: Harper & Row), 1980, p.38.

6. Studies have been done that confirm the differences between bona fide suicide notes and those that were written by experimental subjects. Research conducted by Shneidman and others, for example, entailed a systematic comparison between notes left by people who had committed suicide and notes composed in an experimental setting by individuals who were chosen because they were deemed non-suicidal. The results indicate that real notes tend to be characterized by the presence of specific information, such as names of people and places, as well as by the inclusion of well-defined instructions for the suicide's survivors. Artificial, imaginary notes, in contrast, are more likely to be general and to contain more references of a philosophical, thoughtful nature, "suggesting that the issue of suicide was being pondered, reasoned with, and probably rationalized." (See Daniel Ogilvie, Philip J. Stone, and Edwin S. Shneidman, "A Computer Analysis of Suicide Notes," *The Psychology of Suicide,* eds. Edwin S. Shneidman, Norman L. Farberow, and Robert E. Litman, 2nd ed. [New York: Jason Aronson, Inc. 1976], p. 256.)

The circumscribed nature of authentic notes indicates an apparent contradiction in the suicide's thought process: on the one hand, he/she has accepted not being present in the future. On the other hand, to issue directives implies the desire to maintain control, to have an impact even after death—and that signifies a profound denial that the self will cease to be. (See Edwin S. Shneidman and Norman L. Farberow, "The Logic of Suicide," *Clues to Suicide,* eds. Edwin S. Shneidman and Norman L. Farberow [New York: McGraw-Hill Company, Inc., 1957], pp. 31–40.) On a different level, the obsession with details reflects the narrowed horizon, the loss of perspective that is common in the suicidal state.

Chapter Three

1. H.D. Nomberg, *Ertseylungen,* vol. 2 (Berlin: Klal-Farlag, 1922), pp. 89–100. All references to this work will be cited in the text.

2. Despite the fact that the reader has, theoretically, a more direct access to Moritz/*zun,* in *Fir doyres—fir tsavoes,* than to Felye,

due to the first-person narrative form, he remains a more distant figure than does she. This impression is at the very core of the difference between the stories themselves. For, Nomberg has found a way, by rendering Felye's obsessive self-preoccupation, to chronicle the increasing break with reality that she undergoes before her final confrontation with herself. Peretz' characterization, in contrast, lacks this fluid quality. It is almost as if Moritz/*zun* and, perhaps, Peretz, do not possess the concentration necessary for the suicidal act or the description thereof. In contrast, Nomberg succeeds in composing a suicide note that convinces precisely because it cannot be completely understood and its author reacted to with full empathy. Nomberg's achievement underscores the fact that a form, i.e., the use of a suicide note, does not cause a work to fail.

3. The question of sibling rivalry arises here: is Felye's suicide an unconscious determination not to be replaced or unseated once again by her younger sister, as she had been at the latter's birth? Certainly this is a tempting interpretation which must, however, remain a speculation because there is no direct data to confirm or invalidate it.

4. Dovid Bergelson, *Verk,* vol. 2 (Berlin: Farlag Vostok), 1922, pp. 113–147. All references to this work will appear in the body of the text.

5. Although *Der toyber* was written prior to the Bolshevik Revolution, Bergelson's post-1917 Marxist sympathies led him to adapt the novella for the stage; the new version focused on the exploitation of the deaf man by his bourgeois employers. While the original plot certainly allows for a recasting of the sort attempted by Bergelson, this should not dictate a political interpretation of the earlier work. It is inviting, specifically, to view the protagonist's deafness retroactively, as a physical manifestation of his proletarian alienation. This seems unduly simple. Rather, when viewed from the perspective of its psychological effect on the man himself, the disability immediately suggests multiple meanings. The deafness does not merely force the deaf man to suffer at the hands of his various exploiters, nor does it suggest only that he cannot communicate when he wants to. Rather, to cite just two examples, his perception of the silence around him allows the deaf man to avoid responsibility and action and, furthermore, achieves for him the secondary gain of being pitied by others.

6. I employ the term narrative voice here in order to underscore Bergelson's technique of merging the traditional functions served by omniscient narrative and internal monologue.

7. In 1900, Freud said of dreams in literature that: "Most of the artificial dreams constructed by imaginative writers are designed for a symbolic interpretation . . . They reproduce the writer's thoughts under a disguise which is regarded as harmonizing with the recognized characteristics of dreams." He pointed out that authors who presented dreams in their work neither intended nor attempted a mimetic portrayal; that is, they did not recreate the manifestly confused and confusing material that comprises the dream in everyday life. See Sigmund Freud, *The Interpretation of Dreams* (Leipzig and Vienna, 1900; rpt. Avon Books, 1965), p.129.

Nonetheless, to the extent that Bergelson invested this literary dream with a full range of conscious, subconscious, and unconscious processes, the result is rich in available insights. The dreams that occur in this work and others prove informative when analyzed psychoanalytically, according to current clinical theories of dream interpretation. These include probing not only the circumstances surrounding the dream, but the affect state(s) experienced in the dream and afterwards.

9. It is not possible to know how much of this complex material was written by Bergelson with the awareness of how he was portraying the deaf man's conflicts. Whatever the author's conscious understanding, the material itself calls for some explanation. Furthermore, since this is the only mention of the relationship between husband and wife, it thus assumes the quality and significance of a summary. Finally, this flashback is followed immediately by an account of Esther's second visit to her father, a narrative hint that she is to be considered in the context of her father's anger and disappointment at women for not satisfying his needs.

10. The deaf man has chosen an essentially passive approach to life, with men as well as with women. His violence may be viewed as a last resort, employed when all else fails. The question of how he came, unconsciously, to favor this mode of behavior over other, more effective ones, is not illuminated by the text and therefore cannot be answered.

11. Current psychoanalytic theory focuses centrally on the relationship between parents and children as decisive for psychological health or pathology. One result of this perspective has been the recognition that parents whose own early needs for nurturing have been unmet often attempt to correct this deficit through their children. For an eloquent summary of this pattern, see Alice Miller *The Drama of the Gifted Child,* originally published in German as *Das Drama des*

begabten Kindes, 1979, translator Ruth Ward (New York: Basic Books, 1981), pp.7–8.

12. Y. L. Peretz, *Zindik blut,* in *Verk,* vol. 8 (New York: Farlag Yidish, 1920), pp.24–36. All references to this work will be cited in the text.

13. In fact, it is a standard feature of the *tkhine,* the genre of prayer composed in Yiddish and designed to be recited by women.

14. Early deficiencies of parental care do not mean that the growing child will fail to continue passing through developmental stages. At issue is the degree of success with which the emotionally deprived child can confront them.

15. Psychoanalytic investigation suggests that overt sexuality may hide infantile motives. For a seminal discussion of this idea, see Judd Marmor, "Orality in the Hysterical Personality," *Journal of the American Psychoanalytic Association,* vol. 1, October 1953, pp.656–671.

16. The figure of the benign nurse in this story bears some attention, for she may be seen as an analogue of the lost mother for Manye. She is pure and chaste, yet she seems to be having a flirtation with the doctor; her response when she hears about the religion teacher is one of shock: "Impossible!—she exclaims" (p.29). But she remains fascinated by the story in all its details.

17. Sholem-Aleykhem, *Gants tevye der milkhiker, Ale verk fun sholem-aleykhem,* 2nd ed., vol. 5 (New York: Sholem-aleykhem folksfond), 1918. All references to this work will appear in the body of the text.

18. The straightforward use of this expression occurs in the *eyl moley rakhamim* [*el maley raḥamim*], the Hebrew memorial prayer for the dead. It appears as well in *Ecclesiastes 12:5.*

19. The *Unsane toykef* [*unetane tokef*] is a hymn recited on the Jewish High Holidays. It describes the Day of Judgment and the various fates which will be meted out during the coming year.

20. A recent study suggests that there may be a link between suicide attempts by adolescents and the self-image of their parents. The results indicate that the parents of adolescents who attempt suicide manifest lower self-esteem, greater depression, higher anxiety and significantly greater entertainment of suicidal ideas than parents of a control group. These findings include an unusual observation,

namely that the first two characteristics (low self-esteem and depression) were common among *fathers* while the second (suicidal ideation and anxiety) were more common among the *mothers* of suicidal adolescents. (See Carl L. Tishler and Patrick C. McKenry, "Parental Negative Self and Adolescent Suicide Attempts," *Journal of the American Academy of Child Psychiatry,* vol. 21, no. 4 (1982), pp. 404–408.

21. It is interesting that the translation (by Julius and Frances Butwin) of this story which appears in Irving Howe and Eliezer Greenberg, *A Treasury of Yiddish Stories,* New York: Schocken Books, 1973 and elsewhere, omits this passage. It is the only such deleted section I have discovered in the English rendition and it is tempting to speculate that the translators, who elsewhere have not shied away from the subject, nonetheless felt here that the passage was more trouble than it was worth.

22. Erik H. Erikson, in his pioneering essay, "The Problem of Ego Identity," presents a vignette of a young girl whose mother "had repeatedly expressed the thought that she would rather see her daughters dead than become prostitutes; at the same time she suspected 'prostitution' in the daughter's every move toward companionship with boys." In the end, the girl—treated as a prostitute by outside authorities as well—took her own life. In Erikson's terms, she had chosen a "negative identity." That is, the notion of being a prostitute and, therefore, in her mother's eyes better off dead, had become the "most undesirable or dangerous, and yet, also . . . most real" way to be. I am suggesting that Tevye transmitted this kind of message to his daughters—especially Shprintse—and that it influenced their actions. (See Erik Homburger Erikson, "The Problem of Ego Identity," *Journal of the American Psychoanalytic Association* vol. 4, no. 1 (1956), pp. 56–121, and especially pp. 82, 87.

23. Pirke Avot is one of the sixty-three treatises that comprise the *Mishnah* (the code of Oral Laws). It is read on Sabbath afternoons between Passover and the New Year and therefore appears in prayer books. Tevye, although he delights in boasting of his learning, actually refers mostly to phrases that occur during the course of prayer. This particular quote, from *Avot 4:29,* occurs in the following context: "Know that for all there is an accounting. Let not your desire tell you that the grave will be an escape for you, for involuntarily you were created, involuntarily you were born, involuntarily you are alive, involuntarily you will die, and involuntarily you are destined to give an accounting before the supreme King of kings, the Holy One,

blessed be He." I have taken this translation from David De Sola Pool, editor and translator, *The Traditional Prayer Book for Sabbath and Festivals* (New York: Behrman House, Inc.) 1960, p. 686.

24. Rokhl Faygnberg, *Af fremde vegn* (Warsaw: Farlag Tsentral), 1925. All references to this work will be cited in the body of the text.

25. Just when they are about to become lovers, Borekh talks to her in a "fatherly-harsh" voice (p.187).

26. The question arises whether Sheyndl and Leyzer are involved in a complicated—or perhaps rather simple—acting out of an unresolved oedipal conflict. It may indeed be so that Sheyndl's choice of love is rooted in her unfulfilled and unassuaged desire to claim her father for herself; and it is possible that Leyzer, for his part, is aroused in some fashion by this provocation. However, the overwhelming evidence from the text itself does not lean in the direction of sexual urges per se but, instead, tends towards the wish for acceptance and self-respect.

27. Sheyndl feels most affected by Leyzer's eye contact. Later, with the man who becomes her father-in-law, this form of communication turns into an obsessive horror for Sheyndl.

28. The connection in Sheyndl's mind between her father and Borekh is made clear here, too, as the narrator follows her train of thought from Leyzer's forthcoming invitation directly to the impatience with which she awaits Borekh whom, like her father, she has not seen since her wedding.

29. Again, the question of Sheyndl's unconscious longing for her father as husband, i.e., her oedipal strivings, must be entertained, especially since she had previously connected the notion of marriage with him. Indeed, it is plausible that there is some element of that conflict in her situation. However, the truly oedipal longing involves sexuality, and, in her marriage, Sheyndl is anything but sexual. This may be a defense, but the content of her fantasies suggests that the presence of Leyzer serves one of two purposes, or both simultaneously: the wish to have him help Benye in magically solving her problems, and/or the hope that her father will rescue her from her plight. Such a direction to her feelings would indicate an earlier, pre-oedipal stage of development.

30. See, in particular, Heinz Kohut, "Thoughts on Narcissism and Narcissistic Rage," *Psychoanalytic Study of the Child,* vol. 27 (1972), pp. 360–400, and particularly p. 385.

31. Khaim Grade, *Di agune* (Los Angeles: Yidish-natsionaler arbeter-farband), 1961. All references to this work will appear in the body of the text.

32. For Merl, Reb Dovid closely resembles an "idealized parent imago," someone "to whom the child can look up and with whom he can merge as an image of calmness, infallibility and omnipotence." Heinz Kohut and Ernest S. Wolf, "The Disorders of the Self and Their Treatment: An Outline," *International Journal of Psychoanalysis,* vol. 59 (1978), p.414.

33. Gute and Golde call Merl a wild goat, yet there is no evidence that she has ever been wild. Indeed, when she thinks about her life as a single woman, she compares herself to her niece, Zelde, whose search for love is connected to a desperate hunt for a husband who will grant her stability and security.

34. Merl and Kalmen had met at a cemetery, and the discussion with her sisters occurs in the old-age home where her mother lives.

35. Merl's sisters, Gute and Golde, complain ceaselessly about their husbands. Moreover, in one of the novel's few light moments, Gute's two daughters reveal their amorous techniques; one is painfully clingy, whereas the other is cold and depreciating. Clearly, but for reasons unexplained in the novel, the women in Merl's family do not achieve harmonious, satisfying relationships with men. It is small wonder, therefore, that Merl herself experiences difficulties.

36. This is not the same image, in terms of its metaphoric meaning, as that of Sheyndl split off from herself, but it is a similar technique, i.e., that images represent the inner states that the authors are attempting to convey.

37. As Merl reveals in an interior monologue when thoughts of suicide are already in her mind, neither Kalmen nor Itsik had interested her sexually:

> . . . that her body was like a piece of wood, a piece of clay with him—[Kalmen] neither understood nor felt. To be honest, she had also not loved her first husband enough so that her affection for him gave her joy, made her long for him to embrace her until she ached and was intoxicated (P.236).

38. One way of understanding Merl's fantasies is that, in the case of her mother, a fusion fantasy is at work, whereas with Dovid, it is a wish to be incorporated: by giving up her body, she will become part

of his now more powerful self. In both cases, she is spared the fate of being alone.

39. The English translation of *Di agune,* by Curt Leviant (p.175), does not contain this discussion of Merl's worshipful love for the rabbi. It is a further example of how the reading public—including, unfortunately, translators—seems to conspire to keep stereotypes alive, in this case, apparently, that a woman should not bear a taboo love for a man of God.

Chapter Four

1. Borekh Glazman, *Di mishpokhe pikuda* (Warsaw: Farlag Peretz-bibliotek), 1923. All references to this work will be cited in the body of the text.

2. The narrator adopts a sharply ironic tone when discussing the suicides of Zakhari's siblings. It may be, however, that the tone is meant to reflect the views of Beyle, Zakhari's wife, since the information about these suicides comes as a loose connection to her musings on the matter.

3. One of the punishments for suicide is burial outside the boundaries of the cemetery.

4. Zakhari's self-absorption can, in retrospect, be seen as a slow unfolding of the suicidal constriction that Shneidman describes and that emerges so clearly in the case of Nomberg's Felye.

5. The name of an edition of the *sidur* ("the prayer book") with a Hebrew text and a Yiddish translation.

6. I am not talking here specifically about a relationship of sexual acceptance, but it is significant that the battle between Raye and Zakhari occurs—according to the terms of Freudian theory—during the oedipal period.

7. The image of water plays a very large role in *Di mishpokhe pikuda;* both Zakhari and Raye are drawn to the ocean and spend a good deal of their time either at the shore or contemplating it. When Zakhari decides to commit suicide, he is sitting by the Schuylkill River in Philadelphia; Raye is by the ocean when Zakhari comes to her. The bathing and washing that the two engage in has obvious psychological ramifications which may or may not be connected with the geographical bodies of water that absorb them and link them

in some way. While compulsive washing is traditionally interpreted as a desire to wash away guilt or "undo" some unconscious impulse, the wish to be immersed in warm water of course suggests a striving to recapture the prenatal period, to return to the womb. Insofar as Zakhari has evidently spent his entire life in the pursuit of some early love that has been denied him, his behavior in the end is characteristic.

8. D. W. Winnicott, "Further Thoughts on Babies as Persons" (1947), *The Child and the Outside World* (London: Tavistock), 1957, p.137.

9. Zakhari also creates a link between himself and his older brother, Naum, by employing the same method of suicide. This is another attempt at fusion, but, unlike the gesture towards Raye, it apparently does not become conscious.

Chapter Five

1. Zalmen Shneyur, *A toyt: shriftn fun a zelbst-merder a tiref* (Warsaw: Farlag Hashakhar), 1913. The date at the conclusion of the text is August 1905. All references are from this edition and will be cited in the body of the text.

2. Nekhome is also a Yiddish word meaning "solace."

3. See D.W. Winnicott, "Transitional Objects and Transitional Phenomena," in *Playing and Reality* (London: Tavistock Publications, 1971; rpt. Penguin Books, 1982), pp. 1–30. This version contains Winnicott's original 1951 paper and includes an update. For a recent discussion of Winnicott's concepts, see Arnold H. Modell, "The Works of Winnicott and the Evolution of His Thought," *Journal of the American Psychoanalytic Association,* vol. 33 (Supplement), 1985, pp. 113–137, and especially pp. 124–130. For a theoretical and clinical explanation of the developmental importance of affect recognition and management, see Daphne D. Socarides and Robert D. Stolorow, "Affects and Selfobjects," *Annual of Psychoanalysis,* vols. 12–13, 1984–85, pp. 105–119.

4. H. D. Nomberg, *Ertseylungen* (Berlin: Klal-Farlag, 1922), vol. 2, 11–30. All references to this work will be cited in the body of the text.

5. In this matter the narrator is sharply ironic, indicating that Fliglman *is* open with Levantkovski and then introducing, as an ex-

ample, Fliglman's monologue about the moon (p.13).

6. One of the interesting characteristics of this work is its use of Brecht-like chapter summaries.

7. It is intriguing that Fliglman has an experience of disorientation, yet one that supplies some sense of connection as well, while in bed. At this point in the story, the early memory of being left in bed by his father has not yet occurred, but, in retrospect, the connection between longing and lying in solitude is clear.

8. Interestingly, Fliglman's calmest moments are at night, when he can feel near the moon, which he perceives almost as an object with which he is merged. As he puts it to Levantkovski: "It often happens that I feel that I and the sky and the moon are all one, one absolute, you understand, but in various forms . . ." (p.14). He is trying to sound philosophically sophisticated, but in doing so he reveals how desperately he longs for contact.

9. In the context of Fliglman's growing sense of emptiness, his subsequent mirror-gazing while visiting the homely dentist assumes a new significance. Fliglman is not only looking for a sign that he is accepted and admired for who he is but also attempting to reassure himself of his actual existence, of the fact that he is tangible, real. In such a frame of mind, of course, there can be no room left for appreciating someone else, and this situation leads him to react to the young woman with what appears to be self-absorbed and boring chatter. In terms of Fliglman's own predicament, however, it is a formidable effort at keeping himself phychically whole, at preventing emptiness and its attendant panic from taking over.

10. This is, of course, a very different interpretation from that of classical Freudian psychoanalysis, where compulsive repetition is seen as representing an endless cycle of aggressive fantasies and the attempt to undo them.

11. Kohut's comment in one of his final essays illuminates this idea. Talking about the Spartans who gave up their lives at the Thermopylae, he observed: "They lost their lives, but only their lives. That was their feeling. If you're thinking in terms of biology, of course, then they lost their lives, but if you think in terms of psychology they didn't lose their selves." " 'Stranger, Take Word to Sparta: Here We Lie, Obeying Her Orders'," in Heinz Kohut, *Self Psychology and the Humanities: Reflections on a New Psychoanalytic Approach.* Edited with an introduction by Charles B. Strozier (New

York: W.W. Norton & Company, 1985), p. 264. I am reminded also of a clinical vignette: the patient, coming to a session after a regular one-day hiatus in his analysis, announced: "I think I feel better now, but yesterday and Monday night I just felt so dead, it just felt awful. I felt like killing myself, but even that felt redundant."

12. Borekh Glazman, *Okean,* in *Baginen* ["*Morning*"] (New York: Farlag Kultur), 1921, pp. 203–224. All references to the work are from this edition and will appear in the body of the text.

13. Although it is not clear to what end, Glazman has given his characters names that are, or at least resemble, Yiddish words. Kreynin is similar to the verb *kreynen* "to crown"; Vaysgal means "white bile"; and Lamdn signifies "scholar."

14. Vaysgal's longing, like Merl's in *Di agune,* corresponds closely to what Kohut terms the child's need to feel united with an idealized parent imago. From this experience the child gleans the "basic idealized goals" that become a guiding force throughout life. See Heinz Kohut and Ernest S. Wolf, "The Disorders of the Self and Their Treatment: An Outline," *International Journal of Psycho-Analysis,* 59 (1978), pp.413–425, and especially p.414. Glazman's text does not provide information about the early lives of his characters, but the work does hint at the doctor's continuing lack of inner security.

15. Isaac Bashevis Singer, *Der kuntsnmakher fun lublin* (Tel-Aviv: Hamenora Publishing House), 1971. All citations of this work are taken from the English translation by Elaine Gottlieb and Joseph Singer (New York: Fawcett Crest) and will appear in the body of the text.

16. See, for instance, Irving Buchen's treatment in *Isaac Bashevis Singer and the Eternal Past* (New York: New York University Press, 1968, pp. 101–113) or Irving Saposnik's essay "Yasha Mazur and Harry Houdini: The Old Magic and the New," in *Studies in American Jewish Literature,* 1, Daniel Walden, ed. (Albany: State University of New York Press, 1981, pp. 52–60).

17. Singer makes extensive use in this novel of interior monologue and stream of consciousness. These devices, albeit distancing because of their indirectness, manage simultaneously to underscore the importance of Yasha's mental productions as they clash—less and less as the work progresses—with his actions.

18. It is not contradictory to post-Freudian theory that Yasha could be developmentally arrested and yet pass through an oedipal period. At issue is the child's ability to successfully negotiate this natural phase. The prognosis is less favorable than if previous emotional challenges have been satisfactorily met.

19. Yasha's decision to accomplish magic with locks is thus revealed as stemming from an archaic effort to gain his father's admiration—coupled with the attempt at union with this longed-for parent—rather than an oedipal competition.

20. This situation brings to mind Judd Marmor's statement about the sexuality of hysterics:

> The sexuality of the hysteric is indeed a sham, but primarily *because it expresses a pregenital oral-receptive wish rather than a genital one.* The distress and surprise of the hysterical woman when her seductiveness leads to her being approached genitally is consequently understandable. She is being approached as a woman when what she really wants is to be taken as a child.

From Judd Marmor, M.D., "Orality in the Hysterical Personality," in *Journal of the American Psychoanalytic Association,* vol. 1, no. 4 (October 1953), p. 667.

21. That is, the process "by which an unacceptable impulse is mastered by exaggeration . . . of the opposing tendency" (Charles Rycroft, *A Critical Dictionary of Psychoanalysis* (Nelson, 1968; rpt. Penguin Books Ltd., 1983, p. 136).

22. In a conversation on October 12, 1983, the author told me, in response to my question, that Magda had killed herself because she had called Yasha "dirty Jew" and she knew he would never forgive her. But when I asked why she had killed his animals, Mr. Singer replied that this had to do with her desire for vengeance.

23. It is traditional to perform a pre-Yom Kippur atonement ceremony, in which a chicken is used to represent the original scapegoat of ancient times.

24. Here, as for example with Merl and Tsirl in *Di agune,* the author's position as creator of all the characters becomes important. The connection between Yasha's thoughts and Magda's actions finds its ultimate existence in Singer's imagination. Moreover, Magda's

death solves an authorial problem as well: how to extricate Yasha from his complex milieu without destroying him.

25. Yasha's superficially active act of marriage is from the beginning a very limited attainment. Yasha thus resembles the other passive and suicidal males studied here, although at first he seems entirely different in this regard.

26. The Yiddish original reads: "His father speaks elevated talk to him, he kisses him, warns him, reproaches him . . ."(p.68).

27. Yasha joins the majority of the characters observed in these pages, who suffer because they have not been raised in an intact family. Usually it is the mothers who survive, but because everyone's role is limited to certain circumscribed areas which, taken together, are supposed to constitute a full upbringing, deprivation will be the likely result when any part of that whole is lacking. Yasha longs for an early state of satisfaction with his mother. And, when Magda suddenly abandons him forever, he is catapulted back to the most primitive realization of that longing—and its inevitable frustration.

Chapter Six

1. The novel was published in Yiddish between Friday, February 11 and Saturday, August 13, 1966, in the pages of the *Jewish Daily Forward.* It has never appeared in book form in the original Yiddish. The passages quoted here are from the English translation by Aliza Shevrin and Elizabeth Shub (New York: Farrar, Straus & Giroux, Inc., 1972; rpt. New York: Fawcett Crest, 1973) and will appear in the body of the text.

2. See, for example, "Hanka," "Old Love," "The Admirer," "The New Year Party," all from Singer's English language collection, *Passions* (New York: Farrar, Straus & Giroux, Inc., 1975; rpt. Greenwich, Connecticut: Fawcett Crest, 1976) and "Elka and Meir," "Two Weddings and One Divorce," and "The Bus," from his English language collection, *Old Love* (New York: Farrar, Straus & Giroux, Inc., 1979; rpt. New York: Fawcett Crest, 1980). These are only several of Singer's frequent but passing references to suicide.

3. It is telling, in this context, that Singer's Author's Note appears only in the English translation of *Sonim.* Clearly, he perceives that he has a special message for his English readers that might not fit his Yiddish audience. For more about this subject, see my article,

"The Double Life of I.B. Singer," in *Prooftexts,* vol. 5 (1985), pp.165–181.

4. The name of Shifrah Puah stands out because it combines the names of the two Biblical midwives who refused to follow Pharoah's command that they kill all Hebrew males whom they delivered. Because of their faith and courage, God was kind to them, and the people of Israel grew and became powerful (*Exodus, I:15–20*). Shifrah Puah, with her dreadful memories and constant lament that she would be better off dead is, in a way, an ironic comment on the Biblical text and on redemption itself. At the same time, however, Shifrah Puah does act as a lifeline for her daughter and, thus, indirectly for Herman as well.

5. Herman does, in fact, avoid Masha for a short period before their marriage, after her previous husband had indicated that she had obtained her divorce by agreeing to have sexual intercourse with him one last time.

6. This reaction of Herman's does not appear in the Yiddish original. There, Masha refuses to go away to the country with Herman and only later, in the epilogue, is his disappearance revealed.

7. In general, the survivor characters in this novel talk freely about suicide in situations that are not life-threatening. Thus, for example, Tamara asks Herman whether he is trying to commit suicide when he leaves the house without galoshes (p.188). This can be understood as part of a pervasive mood amongst these characters, namely that the very nature of life and death has been transformed so that neither has the meaning it possessed previously.

8. The irony here in terms of marriage is extraordinary: the lovers consider a single incident with an estranged spouse to be infidelity, never once considering that their own relationship bespeaks unfaithfulness to those original partners. Moreover, Herman's continuing sexual bond with Yadwiga appears not to be problematic. Compare Masha's evidently unruffled reaction to Yadwiga's pregnancy with Sheyndl's disintegration after Mine's third child is born.

9. Masha wants this marriage very much for herself and creates a hysterical pregnancy in order to achieve her aim. Yet it is characteristic of Masha to attribute her own feelings to her mother, since this is a part of their typical interaction.

10. This conclusion, too, is absent in the Yiddish original.

Index

A tog-bikhl fun a farfirer (Der Nister), 15–16, 18–21, 22, 43, 201–2
A toyt: shriftn fun a zelbst merder a tiref (Shneyur), 119–35, 156, 177, 210
Abandonment, 85, 91–92, 93–94, 103
About Fligtman's First Love (Nomberg). *See Fligtman*
Abraham Nissen Yaroslaver, Reb (*Sonim*), 180
Af fremde vegn (Faygnberg), 55–84, 140, 166, 179, 180, 186, 207, 215
Aggression, 109–10
Aloofness, 24–25
Anger, 42–43, 77, 103, 167
Anna (*Af fremde vegn*), 75–76
Anna (*Shvayg, shvester*), 25, 26
Anomie, 53, 198
Arrogance, 154
Ashkenazi (*Af fremde vegn*), 80
Atwood, George E., 200
Author: as creator of characters, 99, 213–14; as translator, 9; and unconscious material, 7, 204; woman's perspective, 55

Basye (*Af fremde vegn*), 65, 67
Bendetzon, Moritz (*Fir doyres-fir tsavoes*). *See* Moritz Bendetzon
Bendetzon, Moritz/zun (*Fir doyres-fir tsavoes*). *See* Moritz/zun
Benye (*Af fremde vegn*), 62, 69, 71, 74, 207; marriage of, 77–79, 80, 81, 82
Bergelson, Dovid, 27–38, 55, 166, 203–5
Beyle (*Di mishpokhe pikuda*), 103, 105–6, 109, 112–13, 121
Beylke (*Tevye der milkhiker*), 43
Bik, Mendl (*Der toyber*). *See* Mendl Bik
Binyomin, Reb (*Fir doyres-fir tsavoes*), 16–17
Bolek (*Der kuntsnmakher fun lublin*), 167
Borekh (*Af fremde vegn*), 55, 80, 82, 179; as father, 61, 207; and Gitl, 81, 83; and hedonism, 76; Leyzer's attitude towards, 64–65, 67–68; and Mine, 71–72, 180; Sheyndl's obsession with, 56–58, 61, 66, 72; social standing of, 61; as trapped, 84
Broder, Herman (*Sonim*). *See* Herman Broder

Childhood: emotional deficit in, 5, 13, 105, 106, 173–74, 200, 205; incomplete family in, 214; influences during, 7; mirroring function of parents in, 82; Oedipal conflict during, 4, 5, 209, 213
Communication, lack of, 28, 29, 37, 121, 148
Compulsive repetition, 148, 211
Criticism, 121–22, 129

Davidke (*Af fremde vegn*), 67
Death: fantasy of, 52, 164–65; preoccupation with, 44–47, 48–49, 54. *See also* Suicide
Death in Venice (Mann), 12
Der kuntsnmakher fun lublin (Singer), 157–76, 178, 181–85, 186, 191, 194, 212, 214, 215
Der Nister, 15–16, 18–21, 22, 43

Der toyber (Bergelson), 27–38, 55, 166, 203–5
Di agune (Grade), 84–100, 178, 208–9, 212, 213
Di mishpokhe pikuda (Glazman), 101–18, 120, 121, 134, 135, 150, 156, 177, 209–10
Disability, psychological effects of, 28, 203
"Dos groyse gevins" (Sholem-Aleykhem). *See Tevye der milkhiker*
Dos Tepl (Sholem-Aleykhem), 102
Dovid Zelver, Reb (*Di agune*), 85–86, 87–88, 89–91, 92–93, 98, 208–9
Dreams in literature, 7, 30–32, 145–47, 148, 204
Durkheim, Emile, 1
Dvoyre (*Af fremde vegn*), 55–56, 72–75

Eliezer Khaykls, Reb (*Fir doyres-fir tsavoes*), 16
Elzbieta (*Der kuntsnmakher fun lublin*), 166–67, 181
Emilia (*Der kuntsnmakher fun lublin*), 158, 161, 162, 164
Emotions, denial of, 25, 138, 158–60, 171–72, 175–76
Esther (*Der kuntsnmakher fun lublin*), 158, 161, 162, 164, 165
Esther (*Der toyber*), 27–38, 55, 166
Eydl Zelver (*Di agune*), 87

Family: incomplete, 214; isolation in, 101–2. *See also* Father, Mother, Parents
Fantasy: of death, 52, 164–65; fusion, 208–9; jealous, 83; of mother, 121, 131, 134, 173–74; paranoid, 122; of poverty, 53; of romance, 58, 90, 93, 124–25, 132, 139, 140, 143, 151, 155
Father: blaming, 46; and daughter's sexuality, 27, 31–33, 35, 36, 65, 68, 94, 96–97; dependence on, 66–67, 69, 70, 78; as deserter, 38, 39, 113; and female roles, 44, 47–48, 50; fusion with, 114, 116, 117–18; hostile, 16–17, 47, 51–53, 59–60, 107–8, 110; identification with daughter, 64–65; lack of support from, 28–30, 37–38; masculinity of, 50–51, 52, 54; and Oedipal conflict, 41, 207; remarriage of, 120–21; support from, 61–65. *See also* Parents
Faygnberg, Rokhl, 55–84, 140, 166, 179, 180, 186, 207, 215
Felye Faynshteyn (*Shvayg, shvester*), 23–27, 134, 135, 177, 202–3, 209
Female stereotypes, 48, 50
Fir doyres-fir tsavoes (Peretz), 15–18, 20–22, 25, 134, 135, 202–3
Fliglman (Nomberg), 135–49, 156, 210–11
Fliglman (*Fliglman*): aloneness, 156; disintegration, 143–45, 147–49; and Levantkovski, 136, 137–38, 144, 145, 148, 210–11; and past, 141–42, 144; self-absorption of, 135–38, 140; and women, 138–41, 142–43, 146
Free association, 9–10, 44
Freud, Sigmund, 4–5, 11, 12, 199
Freyde, (*Af fremde vegn*), 74–75
Fusion, 92, 116, 117–18, 163, 187–88, 208–9

Gitl (*Af fremde vegn*), 69, 81, 83, 84
Glazman, Borekh, 101–18, 120, 121, 149–56, 177, 209–10, 212
Gnesye (*Di mishpokhe pikuda*), 104–5

God: as father, 40, 41; heretical concept of, 169–70
Golde (*Di agune*), 88, 89, 208
Golde (*Tevye der mikhiker*), 43, 45, 46, 47, 51, 52, 53–54
Goldman, Hillel (*Af fremde vegn*), 63
Grade, Khaim, 84–100, 178, 208–9, 212, 213
Gute, (*Di agune*), 88–89, 208

Haynt, 2
Henye, (*A toyt*), 123–25, 128, 132–33
Herman Broder (*Sonim*), 179–80; disappearance of, 185, 215; and father, 182–83; and marriage, 183, 189–90; and Masha, 184–86, 215; and mother figures, 181–82; as responsible, 183–85
Hillel Goldman (*Af fremde vegn*), 63
Hodel, (*Tevye der milkhiker*), 43, 47–48, 50, 51–52
"Hodel." *See Tevye der milkhiker*
Holocaust: and collapse of social stability, 178–80, 194–96; and integration of past and present, 180–81; and sexuality, 193–94; effects on mother-daughter relationship, 193, 194; suicide as response to, 178
Homosexuality, 199
Hurvitz, Reb Levi (*Di agune*). *See* Levi Hurvitz, Reb
Hurvitz, Tsirl (*Di agune*). *See* Tsirl Hurvitz

Imagos, 7
Internal monologue, 203, 208
Introjects, 7
Irony, 149, 209, 210
Isolation, 57–58, 109–10, 115, 120, 122, 130, 144, 154, 156
Ite (*Af fremde vegn*), 58–59, 60, 62, 66, 72, 74, 82
Itsik (*Di agune*), 85, 91, 92

Jewish religious life, 40–41, 104, 170–71
Jewish social structure: importance of marriage in, 2–3; as trap for women, 76
Jews, suicide among, 1–2, 178, 197–98

Kalmen (*Af fremde vegn*), 73, 74
Kalmen Maytes (*Di agune*), 85, 87–88, 94
Khane (*Af fremde vegn*), 62, 63–64, 66, 67
"Khave." *See Tevye der milkhiker*
Khave (*Tevye der milkhiker*), 43, 46, 47, 48–49, 52, 53
Khaykls, Reb Eliezer (*Fir doyres-fir tsavoes*), 16
Kohut, Heinz, 5, 12, 82, 200–201
Kreynin, Gavriel-Uri (*Okean*), 149–56, 177, 212

Lacan, 3, 198
Lamdn, Dr. (*Okean*), 150, 151, 212
Lamdn, Mrs. (*Okean*), 150, 151–52, 155, 212
Lampert (*Sonim*), 185
Leon (*Af fremde vegn*), 75, 76
Levantkovski (*Fliglman*), 136, 137, 139–40, 144, 148, 210–11
Levantkovski, Mrs. (*Fliglman*), 137
Levi Hurvitz, Reb (*Di Agune*), 92, 94–99
Leyzer (*Af fremde vegn*), 58–60, 207; and Borekh, 64–65, 67–68; and Ite, 72; and Sheyndl, 60–65, 66–71, 78; and social standing, 60–61
Literarishe bleter, 2

Literary interpretation using psychoanalytic theory, 3–4, 5–13, 177, 198–202
Loneliness, 155–56
Lying, 144, 147

Magda (*Der kuntsnmakher fun lublin*), 158, 161, 162, 164, 165–69, 183, 186
Magic as metaphor, 174–75
Mahler, Margaret, 5
Mann, Thomas, 12
Manye (*Zindik blut*), 38–43, 55, 134, 186, 205
Marianna (*Sonim*), 180, 195
Marriage, 186; collapse of institution, 179–80, 215; denial of, 172; failure to achieve, 2–3, 18; importance of, 196; motivations for, 85, 87; as price of acceptance, 70–71; refusal of, 61; as trap, 76–80, 82, 83, 104; women's roles in, 71–76
Masculinity, 50, 52, 54, 125–26
Masha (*Sonim*), 178, 179, 183–94, 195; as child, 190; effects of Holocaust on, 193–94; and Herman, 190, 191–92; and marriage, 189–90, 215; suicide of, 185, 186; symbiosis with mother, 186–93, 215
Maytes, Kalmen (*Di agune*). *See* Kalmen Maytes
Mazur, Yasha (*Der kuntsnmakher fun lublin*). *See* Yasha Mazur
Men: and intimacy, 137, 138–39, 142, 155; need for women, 161–62, 163–65; passive, 3, 64, 101, 108; and sexuality, 122–23, 128. *See also* Father; Masculinity
Mendl Bik (*Der toyber*), 27, 28, 30, 31, 32, 36, 37
Merl (*Di agune*): as caretaker, 86, 88–89, 91; need for parent figure, 88, 91–92, 93, 208, 212; and Reb Dovid Zelver, 85–86, 87–88, 89–91, 92–93, 208–9; and Reb Levi Hurvitz, 98–99; and sisters, 88–89, 208; suicide of, 98; and Tsirl Hurvitz, 94, 98–100, 213
Meyer Vilenkin (*Af fremde vegn*), 61, 65, 75
Mine (*Af fremde vegn*), 56, 68, 69, 77, 180, 215; unhappiness of, 66, 71, 75
Mirkin (*A toyt*), 125–26, 132
Mirror, image of, 81–83, 140, 211
Mishnah, 206–7
Moritz Bendetzon (*Fir doyres-fir tsavoes*), 15, 16–18
Moritz/zun (*Fir doyres-fir tsavoes*), 15, 16–18, 21–22, 25, 134, 202–3
Mother: absent, 104–5, 107, 141, 142, 173; analogue for, 205; attacking, 59–60, 82; disharmony with, 112–13; fantasy of, 121, 131, 134, 173–74; fusion with daughter, 92, 187–93; idealization of, 40, 41–42, 43
Mottele Zelver (*Di agune*), 86, 90, 93
Moysey (*Di mishpokhe pikuda*), 102–3
Moyshke Tsirulnik (*Di agune*), 85, 87, 88, 89–91, 93

Narration in the Psychoanalytic Dialogue (Shafer), 8–9
Narrative distance, 15, 20–21, 27, 43, 169
Narrative techniques: circumspection, 201; first-person point of view, 38, 203; free association, 9–10, 44; imagery, 208; internal monologue, 203, 208, 212; journal entries, 15; stream of consciousness, 212; suicide notes, 15, 203
Narrator: role of, 76; as transmitter of character, 7–8; unconvincing, 21–22
Naum, (*Di mishpokhe pikuda*), 102, 103, 115, 210

Nekhome (*A toyt*), 130, 133, 210
Nomberg, H. D., 23–27, 134, 135–49, 156, 177, 202–3, 209, 210–11
Non-Jews, 31, 165–66

Oedipal conflict, 4, 5, 41, 161, 199, 207, 209, 213
Okean (Glazman), 144–56, 177, 212
Omniscient narrative, 203

Parents: importance of, 204; mirroring function of, 82; rejecting, 121, 126, 129; self-image of, 205–6. *See also* Father; Mother
Passivity, 3, 64, 101, 108, 150
Past, integration with present, 180
Peretz, Y. L., 15–18, 20–22, 25, 38–43, 55, 134, 135, 186, 202–3, 205
Point of view, 38, 203
Projection, 89, 90, 164, 168, 187
Psychoanalytic theory, 11, 199; application to literature, 3–4, 5–13, 177, 198–202; on compulsive repetition, 211; criteria for mental health, 157; data gathering, 6; on overt sexuality, 205; patient's participation, 9; post-Freudian, 4–5, 213

Raye (*Di mishpokhe pikuda*), 101; aggressiveness, 120; fate of, 118; and father, 107–9, 110, 113–14, 116; and mother, 104, 112–13; preoccupation with sexuality, 108, 110–11; self-isolation, 109–10
Reaction-formation, 165, 213
Reader, role of, 9, 199–200
Regression, 157–58, 160–61, 172, 174
Reik, Theodore, 11, 12, 198–99
Repetition, compulsive, 148, 211
Roshe-Leye (*Af fremde vegn*), 58, 61, 66, 73
Rootlessness, 17–18

Sadism, 19
Sadness, failure to express, 142
Schafer, Roy, 8–9, 10
Schultz (*Der toyber*), 31
The Search for the Self (Kohut), 12
Self-absorption, 56, 135–38, 140
Self-esteem, lack of, 69, 140–41, 153
Self-mutilation, 111
Sexuality: addiction to, 163; avoidance of, 23, 24–25, 26–27, 40, 42, 92–93, 173; child's preoccupation with, 108, 110–11; as deadly, 105; father's attitude towards, 27, 31–33, 35–36, 65, 68, 94, 96–97; and fusion, 163, 213; and guilt, 90; and Holocaust, 193–94; and humiliation, 128; lack of interest in, 85, 208; and need for nurturing, 191; need for protection from, 41; overt, 42, 205; and pain, 110–11; positive attitude towards, 179; and regression, 161; women's, 27, 31–33, 35–36, 179
Shakhne (*Af fremde vegn*), 74–75, 79–80, 81, 83
Shayke (*Di agune*), 88
Sheva Haddas (*Sonim*), 180
Sheyndl (*Af fremde vegn*): childhood of, 59–60, 82–83; and father, 60–65, 82, 186; and image of mirror, 81–83; isolation, 57–58; jealousy, 69, 81, 83; and marriage, 71–77, 79–80, 83, 179, 180, 215; and mother, 60; need for father, 66–71, 78, 207; obsession with Borekh, 55–58, 61, 66, 72; and Shakhne, 78–80, 81; suicide of, 76, 83, 84, 166

Shifrah Puah (*Sonim*), 180, 183, 184, 185; effects of Holocaust on, 193, 194; and Masha, 186; as mother figure, 181–82; name of, 215
Shloymke (*A toyt*), 156; ambivalence about suicide, 133–34; childhood of, 119–21, 132; disempowerment of, 127–28; fascination with suicide, 122, 130; and Henye, 123–25; isolation of, 120, 122, 131, 132–33; and men, 125–26; and mother, 130–31; and revolver, 127–29, 130, 133; and sexuality, 122, 123, 128; vulnerability of, 126
Shneidman, Edwin, 21, 209
Shneyur, Zalmen, 119–35, 156, 177, 210
Sholem-Aleykhem, 2, 43–55, 102, 126, 186, 198, 205–7
"Shprintse." *See Tevye der milkhiker*
Shprintse (*Tevye der milkhiker*), 43, 44, 47, 49, 52, 53, 54–55, 186
Shvayg, shvester (Nomberg), 23–27, 134, 135, 177, 202–3, 209
Sibling rivalry, 203
Singer, Isaac Bashevis, 157–76, 178–96, 200, 212–15
Sisters: dependence of, 86, 88–89; rivalry with, 25, 26–27, 69, 81
Social standing, 36–37, 60–61
Sonim, di geshikhte fun a libe (Singer), 178–96, 214–15
Sonya (*Af fremde vegn*), 75
Spence, Donald P., 8, 9–10
Splitting, 90
Stolorow, Robert D., 200
Stream of consciousness narrative, 212
Suicide: ambivalence about, 133–34, 186; among Jews, 1–2, 178, 197–98; and burial, 209; as connection to humanity, 134; as empowerment, 117, 128, 129; fantasy of, 52; as focus of plot, 23; as forbidden, 2, 46, 53; and fusion, 116, 117–18; narrative distance from, 169; preoccupation with, 47, 122, 130, 185–86, 215; as redundant, 149, 211–12; as sacrifice, 167; as safety valve, 24; and self-image of parents, 205–6; and verbal cues, 44–47, 48, 49
Suicide, causes of: abandonment, 91–92, 93–94; anomie, 198; avoidance of sexuality, 23, 24–25, 26–27; desire for reunion with beloved person, 92, 114, 130, 131; economic factors, 2, 17, 198; emotional deficit in childhood, 5, 13, 16, 17, 132, 142; failure to marry, 2; Holocaust, 178; homosexuality, 199; insanity, 2; internal problems of parents, 50–55; isolation, 22, 124, 154, 156; lack of parental support, 28–30, 37, 38, 69; non-communication, 28, 29, 37; pregnancy, 15–16, 20, 54; rigid roles, 54, 76, 83–84; rootlessness, 17–18; sibling rivalry, 203; symbiosis with mother, 187–93; unconscious expectations of parents, 52, 206; vengeance, 165, 167–68, 213
Suicide notes, 15; authenticity of, 21–22, 202, 203
Superficiality, 150–51, 152–53
Synagogue, 106, 170

Tamara, (*Sonim*), 179, 183, 184, 185, 186, 189–90, 195, 215; as mother figure, 182
Tevye (*Tevye der milkhiker*), 43–55; hostility toward daughters, 47–48, 51–53; and masculinity, 50, 52, 54, 125–26; preoccupation with death, 44–47, 48, 49

Tevye der milkhiker (Sholem-Aleykhem), 43–55, 126, 186, 198, 205–7
Torah, 53
Transitional objects, 131–32
Tsaytl (*Tevye der milkhiker*), 43, 48, 49
Tsirl Hurvitz (*Di agune*), 92; and father, 94–96; and Merl, 98–100, 213; and sexuality, 93, 96–97
Tsirulnik, Moyshke (*Di agune*). *See* Moyshke Tsirulnik

Unconscious, denial of, 158–60, 171–72, 175–76
Undzer lebn, 1–2

Vaysgal, Dr. (*Okean*), 150–51, 152, 153–54, 155, 212
Vilenkin, Meyer (*Af fremde vegn*). *See* Meyer Vilenkin

Warsaw, suicides in, 1, 2
Water, images of, 102, 114, 209–10
Wealth, 16, 17
Winnicott, D. W., 5, 116, 131
Wolsky (*Der kuntsnmakher fun lublin*), 162, 173
Women: abandonment by men, 38, 39; and careers, 57, 62–63; freedom from tradition, 3, 62–63; and marriage, 71–76, 180; as mother figures, 161–62, 181; perspective of, 55; sexuality, 27, 31–33, 35–36, 179; traditional prayers recited by, 40
Woytus (*Sonim*), 180, 195

Yadwiga (*Sonim*), 179, 180, 181, 183–84, 195, 215
Yaroslaver, Reb Abraham Nissen (*Sonim*), 180
Yasha (*A toyt*), 127
Yasha Mazur (*Der kuntsnmakher fun lublin*), 181–85, 191; childhood of, 173–74, 215; disengagement of, 168–69; and father, 172–73; forbidden emotions of, 158–60, 171–72, 175–76; image of God, 169–70; injured foot of, 159–60, 174; and Magda, 166–69; as magician, 174–75; mental health of, 157; passivity of, 214; regression of, 157–58, 160, 172, 174; religion of, 169–72; and women, 161–65, 173, 181

Zakhari (*Di moshpokhe pikuda*), 101, 104, 134, 135, 150, 156; childhood of, 103–5, 106, 113; death of, 114–17; isolation of, 115, 117; marriage of, 105–6; and Naum, 210; and Raye, 107–9, 110, 113–14, 116; self-absorption of, 106, 209; and water, 102
Zeftel (*Der kuntsnmakher fun lublin*), 163, 164
Zelver, Reb Dovid (*Di agune*). *See* Dovid Zelver, Reb
Zhenye (*Di mishpokhe pikuda*), 111
Zindik blut (Peretz), 38–43, 55, 134, 186, 205